Dancing in the Dark?
SHINING THE LIGHT ON THE CHURCH

Clive Calver and Steve Chilcraft

with Peter Meadows and Simon Jenkins

with added contributions from
Peter Broadbent, Stephen Gaukroger, Roger Hurding,
David Jackman and Ernest Lucas

LYNX

Spring
Harvest

Copyright © 1994 Spring Harvest

The authors assert the moral right to be
identified as the authors of this work.

Published by
Lynx Communications
an imprint of Lion Publishing plc
Sandy Lane West, Oxford, England

First edition 1994

Acknowledgements
Unless otherwise stated, all scripture is taken
from the HOLY BIBLE, NEW INTERNATIONAL
VERSION. Copyright © 1973, 1978, 1984 by
International Bible Society. Used by permission of
Hodder and Stoughton Limited.

Printed and bound in Great Britain
by Blackmore Press, Shaftesbury

Using this book for group study

This material has been written for use at the Spring Harvest main seminars, which are rather different from church study groups or home groups. But there is a wealth of information here, and plenty of stimulating ideas. So these notes can readily be adapted for any kind of group discussion.

One way might be this:

1. Taking one of the units (e.g. People), decide how many group sessions you will give to it and so which sub-sections you aim to cover each session.

2. Assuming each member has a copy of this book—it's packed with useful knowledge, so it would be unkind if they didn't!—ask them to study that sub-section on their own before the next session.

3. Prepare discussion questions for each session. Some sections have 'Pause for thought' questions in the centre column, which may give some clues as to how to frame yours.

4. Remember these studies are meant to lead to thought and action, not just talk. So why not finish each of your sessions by choosing one or two ways members of the group could take action this coming week, before your next session. Then, next session, begin by sharing how that went.

Contents

People   5

Partners   27

Problems   43

Purpose   69

Introduction to Philippians   92

Philippians – a free translation   93

People
What it means to be human

CONTENTS

Introduction: what is the church?

1   Knowing yourself

2   What does it mean to be human?

3   Twentieth-century versions of 'me'

4   Living in the 'Me' generation

5   Designed by God

6   Made for each other

7   Spoiled by sin

8   Brought back to life

Booklist

> **Book of the seminar day:**
> John White, *The Shattered Mirror*, Intervarsity Press

Introduction: what is the church?

The focus for *Dancing in the Dark* is the church. But what is the church? What does it mean to people today? What do we first think of when we hear the word 'church'?

Here are some popular ideas, from Christians and non-Christians, about what the church is...

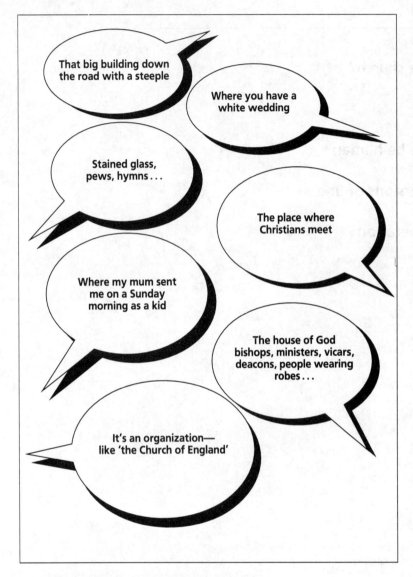

People have very different ideas about what the church is. But how can we get behind these different images to what the church is really all about? If we travel back in time—before the days of cathedrals, pews, stained glass and archbishops—right back to the time of Jesus himself, we quickly discover the bottom line about the church...

'Jesus travelled about from one town and village to another, proclaiming the good news of the kingdom of God. The Twelve were with him, and also some women who had been cured of evil spirits and diseases... These women were helping to support them out of their own means' (Luke 8:1–3).

The simplest definition of the church is this...

▶ the church is people.

More accurately...

▶ the church is the people of God.

 KEY POINT The church is made up of ordinary men and women united in their commitment to follow Jesus Christ, expressed in repentance and faith.

Four angles on the church

Over the next four sections, we will be looking at the church from four different angles...

▶ People
▶ Partners
▶ Problems
▶ Purpose.

The passage in Ephesians 4:12–16 is a good place to start in thinking about these four areas, because all four play a part in it. For example, it talks about...

People—'preparing God's people for works of service...' (verse 12)

Partners—'speaking the truth in love, we will in all things grow up...' (verse 15)

Problems—'tossed back and forth by the waves...' (verse 14)

Purpose—'the whole body... grows and builds itself up in love...' (verse 16).

This first section of these notes explores the 'people' dimension of the church. What does it mean to be a human being? Who am I? How does our culture treat people—and what does it believe? And how can we live as 'the people of God' in today's world?

1 *Knowing yourself*

Human beings have always been fascinated by themselves. Some people find it hard to talk about anything else. 'Well, that's enough about me,' says one person to another over a meal. 'Now let's talk about you—what do you think about me?'

Know yourself!

Since the early 1980s it has become increasingly popular to engage in the process of self-assessment. One writer dubbed the culture of the 1980s the 'Me' generation. Magazine articles, psychoanalysts, adverts and even TV soap operas all tell us that what each individual needs is to 'know yourself'!

There is a great deal of truth in this—but there are also dangers. What angle are we going to take in order to look at ourselves? The viewpoint we take can easily turn out to be incomplete and one-sided. We can end up with a caricature of ourselves, rather than a portrait.

For example, there are two extremes...

Too low a view—a low-esteem that can lead to despair, depression and an unreflecting fatalism which simply accepts whatever life brings to us. There is a sense that we cannot change anything in our own lives or in the wider world, so passive resignation becomes the only conclusion. This is the folly of too much *dependence on others*.

Too high a view—a self-opinionation that believes, like secular humanism, that we have everything needed within to change ourselves and the world at large. The argument is, for example, that with more equable distribution of wealth, increasing tolerance and better education humankind can only improve. In the long run everything will be OK. This is the danger of an *arrogant independence*, or autonomy.

Christians believe that there has to be another way of looking at ourselves. We need a second opinion—an objective view of ourselves from 'outside'. We need to see ourselves through God's eyes.

A biblical view—the Bible gives us exactly this way of looking at ourselves. And the church, as the community of those who follow Jesus, is the place where we can be valued—and where we can learn to value others—as human beings made in God's likeness. This is the path of *dependence on God*, and *interdependence* in relating to others.

Why the fuss?

It is so important to get this view of ourselves right.

KEY POINT The Christian view of what it means to be human is so different from the non-Christian views that it makes a great difference to our lives.

This can be seen by looking at just a few wrong views of what it means to be human. The devastating effect of these views on the lives of real people shows that it is not simply theories that are at stake...

▶ **Apartheid** viewed the different races in South Africa as unequal, and was designed to keep white-skinned people in power. This view of human beings has led to enormous suffering for millions of people.

▶ **Rationalism** believes that human reason is the highest function of human beings. In its extreme form, it leads to the idea that emotions are a sign of weakness and should not be shown in public. The view that 'big boys don't cry' has led to a massive distortion of masculinity.

▶ **Secular humanism** denies the reality of God and the spiritual realm and believes (among other things) that human beings are simply higher animals, because one evolved from the other. This leads to far-reaching conclusions on subjects such as abortion, euthanasia, genetic research, fertilization techniques...

A Christian view of humanity leads to very different conclusions about all these areas. Seeing ourselves through God's eyes makes a radical difference to the way we live, and the way we treat other people.

Looking ahead ...

The next sections look at some of the different views there are about human beings. We are going to look at ...

The way our culture sees us—if we are to reach people with the good news of Jesus, we need to understand them first!

The way the Bible sees us—revealing the kind of people God has designed us to be.

This clash between secular and biblical views will help us to explore what it truly means to be a human being—the raw material of God's church.

PAUSE FOR THOUGHT
How would you explain to a Martian why human existence is a mixture of good and bad?

'**M**iserable, wicked me, how interesting I am.'
W.H. AUDEN

'**E**xistential humanism constitutes nothing less than a determined effort to salvage faith in a godless world. God has left the world, the humanists claim, so that man can elevate himself to the level of God.'
JOEL KOVEL

'**I**ntellectual doctrines about the self don't just sit around in unreadable scholarly journals. They wind up in people's heads.'
M. BREWSTER SMITH

2 What does it mean to be human?

'What is man?' asked the writer of Psalm 8. This question has echoed across the centuries of human history.

KEY POINT Each generation has come up with its own answers to the basic questions of human existence.

Versions of me

One of our most basic beliefs is that each individual person is a 'real' personality...

▶ each of us is an 'existent self', separate and distinct from the rest of the world

▶ every individual remains essentially the same throughout the changing experiences of life

▶ at the end of all the feelings of success and failure, hope and despair, fear and faith, I remain the same person

▶ at the end of all the crises and experiences of life, I can be confident in the fact that—*I am me!*

However, we have to ask which 'me' we are talking about. To a very great extent, the culture of our day determines who we are, what we want, and how we define happiness.

Which is me?

Every decade of the twentieth century has given its own bias to the way we see human identity...

In the 1900s I was optimistic—a new century had dawned, the human race was a success, self-assured, I anticipated a rosy future...

In the 1910s I was betrayed—the trenches of the Somme introduced me to man's inhumanity to man. I entered a no man's land of devastation and shattered dreams...

In the 1920s I was an escapist—the images of Hollywood and the Roaring Twenties introduced me to a world of illusions where I could escape from my poverty and pain...

In the 1930s I was depressed—living in fear of the future and in the shadow of economic collapse...

In the 1940s I was a hero—a patriot prepared to die for my country, to suffer for my friends, to build a brave new world...

In the 1950s I was reconstructed—introduced to freedom, prosperity and rock'n'roll, convinced that I 'had never had it so good'...

In the 1960s I was a rebel—part of a new youth culture which rejected materialism, war, oppression, suburbia and middle-age...

In the 1970s I was lost—sold on consumerism, lacking moral purpose and direction, unhealthily introspective, stagnant and bored...

In the 1980s I was a materialist—my new purpose was to get everything I could, as fast as possible, using whatever means were necessary...

In the 1990s I was a technocrat—less frenetic, more caring, but obsessed by my desktop, video and walkman...

Through all the changing scenes of life one heart cry remains the same—I must be me! But which version is the authentic one?

The story so far...

How do we see ourselves? Down through the history of the Western world, people have come up with many different answers. Here are just a few of them...

Pre-500BC—Many ancient civilizations believed that the world was dominated by a number of powerful gods—often in conflict with each other. People tried to keep on the right side of their gods so that they would have good harvests, healthy children, success in battle, and so on.

These early societies did not place any great stress on the individual person—it was the tribe that mattered, with the king at its head. Each person was confined to his or her particular place in the social structure.

Mind and body were closely connected in popular thinking. For example, Egyptian burial customs show this clearly. Egyptian tombs not only contained a body, carefully prepared for life in the underworld, but also the dead person's favourite harp, board games, chariot, food, etc.—they were all going to be needed!

Plato—When the Greeks discovered mathematics, they began to believe that human reason was all-important in gaining knowledge. Plato gave to the world a vision of human nature divided between...

▶ **the material body**, which is involved in the world

▶ **the immaterial mind**, which seeks to know eternal truths

▶ **the immortal soul**, which is caught between the impulses of the mind and the body.

The soul is trapped in the body. True freedom can be found when the soul turns from the physical to pursue eternal truths. Ultimately, the soul is set free at death, when it rises to the eternal world of Ideas.

Plato's view of body and soul had a profound impact on the thinking of the Western world, including the beliefs of the church.

Hippocrates—He was a contemporary of Plato's, and argued that the different temperaments of individuals are the result of differing balances in bodily elements—blood, phlegm, black and yellow bile.

This 'theory of humours' was highly influential right into medieval times.

The Enlightenment—The Enlightenment was a European intellectual revolution which reached its peak in the eighteenth century. It overturned many of the beliefs of the Middle Ages and emphasized the importance of reason and progress. Its ideas are still very powerful today.

The Enlightenment led to a complete change in the way life, the universe and everything were seen...

▶ many Enlightenment thinkers were hostile to religion

▶ they explained human abilities like perception, memory, imagination and thinking in purely physiological terms

▶ two key ideas of the Enlightenment were the supremacy of human **reason**, and the idea of individual **freedom** of thought and action.

The Romantics—Romanticism was partly a rebellion against the cold reason of the Enlightenment. The

PAUSE FOR THOUGHT
Which is more surprising to you—how good or how bad a person can be?

PAUSE FOR THOUGHT
How often do you think about who you are?

Romantics (who included English poets such as Byron and Keats)...

▶ wanted to break out of reason and respectability and live dangerously instead

▶ said that the only way to discover your true, inner self was through emotion, feelings and experience.

It was only a short step to move from Romanticism to the twentieth-century cult of individuality. From now on the emphasis would be on each individual discovering herself or himself.

Postmodernism—In the twentieth century, Western culture has seen a revolt against the ideas of the Enlightenment, especially in its belief in the supremacy of reason. Postmodernism is not a school of thought, but a mood of rejection against the certainties of the Enlightenment.

Postmodernism attacks...

▶ **Human reason**—by toppling reason from its Enlightenment position, Postmodernists create a climate of pluralism and diversity. This has helped to clear the way for New Age beliefs, pluralistic societies, relativism, and so on.

▶ **Human autonomy**—Many Postmodernists accuse the Enlightenment of inventing the self. They say there is no such thing as the individual. This leads to an increasing focus on consumerism, and a loss of value and meaning for many people.

Where does personality come from?

Fans of the TV science fiction cult serial 'Star Trek' are familiar with the debates which take place between the pointed-eared Vulcan, Mr Spock, and the determined captain of the Starship *Enterprise*, James Kirk.

Mr Spock, being a Vulcan, has no emotions. He judges every issue on the grounds of pure logic. His constant reply to Kirk's headstrong, impulsive actions is 'Most illogical, Captain'. Spock's logic is extraterrestrial in origin; Kirk's irrational behaviour is attractively human.

There is something very appealing in the idea that we have within us a deep-seated well of passionate irrationality. This makes life exciting. We may appear to be cool, calculating individuals, but in fact we are not totally predictable. Instead, we possess the capacity for sudden, instinctive reactions to the situations which we face.

But where do these illogical responses come from? This leads us to encounter some interesting questions. Is our personality...

▶ given to us when we are conceived?

▶ governed entirely by our genetic structure?

▶ simply the product of our experience and environment?

Would I be the same person if I had been born in another place or time? Or if I had had different parents and a different upbringing? What is the real me?

Conditioning human behaviour

There is no simple answer to these questions. Many modern thinkers argue that the truth about it all is a mixture of these ideas. Each 'me' is authentic.

Others argue that our behaviour and identity owe more to external than internal sources. In other words, when we are born, we are like a blank piece of paper. Our background, environment and experiences write their own contributions on the page. The end result is 'me'—the person I discover myself to be at any particular point in my individual history.

> ☞ **KEY POINT** A great deal of popular thinking rejects the idea that each person is born with an inbuilt sense of good and evil, or right and wrong.

Instead, it says that our identity and our morality is formed by a number of external pressures...

▶ our education

▶ the way our parents bring us up

▶ the influence of groups who have power over us

▶ our culture.

Because there are no absolute standards of truth, we have to draw our own conclusions about what is 'right' for us. This modern view considers us to be unique in terms of our own experience, rather than in the innate qualities we possess.

This view has led some thinkers to the conclusion that we can alter personal behaviour by changing the conditions in which people operate.

Such is the depressing conclusion of the society in which we live. Each of us becomes in one sense or another the product of our environment. We are what our culture and temperament determine us to be.

But is this all there is to us? Are we simply rats in a cage, responding to rewards and punishments? Or is there something more to this business of being human?

3 Twentieth-century versions of 'me'

This section outlines some of the more popular views about the 'self' that have been introduced in the last 100

> '*W*hat a piece of work is a man! How noble in reason! how infinite in faculties! in form and moving how express and admirable! in action how like an angel, in apprehension how like a god!'
> WILLIAM SHAKESPEARE

> '*T*he key to understanding the human mind is to see it as a social phenomenon. We arrive in the world with the naked brain of an animal and through the moulding power of speech we become equipped with the thought habits that make us human. The special aspects of the human mind—self-awareness, memory, higher emotion and imagination—are skills we learn rather than faculties that unfold within us like so many budding flowers.'
> JOHN MCCRONE

> '*Y*our problem actually is the fact that you have a lot of what I call "shoulds", "oughts" and "musts"... which unfortunately you were taught when you were very young. You were taught these by your father, your mother, your church... But if you didn't have this concept of ought which unfortunately is nicely defeating your own ends, then you wouldn't believe this—you wouldn't be disturbed.'
> ALBERT ELLIS (A THERAPIST INFLUENCED BY FREUD)

years. It examines four key thinkers of the twentieth century...

▶ Sigmund Freud

▶ Carl Jung

▶ B.F. Skinner

▶ Abraham Maslow

Sigmund Freud

Sigmund Freud is known as 'the father of modern psychoanalysis'.

The subtlety and complexity of Freud's arguments are understood by few people, but his emphasis on the creative struggle between basic human needs, the conscience and the will has widened our understanding of what motivates human behaviour.

He taught that...

▶ each of us is a bundle of a life-enhancing or sexual energy—which he termed the libido

▶ we are sexual animals from birth

▶ social order depends to a large extent on the repression of these sexual urges

▶ all human neuroses result from this repression, but family and civilization would collapse without it.

Freud later developed his thinking to include an awareness of death and our need to repress the fear of our mortality.

Freud explored the mind by teaching that we all possess...

▶ the economy of the mind—two instinctual forces, sexuality and death

▶ the topography of the mind—conscious, preconscious and unconscious

▶ the dynamics of the mind—id, ego and superego.

He relentlessly explored the realm of the unconscious and introduced to the thinking of his day concepts such as the significance of dreams, the libido, the ego, the Oedipus complex and the dangers of repression.

He denied that religion had integrity because he claimed that it denied people the right to challenge it. Eventually, he believed, we would outgrow our need for God.

His personal contribution to the development of psychoanalysis—now a major feature of life in the Western world—is enormous.

The self—according to Freud

Freud recognized the internal conflict we experience between two forces within our personality...

our instinctive desires—Freud termed the part of our personality that contains these the 'id'.

our conscience—Freud termed this the 'superego'—although this term includes elements from the unconscious and the past, which may differ from our present values.

He attributed our basic human wants, impulses and drives exclusively to a sexual source. Human beings are therefore internally torn apart by the conflict between our basic primitive desires and the standards we pick up from others. It happens in this way...

▶ our id constantly seeks self-expression

The professor and the chalk

This view has led some thinkers to the conclusion that we can alter personal behaviour by changing the conditions in which people operate.

A psychology professor once explained to a class of students the idea that personal behaviour could be changed through conditioning. He pointed out how the behaviour of caged rats could be conditioned by a system of rewards and punishments. While he was lecturing, he would pause to underline a point and lightly toss a piece of chalk into the air.

Without his knowing it, the students agreed that when he flipped the chalk they would 'reward' him by giving him their complete attention. For the rest of the time they would 'punish' him by displaying a complete lack of interest in his lecture.

Gradually, the chalk rose higher. It was tossed more often. Eventually it was bouncing off the ceiling at regular intervals. Now the professor, influenced by the attention of his 'rewarding' audience, was as controlled as one of his own caged rats!

Assessing Freud

Positively, he . . .

▶ gave a valuable psychological framework for the complexity of human nature

▶ popularized the ideas of the unconscious, repressed memories, hidden motives and the importance of dreams

▶ gave some understanding of the formation of conscience, the baser instincts and the conflict between them

▶ pioneered an analytical approach to helping others.

Negatively, he . . .

▶ saw all guilt as essentially neurotic (that is, as a disorder or illness)

▶ saw the sex drive as the explanation of all human motives and behaviour, including child development

▶ held an essentially pessimistic view that human nature is governed by instincts

▶ saw the practice of religion as immature and neurotic.

'They [the sexual instincts] are the true life instincts. They operate against the purpose of the other instincts, which leads by reason of their function, to death; and this fact indicates that there is an opposition between them and the other instincts.'
SIGMUND FREUD

▶ however, our superego is overly strict and severe in imposing on us the concepts it has learned from upbringing and society

▶ when the id is frustrated, the superego becomes the prime cause of mental illness

▶ this is because a repressed id leads to false feelings of guilt

▶ airing your pent-up feelings can help to repair the damage.

Between the id and the superego stands a third aspect of personality . . .

our conscious self—Freud termed this the 'ego'. Unlike the irresponsible id and the strict superego, the ego responsibly umpires the conflict.

Carl Jung

Carl Gustav Jung was a Swiss psychiatrist who collaborated with Freud until their break in 1914. Jung came to disagree with Freud about sexuality as the exclusive cause of psychological problems. After this break with Freud, Jung developed a theory of opposites: these operate within the individual to hold him or her in balance and therefore maintain stability.

He argued that all people have . . .

▶ **a persona** or mask for the different roles they play in life—for an individual man these might include the personas of father, husband, church leader, businessman, and so on

▶ behind this public face lies **the ego**, the person's centre of consciousness

▶ beneath these is our unique and individual **personal unconscious**

▶ within the personal unconscious, **the shadow** represents the darker side of human nature

▶ deeper still lies the **collective unconsciousness**, made up from images and memories drawn from a whole race of people.

With his emphasis on the power of the unconscious to

'Over eighty years after the original publication of Freudian theories there still is no sign that they can be supported by adequate experimental evidence, or by clinical studies, statistical investigations or observational methods.'
HANS EYSENCK

'It is no easy matter to live a life that is modelled on Christ's, but it is unspeakably harder to live one's own life as truly as Christ lived his.'
CARL JUNG

'Suddenly I understood that God was, for me at least, one of the most certain and immediate experiences . . . I do not believe; I know. I know.'
CARL JUNG

---

shape the individual's life, it is not surprising that while Freud saw dreams as repressed wishes, Jung viewed them as the anticipation of future realities. Dreams were the natural outlet for hopes and aspirations that could not be expressed in conscious thoughts and words.

Jung also majored on the importance of experience, and saw religion in terms of our personal encounter with God—especially the 'God within'.

The self—according to Jung

Jung developed analytic psychology. He rejected Freud's view of the sexual libido as the driving force in each of us. Instead, he moved beyond an individual consciousness to a collective unconsciousness.

He taught that our individual behaviour is determined by two factors . . .

▶ our individual and racial history (the personal and collective unconsciousness containing images and memories, known as archetypes, of its ancestral history)

▶ our individual aims and aspirations.

Each of us seeks development, wholeness and completion. Jung believed that dreams can have a predictive function, pointing to where our personal development is leading us. Jung hated church dogma and insisted instead on a personal experience of God through an intuitive awareness of his presence.

At the heart of Jung's thinking lay an emphasis on 'individuation'. Each of us becomes a whole person tempered by the conflict between our conscious and unconscious perceptions.

Jung's influence has been widely felt . . .

▶ he is regarded by many as one of the founding influences in the present-day understanding of psychotherapy

▶ with his emphasis on the supernatural and the 'God within', on symbol and on 'the shadow', Jung has been a strong influence on many Christians, particularly those of a Catholic persuasion

▶ others trace his influence on New Age thinking, especially in the idea of a universal subconsciousness

Assessing Jung

Positively, he . . .

▶ believed in the supernatural and in the experience of God

▶ faced the darker side of human nature—'the shadow'

▶ stressed the importance of image, symbol and the quest for wholeness—'individuation'—in human nature

▶ put forward a theory of personality (extended in Myers–Briggs—see page 15) that is useful for self-awareness, communication and counselling.

Negatively, he . . .

▶ elevated human experience above clear teaching about God and human nature

▶ came close to equating the idea of God with the self

▶ was in danger of introducing occultic contamination through dialogue with unknown figures from the unconscious—'archetypal images'.

which unites all people, and which we can all 'plug' into

▶ his theory of personality has also been modified and carried over in Myers–Briggs workshops, which are a useful tool for self-understanding, communication skills and counselling (see page 15).

B F Skinner

The North American psychologist, B.F. Skinner, was radical in rejecting almost all of the psychological theories that had come before him. Skinner's view is an extreme one—and is known as 'behaviourism'.

Skinner demonstrated how animals can be trained to learn appropriate responses. Placed alone in a box, a creature is provided with buttons and levers which, when pressed or pulled, produce food, water or escape. As a result, behaviour patterns can be established.

Skinner's conclusion is that . . .

▶ all human behaviour is conditioned by the environment in which we find ourselves and the experiences we undergo within it

▶ people are neither good nor bad

▶ we are simply a bundle of conditioned reflexes determined by the rewards or punishments which follow from our actions

▶ none of us is a free being, instead we are entirely at the mercy of our environment.

The self—according to B.F. Skinner

Skinner's behaviourist views were developed after he observed the behaviour of pigeons and rats. He noticed two basic forms of behaviour . . .

▶ **respondent**—behaviour which is a response to an external event

▶ **operant**—behaviour which is not a response to external events, but which is conditioned by its external consequences

These consequences of behaviour—which can be either positive or negative—Skinner termed 'reinforcers'. They reinforce the way we behave.

Skinner's view of the human being is bleak—the person is a machine and our behaviour is the product of evolution. Our environment exercises total control over our actions. Punishment, the law, money, religion—he viewed them all as inadequate in terms of placing a desirable control on people's actions.

Assessing Skinner

Positively, he . . .

▶ stressed the importance of accurate observation of behaviour

▶ introduced theories which have been taken up in useful behavioural techniques in communication, education and counselling.

Negatively, he . . .

▶ reduced people to mere animals or machines through his worldview of 'behaviourism'

▶ saw everything in life, including religion, as entirely subject to behavioural forces—'rewards', 'punishments', etc.

PAUSE FOR THOUGHT

What are the key influences in your life? Over which do you have a choice and which not?

> '*T*hings are good (positively reinforcing) or bad (negatively reinforcing) presumably because of the contingencies of survival under which the species evolved.'
> B.F. SKINNER

> '*T*he picture which emerges from a scientific analysis is not of a body with a person inside, but of a body which is a person in the sense that it displays a complex repertoire of behaviour.'
> B.F. SKINNER

> '*T*he basic needs... the basic human emotions and the basic human capacities are on their face either neutral, pre-moral or positively ''good''.'
> ABRAHAM MASLOW

Skinner not only rejected the idea of a spiritual dimension to humanity, he also rejected the whole notion that we are personal beings.

It is important to distinguish between 'behaviourism' as a worldview, and the study and influencing of human behaviour. Many counselling approaches use behavioural techniques to help people, as in the treatment of phobias and in sex therapy. And Christians such as James Dobson use behavioural principles, such as Skinner's law of reinforcement, in their work.

Abraham Maslow

Abraham Maslow was also an American psychologist. He started out as a humanist, but he came to acknowledge that people are more than a mere product of human behaviour. By the end of his life he believed in the reality of evil and the need to discover something 'bigger than we are'.

During his humanistic phase, Maslow urged that each individual should travel on a journey of self-actualization in order to discover himself or herself. This search for self-actualization can be anything from a superior form of ego trip to an unselfish quest to live out our potential.

However, Maslow's earlier thought typifies the whole concept of 'going it alone' . . .

▶ true independence and individuality are seen in terms of a search within ourselves

▶ we search to discover our 'potentials, capacities and talents'

▶ true fulfilment comes in discovering the unity of ourselves, our security, significance and self-worth

▶ all this is done without help from beyond ourselves.

We can see these ideas all around us today. For example, in the idea of . . .

▶ fulfilling my potential

▶ having my needs met

▶ developing my self-awareness.

These definitions of happiness come at us in adverts, from the pages of magazines, from films, TV and all the other media. Since the early 1960s they have been part of the foundation of Western culture.

Towards the end of his life Maslow went further, and talked about our need for a link with 'a transcendent force'. However, his idea of God falls far short of the Christian belief in the God who has revealed himself in Jesus. Maslow's offer of a link between humankind and some sort of deity needs still to be seen within his framework of basic human need.

The self—according to Maslow

Maslow believed that each individual possesses a hierarchy of human needs. These start with the most basic, and then progress to higher needs . . .

Physical—the lowest level of human need is physical, including the basic requirements for survival: food, drink, sleep . . .

Safety—the next level of need includes other survival elements, such as clothing, shelter and protection from the environment . . .

Emotional—each person needs to love and belong, so this level of need includes friendship, self-esteem, acceptance . . .

Assessing Maslow

Positively, he . . .

▶ valued human nature as special and full of potential

▶ in later life held that people need some power beyond themselves

▶ introduced a hierarchy of human need that fits well with everyday reality.

Negatively . . .

▶ his goal of 'self-actualization' can become self-centredness

▶ people who have 'peak experiences' can be seen as superior to lesser mortals

▶ in his teaching, the human need for God can be seen on an equal footing with everyday needs for 'sunlight, calcium or love'.

Personal fulfilment—Maslow's highest level is self-actualization, where the individual moves beyond the lower needs into personal fulfilment, self-harmony, spiritual awareness . . .

We are living a fully human life when all these levels of needs are met. Maslow believed that we can only move on to the next level when we have completed the previous one. The top level, which few attain, is marked by 'peak experiences' of reality. He cites Abraham Lincoln and Albert Einstein among the few people who display the hallmarks of self-actualization.

While some people are locked in by human fear and cling to safety, others launch out to discover who they really are.

4 *Living in the 'Me' generation*

Since the 1960s, following the rebuilding of society after World War II, the West has become increasingly preoccupied with the individual. In the 1960s and early 70s your growth as a person was felt to be lacking unless you had had an identity crisis! By the 1980s, the inner quest for self-understanding had given way to a search for self-fulfilment through possessions. The 'drop-out' had given way to the 'go-getter'.

Meanwhile, in the USSR and Eastern Europe, the individual human being was an endangered species. Communism believed in putting the masses first, and the individual person frequently suffered. When the Berlin Wall fell in 1989, all this changed.

In the 1990s, in the face of world recession and the collapse of many ideologies, there is a renewed search for personal focus and identity . . .

▶ for many, especially in Eastern Europe and among the poor worldwide, the search is a desperate one—for food, drink, shelter and a living wage

▶ for others, particularly among the wealthier nations, the search is for the true self, looking for ways to mature and grow as a person.

How should Christians evaluate this fresh mood in our culture? Clearly, there are many good things about it, as

> 'Wherever two people meet there are really six people present. There is each man as he sees himself, each man as the other person sees him, and each man as he really is.'
> WILLIAM JAMES

> 'Self-awareness is the ability to step back from the canvas of life and take a good look at yourself as you relate to your environmental, physical and mental worlds. It is the ability to accept yourself as a unique, changing, imperfect and growing individual. It's the ability to recognize your potential as well as your limitations.'
> DENIS WAITLEY

well as certain dangers.

This section explores five of the areas marked out for personal growth today and seeks to give a Christian response to each . . .

▶ self-awareness

▶ self-image

▶ self-motivation

▶ self-expression

▶ self-discovery

Self-awareness

KEY POINT **Self-awareness is how people see themselves.**

This is rarely a fixed view. Think how differently you see yourself when you are . . .

▶ lying back in a dentist's chair

▶ sitting at the wheel of a fast car.

In the one you may see yourself as a trembling coward, in the other as powerfully in control of life.

Self-awareness is concerned with every aspect of who we are: the physical, mental, emotional, relational, etc. The cultural pressures which surround us today can drive us towards . . .

▶ 'the body beautiful', as seen in adverts

▶ competitiveness, and the belief that positive thinking can solve anything

▶ the idea that all our emotions—even the destructive ones—must be expressed, regardless of others

▶ the view that self-knowledge can give us a licence to manipulate those to whom we relate.

Rightly seen, self-awareness is a consciousness . . .

▶ that we are made in God's image

▶ that we are sinful men and women who are redeemed by Christ

▶ that we can become more like him through the work of the Holy Spirit.

It is God himself who can help us to see ourselves in the right way—with all our strengths and weaknesses—as we pray for greater self-awareness . . .

'Search me, O God, and know my heart; test me and know my anxious thoughts. See if there is any offensive way in me, and lead me in the way everlasting' (Psalm 139:23–24).

Self-image

We may be aware of who and what we are, but how do we evaluate what we see? This raises the question of self-image, or our sense of identity.

We can say that our 'self-image' is made up of . . .

▶ how we see ourselves (self-awareness)

▶ how we evaluate what we see (self-esteem).

A poor self-image (or sense of identity) comes about when we are confused about who we really are, or when we have a low view of our worth. A strong self-image comes from clear self-awareness coupled with an appropriate level of self-esteem.

KEY POINT **Our sense of identity is built up, or pulled down, all through life.**

It starts with how our parents and others relate to us from early childhood, and how we learn to view ourselves. Today we are taught that it is important to develop our self-image by...

▶ accepting ourselves, with little or no self-criticism

▶ improving our feeling of self-worth, rejecting the criticism of others and focusing on success

▶ talking to ourselves, concentrating on what we can be and raising our self-esteem.

We need to see that it is no answer to low self-esteem to indulge in an ego-trip of inflated self-opinion. Instead, we are to evaluate ourselves with 'sober judgment' (Romans 12:3) and understand that the key to a right self-acceptance lies in the call to 'accept one another ... just as Christ accepted you' (Romans 15:7).

In other words, the appreciation that Christ accepts and welcomes us should prevent us from either putting others or ourselves down. He made us, he has redeemed us, he values us. A right self-esteem acknowledges personal sin and yet celebrates the value that God puts on our lives.

Self-motivation

Self-image is not an end in itself. Our self-awareness and self-esteem inevitably affect...

▶ our motives (including self-motivation)

▶ actions (including self-expression)

▶ and our continuing journey of self-discovery.

KEY POINT Self-motivation, the need to stir ourselves into action, is an essential ingredient for human life.

Our present culture, with its competitive drives and commitment to results, is highly committed to understanding and using self-motivation. For example...

▶ **market research** continually looks at what motivates the consumer to buy certain products

▶ **the world of business** urges realistic goal-setting and careful time-management on its employees

▶ **in every walk of life** we are encouraged to consider the possibilities and strive for greater achievement.

The list of 'Twenty hallmarks of maturity' (see the box), gives the flavour of today's assessment of the well-motivated individual.

It is important to recognize that self-motivation is part of what it means simply to be human—it helps us to achieve our legitimate daily pursuits. And a great deal of our culture's emphasis—on planning ahead, setting goals and making strategies—makes sense in helping us to face the realities of life.

However, there are real dangers in how self-motivation is seen today. We can become driven and stressed people...

▶ caught up with power games or cut-throat competition

▶ motivated to reach the top at all costs

▶ believing that the end result justifies any means, however ungodly, un-neighbourly, or against our own integrity.

The Bible has a great deal to say about fallen human motivation and our need to line up our desires, motives and plans with God's blueprint for our lives. The yardstick for right motivation is summed up by the New

> **'O**ur self-image is... dictated by others, put together over the years in bits and pieces. Parents, childhood playmates and schoolmates, teachers, relatives, athletic coaches, friends, fellow workers, bosses, ministers, priests and rabbis all contribute.'
> JOEL WELLS

> **'G**od is not a theological means to a higher psychological end. God is not a means to any other end. God is the Alpha and Omega, the beginning and the end. Our true identity is found in accepting our status as creatures of this infinite Creator God and in rooting our sense of identity in his. Our identity is an identity derived.'
> DICK KEYES

> **'T**he quest for identity is sometimes incorrectly defined as an introspective retreat from others, a kind of examination of one's psychic navel. However, to attempt to find self apart from others is to fail to find our true selves. True selfhood is a gift we receive from others; in relationship to others we find who we truly are.'
> DAVID BENNER

Twenty hallmarks of maturity

1 personal security

2 ability to discriminate between means and ends

3 a knowledge of oneself

4 diverse hobbies and interests

5 a respect for others regardless of gender, race or creed

6 fresh appreciation of things

7 a sense of self-worth

8 individual judgment, free of cultural processing

9 acceptance of oneself, others and nature

10 ability to distinguish reality, and that which is important in life

11 profound interpersonal relationships

12 freedom to experiment with fresh ideas

13 creativity

14 tendency to mystical spiritual experiences

15 commitment to the environment

16 tolerance and adaptability

17 sense of humour

18 comfort when alone, in solitude

19 spontaneity

20 a knowledge of personal significance

Testament as 'the royal law' (James 2:8), in which we...

▶ live out the priority of loving God with all our being

▶ love others with the same care, acceptance and esteem we give to ourselves.

This teaching is reflected throughout the Bible—see Leviticus 19:18; Matthew 5:43; 19:19; 22:39; Romans 13:9; 15:2; Galatians 5:14.

Self-expression

Who we are has to spill over into self-expression. Sadly, though, many in today's society move from right self-expression to *self-projection*—which is a very different thing. In our culture, 'image' is everything: how I look, the clothes I wear, the shampoo I use, the personality I inflict on other people.

It has been suggested that you can always spot a 'winner' when he or she walks into the room. The glow, the sense of presence, self-confidence and self-esteem are obvious to everyone.

The confidence to project ourselves originates in a sense of self-expectancy. The idea is that whatever we devote most to in terms of thought and energy will be fulfilled. In other words, self-expectancy will take the thoughts, feelings and images of the subconscious 'you' and commit them to action.

And yet, made in God's image, we are to follow humbly the example of the God who expresses himself. Christ's model is not one of self-advertisement and trying to impress others. He did, of course, impress others but this was simply a by-product of his obedience to the Father. Within his call to express who he was as a servant (John 13:1–17), he also knew when to hold himself back from other people—at times he 'would not entrust himself to them, for he knew all men' (John 2:24).

KEY POINT We too are to express ourselves within right limits...

▶ as God's servants, in the call to 'one-anotherness' within the church

▶ as his ambassadors in the wider community.

Jesus is the Light of the world, but he also said to his followers, 'you are the light of the world... let your light shine before men, that they may see your good deeds and praise your Father in heaven' (Matthew 5:14–16).

Self-discovery

Self-discovery should be seen as a rightful by-product of establishing a healthy self-image, self-motivation and self-expression. Sadly, today's quest is often for self-discovery as life's goal rather than life's by-product. In other words, the heart of human existence for many is defined in terms of the two-letter word: 'Me'.

In myself lies all that I need for a successful life. However, external factors have damaged my relationship with myself and I therefore need to embark on an exciting exploration of self-discovery. This is the conclusion of a multitude of textbooks, handbooks and popular guides to everyday living. The argument is simple—start the journey, find yourself.

Because each person is an individual it is recognized that he or she will encounter different signposts on the road. Some of these are shown on the 'Self-help techniques' chart.

It is important to acknowledge that although many of the routes shown on the chart are potentially routes that begin and end in the self, people have found a liberation from self-centredness on some of these journeys. For example, self-help groups such as Alcoholics Anonymous can be a powerful resource for a God-given sense of belonging—and many have found that their times of 'retreat' are actually times of advance in their obedience to Christ.

 KEY POINT Jesus showed that the way to legitimate self-discovery is the way of self-denial.

He said to the crowd and his disciples: 'If anyone would come after me, he must deny himself and take up his cross and follow me' (Mark 8:34).

It is important to see what comes before and after this challenging statement...

Before—Peter had just been rebuked for not having 'in mind the things of God, but the things of men'—in other words, Peter is challenged for being self-centred rather than God-centred.

After—following his call to self-denial, Jesus says, 'For whoever wants to save his life will lose it, but whoever loses his life for me... will save it'—if we put self first as our way of living, we will lose ourselves; if we put Christ first we will find true life, our essential selves, secure in him.

Personality and temperament

The Apostle Peter's concept of a 'holy nation' was linked to his teaching that we needed to become a people who belong. All of us need this sense of belonging—not just 'somewhere', but 'to someone'. The purpose of the church is to be a people who belong to God (1 Peter 2:9).

Self-help techniques

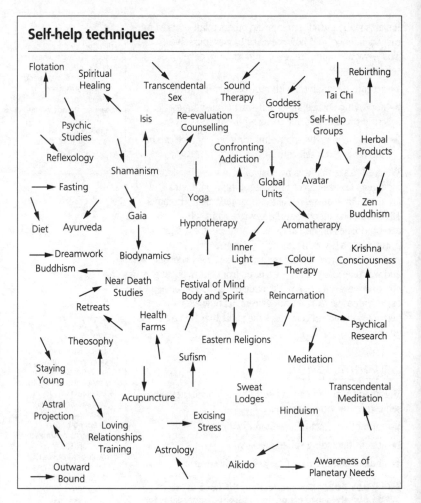

Flotation · Spiritual Healing · Transcendental Sex · Sound Therapy · Rebirthing · Tai Chi · Goddess Groups · Self-help Groups · Psychic Studies · Isis · Re-evaluation Counselling · Herbal Products · Reflexology · Confronting Addiction · Shamanism · Global Units · Avatar · Zen Buddhism · Fasting · Yoga · Gaia · Aromatherapy · Diet · Ayurveda · Hypnotherapy · Krishna Consciousness · Dreamwork · Biodynamics · Inner Light · Colour Therapy · Buddhism · Near Death Studies · Festival of Mind Body and Spirit · Reincarnation · Retreats · Health Farms · Psychical Research · Theosophy · Eastern Religions · Meditation · Staying Young · Sufism · Sweat Lodges · Transcendental Meditation · Astral Projection · Acupuncture · Excising Stress · Hinduism · Loving Relationships Training · H. · Astrology · Aikido · Awareness of Planetary Needs · Outward Bound

'**W**hen a man is wrapped up in himself, he makes a pretty small package.'
JOHN RUSKIN

This would be a relatively easy concept if we were all the same as one another, but that is far from being the case! Each of us has a different temperament and personality, and each is designed to respond separately and uniquely to God's direction.

People are different from each other in terms of the way in which they feel most comfortable doing things. For example...

▶ some plan ahead in detail—others keep their options open

▶ some like their own company—others thrive on being with friends

▶ some let their head rule their heart—others let their heart rule their head

▶ some are always looking for new ways to do things—others stick to the tried and tested.

It is not that any of these ways of doing things is 'right' or 'wrong', any more than being right-handed or left-handed is 'right' or 'wrong'. However, problems arise when we believe and behave as though...

▶ what works for one person will work for everyone

▶ our way is *the* way and others had better shape up

▶ we fail to understand that our way of doing things can create problems for others.

KEY POINT An understanding of our temperament, and the temperament of others, will improve both our own effectiveness and that of the other people to whom we relate.

In particular, those who work together ignore the significance of temperament at their peril.

The Myers–Briggs Type Indicator

The most widely used method to identify the different kinds of temperament and their implications is the Myers–Briggs Type Indicator.

Starting in the 1920s, two US women, Katherine Cook Briggs and her daughter, Isabel Briggs Myers, developed an inventory to help people understand themselves and others. Using a self-analysis questionnaire, they helped people to identify what they would most naturally do in a hypothetical situation.

By this method, they identified two alternative preferences for each of four basic ways in which we focus our attention on the outer or inner world.

These are as follows…

1 What is your preferred world of activity?

▶ or the outer world of people and things— **Extroversion**

▶ the inner world of ideas and concepts—**Introversion**

CHARACTERISTICS

Extroversion	Introversion
outward orientation to people and things	inward orientation to concepts and ideas
want to change the world	want to understand the world
relaxed and confident	reserved and questioning
after-thinker	forethinker
action orientated	quiet and concentrated
blurt it out	keep thoughts to oneself
value breadth	value depth

E ◀————————————————▶ I

Extroversion   **Introversion**

2 What is your preferred way of gathering information?

▶ using the five senses—**Sensing**

▶ or using your intuition and noticing what might be or could be rather than what is—**Intuition**

CHARACTERISTICS

Sensing	Intuition
use the five senses	use 'sixth sense' plus possibilities
details	the big picture, patterns
practical	theoretical, innovative
present orientation	future possibilities
facts	insights
step by step	jump about
live life as it is	want to change life

S ◀————————————————▶ N

Sensing   **Intuition**

3 What is your preferred way of evaluating information and making decisions?

▶ using logic, analysis and objectivity—**Thinking**

▶ or subjectively, appreciating the particular circumstances and your values—**Feeling**

CHARACTERISTICS

Thinking	Feeling
head	heart
logical	human values and needs
objective	subjective
things	people
truth	tact
justice	mercy
principles	harmony
impersonal / brief	personal / friendly
reason	empathy
exposes wrong	care and concern for others

T ◀————————————————▶ F

Thinking   **Feeling**

4 What is your preferred way of living?

▶ having everything structured, planned, organized and decided—**Judging**

▶ or being more spontaneous, flexible and open— **Perceiving**

CHARACTERISTICS

Judging	Perceiving
decisive	curious
planned	spontaneous
exacting	tolerant
settled	tentative
purposeful and controlled	adaptable
make quick decisions	postpone decisions
set goals	gather information
organized	flexible
focus on completion	focus on starting
run one's life	let life happen

J ◀————————————————▶ P

Judging   **Perceiving**

Most people have a preference and sometimes it is a very strong one. Either way, the preference is then defined by the appropriate letter in each case. Thus, each person's temperament is defined by a combination of four letters, such as ISTJ, ENTP, ESFJ, etc. This gives sixteen possible combinations. But within each of the sixteen there will still be differ-ences due to the relative strengths of preference that each person has.

The above is a brief and general introduction to a very complex subject. Remember…

▶ a full Myers–Briggs test involves 126 questions and a detailed analysis

▶ some people have very strong preferences, while others do not

▶ it is possible to develop those aspects of our temperament that do not represent our preference

▶ there are no 'good' or 'bad' types—every type contributes special gifts to the world.

Knowing and understanding our type helps us to develop more fully as people, and also to work more effectively with others.

Temperament and prayer

KEY POINT Ways of praying are rich and diverse, and different temperaments respond to different styles of prayer.

Unfortunately, most Christians are probably channelled into a particular form of praying favoured by their local church. Such a restricted approach will suit some temperaments but not others. As a result, some people may even be tempted to give up on prayer altogether.

The following lists give a general impression of the flavours of prayer that correspond to our personality preferences...

Extroversion	Introversion
settles readily with the most suited approach	complex prayer patterns
enjoys prayer with others	enjoys praying in solitude
prayer linked with service and action	prayer non-conforming
'hands on' praying	'background' praying

Sensing	Intuition
puts off prayer if conditions are difficult	may not feel the need for specific prayer time
in touch with real situations	meaning and insight are important
step-by-step approach	importance of creativity (music, poetry, etc.)
concerned with present rather than future possibilities	concerned with future possibilities

Thinking	Feeling
ordered and logical (use of prayer lists, etc.)	needs strong emotional motivation
theological perspectives are important	dedicated to approach of church or organization
considers carefully before making commitment	concerned about issues of injustice, etc.
values clear thinking in prayer-life	values personal feelings in prayer

Judging	Perceiving
needs a settled system of praying	open to different styles of prayer
can persist with even unsuitable approaches	takes risks with unfamiliar types of prayer
finds uncertainty over times for prayer difficult	comfortable with uncertainty over times of prayer

It is helpful to identify what forms of prayer suit us most and major on these. We also need, from time to time, to experiment with other types of prayer as these may lead us to a new awareness of God.

Some approaches deliberately try to cater for different aspects of the personality. For example...

▶ careful study of a passage from the Bible (Sensing)

▶ a time of meditation on what God is saying to me (Thinking)

▶ allowing what God has said to stir me into intercession (Feeling)

▶ a concluding time of stillness, perhaps with reflective music, in which God is contemplated (Intuition).

Temperament and worship

Similarly, although God calls us to worship him with our entire being, our various temperaments respond more readily to certain forms of worship than others. As in prayer, it is important...

▶ to understand why certain types of worship appeal to us

▶ to learn, from time to time, to develop our more neglected responses.

The following give only some general pointers to our preferences...

Extroversion	Introversion
big gatherings	smaller gatherings
opportunity to relate to others	opportunity for quiet reflection
enjoys participation	prefers anonymity
links worship to action	links worship to experience
values God's closeness (immanence)	values God's beyond-ness (transcendence)

Sensing	Intuition
use of all senses	use of insights and imagination
likes detail and specifics	likes broader perspectives and possibilities
secure in known patterns of worship	likes change in patterns of worship
links worship to what can be seen, handled, etc.	values symbols and metaphors
values God's reality in the everyday (incarnation)	values God as Spirit (the mystery of God)

Thinking	Feeling
use of reason and speculation	expression of emotions
values theological emphasis	values relationships within worshipping community
likes to understand principles of worship	emphasis on the personal and immediate
values acquisition of knowledge	importance of values and ideals
values God as source of all truth	values God in personal relationship (Father, Friend, etc.)

Judging	Perceiving
values order and discipline	values spontaneity and element of fun
likes worship to have definable results	enjoys the process of a time of worship
emphasis on the response of the will	emphasis on awareness
values initiative in worship	values responsiveness in worship
values God as Ruler and Judge	values God as Redeemer and Healer

Temperament and teamwork

KEY POINT Myers–Briggs not only helps us with self-awareness, it is also useful in understanding interaction, decision-making and the handling of conflict within groups.

Here are some of the ways that different aspects of temperament respond in teamwork...

Extroversion	Introversion
prefers action	prefers ideas
energized by what is going on	energized by quiet reflection (value of coffee breaks!)
focus on world of people and things	focus on inner world

Sensing	Intuition
interested in facts	interested in possibilities (brainstormers)
emphasis on what will work	good at making links in problem-solving
adopts step-by-step approach	likes new projects, new perspectives

Thinking	Feeling
analyses impersonally	analyses personally
counts the cost of strategies	weighs up alternatives as to how deeply felt they are
sticks to ground-rules and principles	sticks to values and how people feel

Judging	Perceiving
decisive	flexible
orderly	spontaneous
controlling	understanding

In Western society, the ESTJ personality is highly valued (Extroversion, Sensing, Thinking, Judging). He or she is...

▶ action-oriented

▶ concerned with the facts

▶ logical and decisive

▶ often found in executive positions.

KEY POINT For teamwork, though, all temperaments are needed.

Other personality types should be seen as equally valuable in the process of planning, clarifying and decision-making.

For example, those who have **introverted** and **intuitive** preferences are needed to...

▶ generate new ideas

▶ look at unexpected possibilities

▶ see wider implications.

Those with **feeling and perceiving** preferences are essential because they...

▶ remember that people matter

▶ challenge the team to take note of personal values

▶ encourage flexibility and spontaneity.

Often, the extrovert dominates the early stages of a team's meeting by talking readily. It is essential that the leader encourages the more reflective introvert to express ideas too. See the box, 'Teamwork', for an example of a team situation.

Teamwork

Eight Christians are planning a mission to an urban area with high unemployment and poor housing.

▶ **Dave** is the team leader. He has wide experience of similar situations, and has thought through a plan very thoroughly. He is determined, though, to give his less experienced team a fair hearing.

▶ **Jane** has a lot to say, but tends to speak before thinking things through.

▶ **Nick** is irritated by her talkativeness and longs for a coffee break to get his ideas together.

▶ **Jim** is the 'hands on' man. He is very practical and keeps saying to Dave, 'Come on, you're the one who knows how these missions tick—what will actually work when we get down to it?'

▶ **Sue** has great vision for the needs of the estate they will visit, and is full of creative (but sometimes impractical) suggestions.

▶ **Liz** feels that all the talk, all the ideas, all the practicalities, all the words about the meaning of mission, leave out how the people of the estate will feel when this lot barges in.

▶ **Sarah** is enjoying the discussion and just wishes some of the team members wouldn't be so rigid in their approach. She reckons they must keep an open mind and feel their way with people on the estate.

▶ **John** thinks that Dave should exercise more control over the meeting and bring the whole thing to a conclusion by 10 o'clock prompt.

Which members do you identify with in this team? How would you allow for the varieties of approach in working out a strategy and reaching decisions?

Psychometric testing

There are a number of other psychometric tests which identify temperament and aptitude. These have become extremely popular in both business and general management training. Many Christian organizations and missionary societies now use tests in their selection

---

MEMO

To: Jesus, Son of Joseph, Woodcrafters' Carpenter Shop, Nazareth 25922

From: Jordan Management Consultants

Dear Sir,

Thank you for submitting the resumé for the twelve men you have picked for management positions in your new organization. All of them have now taken our battery of tests.

We have not only run the tests through our computer, but also arranged personal interviews for each of them with our psychologist and vocational aptitude consultants. The profiles of all tests are included, and you will want to study each of them carefully.

As part of our services for your guidance, we make some general comments. It is the staff's opinion that most of your nominees are lacking in background, education and vocational aptitudes for the type of enterprise you are undertaking. They do not have the team concept. We would recommend that you continue your search for persons of experience with managerial ability and proven capabilities.

Simon Peter is emotionally unstable and given to fits of temper.

Andrew has absolutely no qualities of leadership.

James and John---the sons of Zebedee---place personal interests above company loyalty.

Thomas demonstrates a questioning attitude that would tend to undermine morale.

We feel it is our duty to tell you that Matthew has been struck off by the Greater Jerusalem Better Business Bureau.

James, the son of Alphaeus, and Thaddaeus definitely have radical leanings, and they both registered a high score on the manic-depressive scale.

One of the candidates, however, shows great potential. He's a man of ability and resourcefulness, meets people well, has a keen business mind, and has contacts in high places. He is highly motivated, ambitious and responsible. We recommend Judas Iscariot as your comptroller and right-hand man.

Jordan Management Consultants

PAUSE FOR THOUGHT

What are the implications of the modern ideas about temperament for evangelism?

process or as part of staff development. These tests may:

▶ help self-understanding and increase tolerance of those who are different

▶ help people to identify their strengths and potential strengths which may have been stifled by others or by circumstances

▶ illustrate weaknesses and areas of life that need attention

▶ encourage teamwork.

Testing of this kind, however, has its critics. It is often seen as only being relevant to Western culture. Psychometric testing only produces generalizations and cannot fully reflect the uniqueness of the individual. For many Christians it fails to acknowledge the unpredictability of the Holy Spirit's activity to change and equip the life of the believer.

Just as there is unlikely to be a reason for the Holy Spirit to alter someone's preference to right-handedness, the same is no doubt true for someone's temperament. After all, it was God who made the essence of who we are!

5 Designed by God

Despite our own humanity, the Christian doctrine of what it means to be human is perhaps the one we least understand. Yet it is of critical importance to each one of us.

The whole of this century has been haunted by the question of what it is to be a human being. Debates have raged about the origins of life, evolution, genetic research, euthanasia, and many others—and they all stem from this central question.

KEY POINT More than ever, Christians should be able to give strong biblical answers to the big questions of human life.

Our secularized, materialistic society, currently under invasion by New Age beliefs, needs to hear an alternative view of life—as designed by God.

This section explores what the Bible has to tell us about being human, starting with the creation accounts of Genesis 1.

Designed to crown God's creation

The creation of men and women by God is told in Genesis chapters 1 and 2. The story is both humbling and inspiring.

The origins of humankind are rather humbling...

▶ women may object to the idea of being created from Adam's spare rib...

▶ but the male of the species has little reason to feel superior—he is made from the dust of the ground (Genesis 2:7).

In the light of the awesome character of creation, and its Creator, human beings are put firmly into perspective.

However, God does not leave them there, because he made humankind to be uniquely different to the rest of the creation. Instead of a mere physical and emotional

> '*L*et us make man in our image, in our likeness...'
> GOD SPEAKING IN GENESIS 1

> '*T*here would be no absolute loss if every human being were to die tomorrow. Man is the mistake of creation.'
> D.H. LAWRENCE

being, the man (and from him, the woman) is created as 'a living soul' (Genesis 2:7, AV), in the image of God himself (Genesis 1:27).

KEY POINT The Bible does not see humankind as a mistake or a moment of madness on God's part, but as the crowning glory of his created order.

As one Bible writer expresses it: 'You made him inferior only to yourself; you crowned him with glory and honour. You appointed him ruler over everything you have made; you placed him over all creation...' (Psalm 8:5–6).

Designed in God's image

The Genesis story uses a striking phrase in describing the creation of men and women: 'Then God said, "And now we will make human beings; they will be like us and resemble us..." And so God created human beings, making them to be like himself. He created them male and female...' (Genesis 1:26–27). Older versions of the Bible describe human beings as being made in the 'image' of God.

What does it mean to be made in God's image or likeness? How are we a reflection of God? Some people have asked whether 'the image of God' refers to a physical likeness...

▶ **in ancient Babylonian myths** man is described as being made in the physical likeness of his gods

▶ **in the Book of Genesis** Adam's son Seth is said to be 'a son in his own likeness, after his image' (AV)

▶ **one or two early church writers** such as Irenaeus believed the 'image of God' was a physical likeness— he believed all human beings bear a physical resemblance to God, but only those made perfect by the work of the Holy Spirit reflect God's moral nature.

However, the idea of a physical resemblance is very much a minority view. God is Spirit—he is way beyond anything that we can think or imagine.

There are several positive ways in which we can think about being made in God's image...

A mark of ownership—words such as 'image' and 'likeness' were carved into the statues of the kings of Assyria in the time of the Old Testament. The statues were then set up to proclaim the ruler's ownership of a territory and his authority over it. By saying that we carry God's image, the Genesis account declares that we are God's representatives on earth, put here as a mark of his ownership of the earth and to rule it in his name. God gives us some of his attributes—such as justice, wisdom, creativity, love—so that we can rule the earth as he would.

A unique gift—in the Bible, it is only men and women who are described as being made in God's image. In contrast to modern, secular views of humanity, the Bible teaches that we are different from the animals. We are different not just because we do things differently, but because of who we are.

Knowing and loving God—human beings are created so that they can know God and respond to him in love. Our sense of right and wrong is not merely learned by experience, it is something that God has planted in us.

Sharing God's creativity—God has created us with minds that can learn about and explore God's creation. We are also created so that we in turn can create—in music, painting, writing, and through our relationships

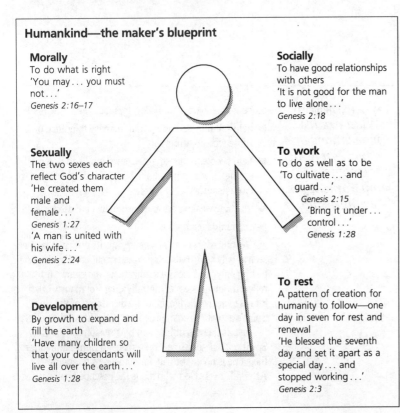

Humankind—the maker's blueprint

Morally
To do what is right
'You may... you must not...'
Genesis 2:16–17

Sexually
The two sexes each reflect God's character
'He created them male and female...'
Genesis 1:27
'A man is united with his wife...'
Genesis 2:24

Development
By growth to expand and fill the earth
'Have many children so that your descendants will live all over the earth...'
Genesis 1:28

Socially
To have good relationships with others
'It is not good for the man to live alone...'
Genesis 2:18

To work
To do as well as to be
'To cultivate... and guard...'
Genesis 2:15
'Bring it under... control...'
Genesis 1:28

To rest
A pattern of creation for humanity to follow—one day in seven for rest and renewal
'He blessed the seventh day and set it apart as a special day... and stopped working...'
Genesis 2:3

with others. We are also 'sub-creators' with God in the creation of children.

The imprint of love—the Bible specifically includes both man and woman as made in God's image (Genesis 1:27). This means that our sexuality and our ability to give and receive love also reflects the character of the God who made us.

An eternal relationship—being made in God's image also means that we are made for eternal life with God. This is one of God's original gifts to us as human beings. Almost immediately after the creation of men and women, the Bible moves on to the story of how they rebelled against God. When this happened, the image of God was defaced and spoiled. Each of the above areas of the image of God was affected.

However, it is important to remember that even after the fall, human beings were still divine image-bearers (Genesis 9:6; James 3:9).

> **KEY POINT** The biblical view is that we are no mere cosmic accident. Humankind is the pinnacle of God's creation. We are different from all that has gone before and represent the fulfilment of God's plans and purposes.

Designed for a reason

What is the place of humankind in creation? There are two elements to bear in mind here...

Humility—human beings are less than God. We are finite and small (Psalm 8:3–4; 103:15–16), especially in comparison to him (Psalm 8:1–2).

Greatness—we are superior to the rest of creation because God has uniquely loved and gifted us to rule over all that he has made (Psalm 8:4–8). In this sense, there is a God-given greatness about being human.

We have to hold these two elements in tension when thinking about how God created us. On the one hand we should not reject our dignity and uniqueness. But on the other, we must not overlook God's absolute authority and supremacy. We are what we are because of God.

> **KEY POINT** God has entrusted us as caretakers of this world.

We are to be governors of the planet, but this fact never gives us a licence to exploit it. We are here not only to be environmentally aware, but to act as custodians of God's created order.

Adam and Eve were not created for an idle life...

▶ before their expulsion from the Garden of Eden they were responsible for its care and upkeep—they were accountable to God for it (Genesis 2:15)

▶ Adam was given the task of naming the animals (Genesis 2:19–20)

▶ There was to be fulfilment and satisfaction in purposeful work—work was always intended to constitute an essential part of our humanity.

Designed as whole persons

One Bible writer worships God by saying: 'I praise you because I am fearfully and wonderfully made' (Psalm 139:14).

> **KEY POINT** The Bible reflects the intricacy of our creation by using a wide variety of words to describe us.

The effects of 'the fall' are described in more detail on page 22.

PAUSE FOR THOUGHT

Are you a good reflection of God?

> '**S**ince God has made man in his own image, man is not caught in the wheels of determinism. Rather man is so great that he can influence history for himself and for others, for this life and the life to come.'
> FRANCIS SCHAEFFER

> '**U**nderstand that you have within yourself, on a small scale, a second universe: within you there is a sun, there is a moon, and there are also stars.'
> ORIGEN

These words describe human beings as they act, think, feel, decide, reflect on themselves—and as they simply are. A number of these words are explored below. In looking at them, it is important to remember...

▶ The Bible sees us as whole persons—and not as creatures of many different bits and pieces (body, soul, mind, etc.).

▶ Each of the different words used to describe us gives a different angle on the whole personality, rather than describing separate parts.

▶ A rich variety of words is used. In the past, Christians have debated whether human beings are made up of body and soul, or body, soul and spirit. However, neither of these models does justice to the range of descriptions used in the Bible.

▶ Many of the words overlap each other in meaning. Paul, for example, often uses 'soul' and 'spirit' to describe the same thing, and sometimes even does this with 'flesh' and 'spirit'. The Bible does not set out a scientific description of how human beings are made up.

> **KEY POINT** A number of key words used in talking about human life are as follows...

Flesh

This word points to our physical existence as men and women created by God. It is used in a number of ways in the New Testament...

Physical existence—the person seen purely as a physical being, without the spiritual dimension

Part of the created order—belonging to the human race, the Jewish race, and so on ('flesh' is used in 1 Corinthians 10:18 and Philippians 1:24, although not in modern translations)

Our otherness from God—the flesh in itself is not sinful (after all, God made it, and the Word 'became flesh'—John 1:14), but if we live only 'in the flesh' and not 'in the Spirit', then we fall into sin and cannot please God (Romans 8:8).

The Greek word for 'flesh' is *sarx*—from which we get 'sarcophagus', 'sarcastic', etc.

Body

The Bible is 'friendly' towards the body, teaching that God made it and that the body is an essential part of who we are...

The body is good—some heresies have taught that the body is in itself evil, but the Bible tells us that God was pleased with his creation of the body (Genesis 1:31)

To glorify God—the body (like all the other aspects of ourselves) can be used for sin, but it is meant to be used 'for the Lord' (1 Corinthians 6:13), and in our worship of God (Romans 12:1)

The spiritual body—Paul teaches that at the resurrection, our bodies will be raised as 'spiritual bodies' (1 Corinthians 15:42–44)—our future hope is not that our souls will be released from our bodies, but that we will be raised as Christ was.

The Greek word for 'body' is *soma*—from which we get 'psychosomatic'.

Conscience

This word originally meant 'joint-knowledge' with another person. In the New Testament, it means knowledge of ourselves, the ability to judge our thoughts and actions against external standards. The New Testament letters teach...

To be taken seriously—conscience is God-given and must be obeyed, even when it is weak (Romans 13:5; 1 Corinthians 8:12)

Clear conscience—a clear conscience is essential in living as a Christian (Romans 9:1; 1 Timothy 1:19; 1 Peter 3:16)

It is limited—God is the final judge of our actions, and our judgment of ourselves can either fall short or be misguided (1 Corinthians 4:4–5).

The Greek word for 'conscience' is *suneidesis*.

Soul

In the Bible, the word 'soul' does not describe a separate part of us, but instead means 'vitality' or 'life' itself. The Old Testament word for 'soul' is *nephesh*, which came from the word for 'throat'—connecting it with the idea of breath. It is a flexible word and is used in a number of ways...

The whole person—'Bless the Lord, O my soul' (Psalm 103:1, AV) means 'Let my whole self bless the Lord'

A focus of feeling—it is the soul which expresses our deepest feelings and which longs for God (this comes especially in the Psalms—see Psalm 31:9; 42:1–2, 5; 94:19)

The eternal dimension—'soul' is used to express our ultimate value as human beings, the aspect of us that we must not lose, whatever the cost (Matthew 10:28; 16:26; Hebrews 6:19).

The Greek word for 'soul' is *psuche*—from which we get 'psychology', 'psychopath', etc.

Mind

For the Greek philosophers of Paul's time, the mind was the part of us where abstract thought takes place. However, Paul's picture of the mind is very different...

The active mind—the mind is the place of thinking, but it is the sort of thinking which leads to action (Romans 12:2)

Area of the will—the mind decides between good and evil, leading us to willing acts that either take us into the darkness (Romans 1:21) or into a renewal of our minds (Ephesians 4:23)

The mind of God—to know God's mind is to receive a revelation of his will and to have insight into the depths of God (Romans 11:34; 1 Corinthians 2:16).

The Greek word for 'mind' is *nous*—from which we get 'nous', meaning 'common sense'.

Heart

The New Testament often uses 'heart' in exactly the same way as 'mind' in describing human thinking and willing. 'Heart' contains all the meaning of 'mind', but it goes beyond it in a number of ways...

The emotions—the main feature of the heart is that it is moved by feelings of love, pain, and so on (Romans 9:2; 2 Corinthians 8:16)

> '**M**an is nothing but fat enough for seven bars of soap; iron enough for one medium-sized nail; sugar enough for seven cups of tea; lime enough to whitewash one chicken coop; phosphorus enough to tip 2,200 matches; magnesium enough for one dose of salts; potash enough to explode one toy crane; sulphur enough to rid one dog of fleas.'
>
> PROFESSOR C.E.M. JOAD

> '**T**his description of man as soul and spirit must not, of course, be misconstrued as implying that man is composed of different and self-contained compartments. It is clear that the biblical authors wrote and spoke on the firm assumption of man's psychosomatic unity.'
>
> GEORGE CAREY

For further teaching about the Trinity and relationships, see pages 35–37.

Our true selves—what people are at heart is often used in contrast to what they appear to be from the outside: a desire from the heart is a true and deep desire; an event in the heart is a significant event; a state of the heart is a real state, despite outward appearances (Jeremiah 29:13; Romans 10:9; 2 Corinthians 5:12; 1 Peter 1:22)

God and the heart—God deals directly with the human heart (2 Corinthians 4:6); his law is written on our hearts (Romans 2:15); he creates in us new hearts which respond to his Spirit (Ezekiel 36:26).

The Greek word for 'heart' is *kardia*—from which we get 'cardiac', etc.

Spirit

The Bible's use of 'heart' overlaps considerably with its use of 'spirit'. However, there are differences between the two words. More than any other in the Bible, 'spirit' is used to describe our deep, inner selves, the aspect of us that relates 'upwards' to God...

Breath of God—the Old Testament word for 'spirit' is *ruach* and is the same word that is used for 'wind' or 'breath'—it is the spirit that gives us life and animation (Job 34:14–15; Ecclesiastes 12:7; James 2:26)

Inner being—Paul contrasts the spirit and the flesh: the flesh gives us a superficial, external view of ourselves, while the spirit shows us our true, inner depths (Philippians 3:3; 1 Corinthians 2:11)

Spirit of God—the spiritual aspect of us is able to perceive God at work—more than the mind or even the soul (1 Corinthians 14:14), and life lived in the spirit is life directed towards God (1 Corinthians 2:15–16) because God himself is Spirit.

The Greek word for 'spirit' is *pneuma*—from which we get 'pneumatic' and 'pneumonia'.

6 *Made for each other*

KEY POINT God has not designed us as solitary and separate individuals. We can only be fully human when we are in community with others.

By giving us emotional and spiritual dimensions God not only distinguishes us from the rest of creation, but gives us the capacity to love and enjoy personal relationships with others and with himself. This is part of what it means to be made 'in the image of God' (Genesis 1:27).

The basis for our relationships is God himself. The creation account hints at this when it says: 'Then God said, "Let us make man in our image..."' (Genesis 1:26). God is spoken of in the plural here—'us'—and this points forward to the Christian idea of God as a Trinity...

▶ God is a 'community' of three equal persons

▶ these three persons relate to each other in love (John 17:24)

▶ God is 'three persons in one substance': the community is also a unity.

The being of God himself will always be a mystery to us. We can never fully comprehend God—if we could, he would not be God. However, the Bible's teaching about the Trinity is the foundation for all our relationships. God is a personal God; he relates to others. As we reach out and relate in love to other persons, we start to find our true identity.

Hungry for God

> **KEY POINT** Human beings are created with a longing for God.

We are made to live in relationship to him. We only find true value and meaning as people when we find God for ourselves. This hunger for God can be seen in many ways...

▶ in the vast variety of religions in the world which search for God in different ways

▶ in the sacrifices people make in pursuing the different religious faiths

▶ in the emptiness and despair of the twentieth-century thinkers, writers, artists and politicians who have rejected belief in God.

This hunger for God runs throughout the Bible. It comes up against the fact of human sin, which blocks our relationship with him, and which must somehow be overcome. This can be seen in...

▶ the Old Testament system of sacrifices which was designed to cleanse the people's sins and restore their relationship with God

▶ the cry of the Psalms for God's presence and help (Psalm 63:1; 69:16–18)

▶ the great Old Testament hope that all people will know God for themselves (Jeremiah 24:7; 31:34)

▶ Jesus coming as 'God with us' (Matthew 1:23; John 1:14)

▶ the 'new and living way' opened up for us to draw near to God, through the death of Jesus (Hebrews 10:19–22).

The two sexes

The opening chapter of Genesis is full of God's comments on creation...

▶ on every occasion he concludes that it is 'good' (Genesis 1:4, 10, 12, 18, 21, 25) or 'very good' (Genesis 1:31)

▶ in contrast, as God looks at Adam, his reaction is, 'It is not good for the man to be alone' (Genesis 2:18).

Human beings need others. Primarily, this verse is about community—it is not good for anyone, married or single, to be alone. 'Two are better than one', as the writer of Ecclesiastes puts it (Ecclesiastes 4:9–12).

The Bible's teaching about the two sexes includes the following key points...

Man and woman together reflect the image of God—Most Christians agree that God is neither male nor female. His being is beyond sexuality. According to Genesis chapter 1, God did not create woman as an afterthought, but as an integral part of his creation of humanity (Genesis 1:27).

> **KEY POINT** This means that neither sex uniquely bears the image of God. Instead, God's image is shown by both sexes, living in relationship to each other.

This is a very important point, because it shows the fundamental equality of man and woman. When one sex is oppressed by the other, it is a sign of human sinfulness.

Commissioned as partners—In Genesis chapter 2, God creates a suitable partner for Adam. Two short

> '*Y*ou have made us for yourself, and our hearts are restless until they find their rest in you.'
> AUGUSTINE

Hebrew words are used, and together they start to build up a picture of the relationship between the two sexes...

▶ The first word means 'helper' (the Hebrew word '*ezer*). One writer describes this word as 'the embodiment of inner and outer encouragement'. The emphasis here is on the wife helping her husband. Elsewhere in the Bible the balance of the husband helping his wife is given (for example in 1 Timothy 3:3).

▶ The second word means 'suitably opposite him', 'counterpart', or even 'matching him' (Hebrew *kenegdo*). It is only used in scripture this once.

The two words together give a wonderful picture of the ideal relationship between husband and wife, a relationship of equality and complementarity.

Human sexuality is good—The Bible sets human sexuality in the context of relationships. Sex is not something that should exist outside a permanent bond of love, respect and partnership between a man and a woman.

This is expressed strongly in Genesis. The writer comments on the union between the man and the woman with the words later quoted by Jesus: 'For this reason a man will leave his father and mother and be united to his wife, and they will become one flesh' (Genesis 2:24).

▶ the word used for 'unite' is a very strong word—it implies passion and permanence, an even tighter bond than that which previously existed between parent and child

▶ the union is more than just coming together sexually—the sexual act is an essential part of the union, symbolizing the consummation of two people choosing to live as one—but the act of love is not the union itself

▶ the reason for our sexuality is not primarily for the procreation of children, but to bring us into relationship with each other.

Sex is a gift of God—Like every other aspect of our humanity, sex can be misused and lead us into sin. But sex itself is good, given by God for us to enjoy. This has to be emphasized, because the church has frequently taught or implied that sex is shameful, or even sinful.

This largely stems from the time when the church was under the influence of Greek philosophy, which saw the body as evil.

> **The Bible's approach to human sexuality is positive. To take just a few examples...**

▶ Adam and Eve were 'both naked, and they felt no shame' (Genesis 2:25)

▶ the Song of Songs in the Old Testament is a beautifully poetic celebration of erotic love

▶ marriage is seen as the pattern for humankind, and the Bible contains a number of 'love stories'—Isaac and Rebekah (Genesis 24), Ruth and Boaz (the Book of Ruth)

▶ marriage is considered an appropriate image to describe the relationship between God and his people (Hosea 1—3) and Christ and his church (Ephesians 5:22–23).

> '*G*od created man in order to have someone on whom to shower his love.'
> IRENAEUS OF LYONS

A family of relationships

There is no one word used in the Bible which means the same as our word 'family'.

The web of relationships in the Bible stretched out from the immediate family living in the house, to the extended family of grandparents, aunts, uncles and cousins, to the wider clan and tribe, and then to embrace the whole 'house of Israel'.

These relationships can be seen in a number of ways...

The whole community—the people of Israel were taught by Moses to show justice, compassion and respect to all members of the community, especially those in particular need...

▶ widows and orphans (Exodus 22:22–24)

▶ the elderly (Leviticus 19:32)

▶ the poor and foreigners (Leviticus 19:9–10).

The tribe or clan—the nation of Israel was made up of twelve tribes, descended from the twelve children of Jacob. Within the tribes, there were extended family networks, or clans. One such clan, from two villages, numbered at least 600 men (Judges 18:11). Loyalty within these groups often centred on...

▶ the right of individual protection

▶ the obligation to respond to a call to arms in an emergency

▶ the honouring of 'elders', who taught the customs and history of the tribe (Deuteronomy 32:7) and who administered justice (Deuteronomy 25:7–9).

The wider family—the extended family was a great deal more important in the Bible than it is today. Because there was less mobility, people tended to live in the village in which they were born, near to their close and more distant relatives...

▶ in the Old Testament, there were a number of obligations towards relatives (for example, Ruth 4:5)

▶ in the New Testament, the 'household' might include parents, children, relatives, friends, employees and slaves, all living under the same roof (Acts 18:8; 1 Corinthians 16:15).

The immediate family—the relationship between parents and children is very important in the Bible. For parents...

▶ the home was the place where the faith of Israel (and later, the Christian faith) was taught by parents to their children (Deuteronomy 6:7; Ephesians 6:4)

▶ children were to be taught how to live by their parents, and brought up with firm discipline (Proverbs 22:6; 23:13)

▶ church leaders were to manage their children and their household well (1 Timothy 3:12).

For children...

▶ the fifth commandment tells children to 'honour your father and your mother...' (Exodus 20:12)

▶ respect and care had to be shown to parents and grandparents (1 Timothy 5:4).

Friendship—as an issue, singleness is not really tackled in the Bible. Marriage is seen as God's pattern for society, although several passages point to singleness as an alternative pattern...

> '*N*o man is an Island, entire of itself; every man is a piece of the Continent, a part of the main.'
> JOHN DONNE

> '*A* friendship that can cease to be was never a friendship.'
> JEROME

> '*N*o age knows so much and so many things about man as does ours; and yet no age knows less than ours what man is.'
> MARTIN HEIDEGGER

> '*I*n our secular society the focus of man's attention has shifted from heaven to earth, from God to man. In doing so man has created a world where God has been squeezed out and where it is not only increasingly difficult to believe in God but also increasingly unnecessary to do so.'
> DEREK TIDBALL

▶ Jeremiah was called to remain unmarried as a prophetic warning to the people of his time (Jeremiah 16:1–4)

▶ singleness can be a call of God to Christians for the sake of God's kingdom (Matthew 19:10–12; 1 Corinthians 7:7–9)

▶ Jesus himself did not marry.

Friendship is valued very highly in the Bible. This comes across in the teaching of the Old Testament, the life of Jesus, and in the early church...

▶ In the Old Testament, a friend is someone who tells you the truth about yourself (Proverbs 27:6), who offers wise advice and does not fail in times of trouble (Proverbs 27:9–10)

▶ Jesus had three close friends—Peter, James and John (Mark 9:2)—the immediate group of twelve disciples, plus other friendships, including Mary, Martha and Lazarus (John 11:5), who seem to have been unmarried

▶ Jesus was also known as 'the friend of sinners' (Luke 7:34)—he reached out in friendship to people who were outcasts in his day

▶ In the early church, friendships were vital in spreading the good news—the partnerships of Paul and Silas, and later Paul and Barnabas, plus the many friends mentioned in Paul's letters, show how closely Paul worked through friendships (Romans 16:5; Colossians 4:14; Philemon 1).

7 Spoiled by sin

The Bible consistently affirms that we are all the unique creation of God himself (Psalm 139:13–16; Acts 17:25–26).

KEY POINT Something has clearly gone wrong with all the wonderful gifts God gave us at the creation.

Trouble in paradise

This is how just a few of these gifts (described on pages 18–19) have been spoiled...

▶ **Knowing God**—people long for God, but they do not know how to find him. Cut off from the life and love of God, they are also in the dark about their own identity.

▶ **Sharing God's authority**—we have abused our God-given responsibility for Planet Earth: burning rainforests, global warming, endangered species, pollution of the land, air and sea...

▶ **The imprint of love**—we are made to live in relationships, but at every level our relationships break down. Racism, divorce, the rich–poor divide, sexual discrimination, injustice—they all show a chronic failure of what we were created to be.

Genesis chapter 3 tells us what has gone wrong...

▶ Adam and Eve disobey God.

▶ their rebellion leads to their exile from paradise.

▶ they become alienated from God.

▶ they lose their true identity.

▶ they are no longer man and woman as God created them to be.

Giving evil a name

What is sin? Sin assumes many shapes, and has a devastating variety of effects—so much so that the Bible has to use a vast number of words to describe it. Some of the main terms used for sin are . . .

Old Testament words (Hebrew)	Meaning	Reference
chattath chet	missing the mark, erring	Psalm 25:7
pesha	deliberate rebellion	Proverbs 28:13
shagah	going astray	Leviticus 4:13
awon	perversity, to twist (guilt and its consequences)	Genesis 15:16
rasa	to act wickedly	2 Samuel 22:22
amal	mischief done to others	Proverbs 24:2

New Testament words (Greek)	Meaning	Reference
hamartia	missing the mark, failure,	Matthew 3:6
	actual wrong-doing, violating God's law	Acts 7:60
paraptoma	fall, blunder, offence, trespass	Ephesians 2:5
parabasis	transgression	Romans 4:15
asebeia	ungodliness, irreverence	2 Timothy 2:16
anomia	lawlessness	Matthew 7:23
adikia	injustice, doing wrong to neighbour,	
	unrighteousness	Luke 13:27
ptaio	stumble, offend	James 3:2
enochos	guilty (a legal term)	1 Corinthians 11:27
opheilema	debt, what is owing	Matthew 18:29–32

Effects of the fall

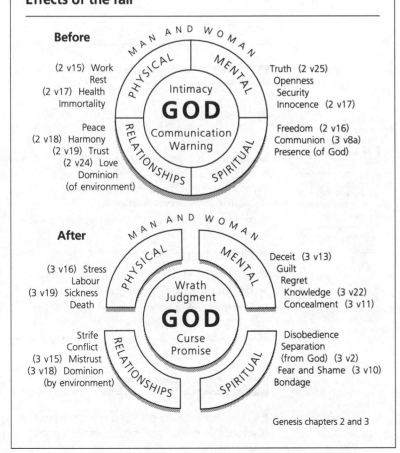

Genesis chapters 2 and 3

 KEY POINT The human race threw it all away. It is not enough for a Christian understanding of humanity merely to look at our creation.

Sin entered our lives and became the dominant fact of human history, introducing devastation, disorder and chaos.

When asked, 'What has gone wrong with our world?', Christians can only point to the reality of human sin. It is universal in its effect and implications. The Apostle Paul says that 'All have sinned and fall short of the glory of God' (Romans 3:23). Its effects are witnessed in the lives of individuals, in society and in the church on a worldwide scale.

All of this shows us that sin is much more than mere human selfishness. All sin is actually an offence against God (see Psalm 51:4; Proverbs 6:16–19; James 4:4). The consequences have been enormous, affecting every area of human life and relationships.

Guilty before God

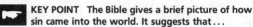

KEY POINT The Bible gives a brief picture of how sin came into the world. It suggests that . . .

▶ sin originated with the deliberate choice of certain angels, under Satan's leadership, to rebel against God (see 2 Peter 2:4; 1 John 3:8; Jude 6; Revelation 12:9)

▶ while the details of this first rebellion are indistinct, their effects are mirrored in the second rebellion, when Adam and Eve give way before the serpent's temptation (Genesis 3:1–7)

▶ by ignoring and rejecting what God has said, the first human beings broke their dependence on God— throughout history this remains the pattern that humankind has followed.

KEY POINT It is important to draw a distinction between specific wrong acts (sins) and the state of fallen humanity (sin—see Psalm 51:5).

We only carry out specific acts of sin because we are in a sinful state. However strong our longing to live as God intended, what happened at the beginning affects us today. Paul stressed this to the Christians in Rome: 'Therefore, just as sin entered the world through one man, and death through sin, in this way death came to all men, because all sinned' (Romans 5:12).

KEY POINT There are two ways in which this transmission of sin has been understood . . .

▶ **Genetically**—the genes of all their descendants were present in Adam and Eve, and therefore the effects and consequences of sin are passed on physically

▶ **By covenant**—Adam, as the representative of the whole human race, broke his agreement with God, and as we are all identified with him we suffer the same consequences.

The end result of sin is always death (Romans 6:23), both physical and spiritual. This happens in many ways . . .

Because we are accountable for our actions to our Creator we are subject to God's judgment. The Bible uses strong language here. The penalty for sin is . . .

▶ eternal separation from God (Matthew 6:23)

▶ facing God's anger (Romans 1:18)

▶ suffering in the hell prepared for the devil (Matthew 25:41).

Our major problem is that we are powerless to solve our most fundamental problem—the fact that we are guilty before God (Romans 5:8; 8:7–8). However, that is not the end of the story.

8 *Brought back to life*

If the Bible stopped at this point, it would have only the most devastating bad news to give to the human race. But it does not stop there.

KEY POINT The Bible tells us about God's response to human sin. It tells us about God's mission to rescue fallen humanity in the life and death of Jesus.

And now the good news . . .

The good news is that . . .

- sin does not have the last word
- God's love for us has not failed
- in the life, death and resurrection of Jesus, God worked to reconcile sinful humankind to himself
- Jesus makes it possible for us to come home again to God
- on the cross, he took the curse of sin upon himself, setting us free from its penalties and power.

Jesus also represents a new start for the human race. Because Jesus was fully a human being (as well as being fully God's Son), and lived a perfect human life, free from sin, he is the head of a new humanity. The Apostle Paul describes it in this way (see Romans 5:12–19) . . .

- **Adam** represents the old human race—fallen and guilty before God
- **Jesus** represents the new human race—reconciled to God, and living fully human lives, as God designed us.

The death and resurrection of Jesus marks the start of a new relationship between God and human beings. God gives us his Holy Spirit, who . . .

- lives in us
- brings the presence and power of God into our lives
- puts us directly in touch with the life and energy of God himself
- transforms us so that we become fully human, fully alive.

Describing the indescribable

The Bible has a vast, dark collection of words to describe human sin.

KEY POINT In the same way, the Bible pours out an extravagant wealth of pictures and descriptions to describe what Jesus has done for us.

We are . . .

- justified by faith (Romans 3:23–26)
- reconciled to God (Romans 5:10)
- saved from sin (Matthew 1:21)
- liberated from captivity (Luke 4:18)
- given the gift of eternal life (John 3:16)
- redeemed from the penalty of the law (Romans 3:28)

> '**S**in: Moral offence or shortcoming, condition of so offending.'
> CHAMBERS ENGLISH DICTIONARY

> "**W**ould you tell me, please, which way I ought to go from here?" asked Alice. "That depends a good deal on where you want to get to," said the Cat. "I don't much care where . . ." said Alice. "Then it doesn't matter which way you go," replied the Cat.'
> LEWIS CARROLL

> '**F**or since death came through a man, the resurrection of the dead comes also through a man. For as in Adam all die, so in Christ all will be made alive.'
> PAUL, IN 1 CORINTHIANS 15:21–22

- forgiven from our sin (Romans 8:1–2)
- sanctified, washed, cleansed (Acts 15:9)
- at peace with God (Acts 10:36)
- adopted by God (John 1:12–13)

We are changed from . . .

- darkness to light (Ephesians 5:8)
- slavery to freedom (Galatians 5:1)
- lost to found (Luke 15:24)
- separation to presence of God (Ephesians 2:12–13)
- death to life (Ephesians 2:5)
- old to new (2 Corinthians 5:17).

And finally, we become . . .

- a saint (Colossians 1:12)
- a child of God (Galatians 3:26; 4:6)
- seated with Christ (Ephesians 2:6)
- a citizen of heaven (Philippians 3:20)
- part of the worldwide church (1 Corinthians 12:12–13)
- united with Christ (1 Corinthians 6:15)
- an inheritor (Romans 8:17)
- a priest (1 Peter 2:9)
- a new creation (2 Corinthians 5:17)
- holy (Hebrews 10:10).

The amazing truth is that we have been chosen by God to be his people. Peter describes this by saying: 'But you are a chosen people, a royal priesthood, a holy nation, a people belonging to God, that you may declare the praises of him who called you out of darkness into his wonderful light' (1 Peter 2:9).

In other words, we have joined a new community of people. This new humanity of Jesus has a name—it is called the church.

Made for the glory of God

A lot of modern thinking is shot through with real despair . . .

- The cold, unfriendly universe of modern thought leaves many people with a sense of hopelessness and cosmic emptiness.
- Others try not to think about it too much. They put their ideas about death and what is beyond it into a 'pending' file which is never opened. Death is not a popular subject in our generation.

Stuart Briscoe speaks about the four articles of belief of modern secular culture . . .

- Man is the centre of the universe
- Time is the extent of our experience
- Earth is the limit of our environment
- Matter is the measure of value.

Armed with these beliefs, it is no surprise that people in today's world either collapse under the weight of despair, or turn to sport and soap operas for comfort.

KEY POINT Christians have a different perspective, because the Bible offers us real hope.

It tells us that we live in this world as strangers and pilgrims. It is a staging-post on the way to eternity

(1 Peter 2:11). While death is still a reality to be faced by Christians, it is not the end. Our journey's end lies beyond it, in the presence of God.

There we will find our true destiny, as human beings made and remade in the image of God...

▶ we will be with Jesus (Colossians 3:4).

▶ our transformed bodies will be like Jesus' body at his resurrection, because we will have traded the old one for an eternal model (Philippians 3:21).

▶ we will reign as co-heirs with Jesus and will share his glory (Romans 8:17; Colossians 3:4).

▶ we will have a greater vision and understanding of God's glory (John 17:24).

▶ our resting place in heaven will last for eternity (2 Corinthians 4:17 and 2 Timothy 2:10).

> '*D*ear Sir, What's wrong with the world? I am. Yours faithfully, G.K. Chesterton.'
> G.K. CHESTERTON, LETTER TO *THE TIMES*

All of this has an impact on how we live now...

▶ the hope we have for the future spills back into our everyday lives in the present.

▶ it tells us that our faith is not a 'privatized' sort of faith—it is not for me alone.

▶ being a Christian is not just another version of the self-fulfilment our culture craves—with a religious flavour.

Instead, true Christian faith opens us up to God and to other people.

Just as Jesus was open to others, so we are to form relationships, make friends, give people our time—and share with them the hope we have discovered. God has entrusted us with the greatest news possible in a despairing world.

Booklist

Adams, J.E., *Competent to Counsel*, Baker
Atkinson, D., *The Message of Genesis 1–11*, IVP
Berry R.J., editor, *Real Science, Real Faith*, Monarch
Blocher, H., *In the Beginning*, IVP
Boice, J.M., *Foundations of the Christian Faith*, IVP
Bullock, A., *The Fontana Dictionary of Modern Thought*, Fontana
Campolo, A., *Partly Right*, Word
Campolo, A., *The Success Fantasy*, Scripture Press
Campolo, A., *Who Switched the Price Tags?*, Word
Carey, G., *I Believe in Man*, Hodder & Stoughton
Chadwick, O., *The Secularisation of the European Mind in the Nineteenth Century*, CUP
Collins, G.R., *Christian Counselling*, Word
Crabb, L., *Inside Out*, Navpress
Craig, E., *The Mind Of God and the Works of Man*, OUP
Dobson, J., *Emotions, Can You Trust Them?*, Hodder & Stoughton
Ferguson, J., *O My People*, Oliphants
Getz, G.A., *The Measure of a Man*, Regal
Getz, G.A., *The Measure of a Woman*, Regal
Hawthorne, T., *Windows on Science and Faith*, IVP
Hirsh, S. and Kummerow, J., *Lifetypes*, Warner Books
Hodgkinson, L., *The Personal Growth Handbook*, Piatkus
Hughes, S., *How to Live the Christian Life*, Kingsway
Hunt, D. and Mcmahon, T.A., *The Seduction of Christianity*, Harvest House
Hurding, R.F., *Roots and Shoots*, Hodder & Stoughton
Hurding, R.F., *The Bible and Counselling*, Hodder & Stoughton
Hurding, R.F., *Restoring the Image*, Paternoster
Jones, G.R., *Naturally Gifted*, Scripture Union
Keay, K., *Men, Women and God*, Marshall Pickering
Keeley, R., editor, *An Introduction to the Christian Faith*, Lion
Keller, W.P., *Taming Tension*, Baker
Keyes, D., *Beyond Identity*, Hodder & Stoughton
Kidner, D., *Genesis*, Tyndale
Lahaye, T., *I Love You, But Why Are We So Different?*, Kingsway
Lahaye, T., *The Spirit Controlled Temperament*, Coverdale
Lyon, D., *The Steeple's Shadow*, SPCK
Mackay, D.M., *The Open Mind*, IVP
Macquarrie, J. and Childress, J., *A New Dictionary of Christian Ethics*, SCM Press

McClung, F., *Holiness and the Spirit of the Age*, Word
McCrone, J., *The Myth of Irrationality*, Macmillan
McDonald, H.D., *The Christian View of Man*, Marshall Morgan & Scott
McDonald, H.D., *I and He*, Epworth Press
McDowell, J. and Stewart, D., *Understanding Secular Religions*, Here's Life
McGrath, A., *Bridge Building*, IVP
McGrath, J. and A., *The Dilemma of Self-Esteem*, Crossway
Meier, P.D. and Minirth, F.B., *Introduction to Psychology and Counselling*, Monarch
Naisbitt, J. and Aburdene, P., *Megatrends 2000*, Pan
Naisbitt, J., *Megatrends*, Futura
Nee, W., *Release of the Spirit*, STL
Oddie, W., editor, *After the Deluge*, SPCK
Pascal, B., *The Mind On Fire*, Hodder & Stoughton
Paynes, L., *The Broken Image*, Kingsway
Pippert, R.M., *Hope Has its Reasons*, Marshall Pickering
Poole, M.A., *Guide to Science and Belief*, Lion
Robinson, H.W., *The Christian Doctrine of Man*, T&T Clark
Russell, B., *Why I am not a Christian*, Unwin
Sargant, W., *Battle for the Mind*, Unwin
Schaeffer, F.A., *The God Who is There*, Hodder & Stoughton
Schaeffer, F.A., *Escape from Reason*, IVP
Sire, J.W., *Discipleship of the Mind*, IVP
Sire, J.W., *The Universe Next Door*, IVP
Skinner, B.F., *About Behaviourism*, Penguin
Stallybrass, G., Trombley, S. and Campbell, E.V., editors, *A Dictionary of Pastoral Care*, SPCK
Tidball, D.A., *World Without Windows*, Scripture Union
Toffler, A., *Previews and Premises*, Pan
Toffler, A., *Future Shock*, Pan
Tournier, P.A., *Place for You*, SCM
Tozer, A.W., *Man, the Dwelling Place of God*, STL
Van Leeuwen, M.S., *Gender and Grace*, IVP
Virkler, H., *Speaking Your Mind*, Hodder & Stoughton
Waitley, D., *Psychology of Success*, Irwin
Walter, J.A., *All You Love Is Need*, SPCK
White, J., *The Shattered Mirror*, IVP
Wichern, F.B., Ratcliff, D.E. and McRoberts Ward, R., *Self-Esteem, Gift From God*, Baker
Zacharias, R.A., *Shattered Visage*, Wolgemouth & Hyatt

Partners
Working it out together

CONTENTS

Introduction: pictures of the church

1 Defining the word 'church'

2 According to the New Testament...

3 The church as a partnership

4 The Holy Trinity and community

5 The body of Christ

6 The bride of Christ

7 The building of God

8 *Koinonia* for beginners

Booklist

Book of the seminar day:
David Watson, *I Believe in The Church,*
Hodder & Stoughton

Introduction: pictures of the church

In our culture, people see the church in a wide variety of ways. It can be seen as:

a useful part of the wider community—as a social club, providing comfort and support for those who need its services

an antiquarian institution—because its buildings, structures and ceremonies have historical significance, it commands a degree of sentimental respect

a grotesque anachronism—the barely surviving relic of a bygone age, no longer relevant in the modern world

a benevolent society—not very efficient, but still a commendable, charitable institution

a gathering of religious people—who need the crutch of belief to carry them through life.

This diversity of views is not unusual. Ever since the church began, people have seen it in different ways. Christians also have different pictures of the church:

a hospital—Jesus once said: 'It is not the healthy who need a doctor, but the sick. I have not come to call the righteous, but sinners to repentance' (Luke 5:31–32). The church has often been seen as a sort of hospital, where people receive their healing from God and are made strong again.

an army—Some prefer Paul's picture of spiritual warfare in Ephesians 6. Martyn Lloyd Jones, the great twentieth-century preacher, once said: 'In the Bible I find a barracks, not a hospital. It is not a doctor you need but a Sergeant Major. Here we are on the parade ground slouching about. A doctor is no good; it is discipline we need. That is the trouble with the church today; there is too much of the hospital element; we have lost sight of the great battle.'

a society of saints—The church has often been seen as a community of people who have turned their backs on sin. This view believes that the church has to take sin very seriously, and it puts a strong emphasis on repentance and church discipline. Some have taken this to extremes. One early church leader, Novatian, taught that if a baptized Christian were to sin, then there could be no forgiveness.

a school for sinners—Some see the church as a place where sinners are welcomed with open arms. They are then taught how to repent and grow in righteousness. The church is like a school—a place where we learn how to live as Christians. It is a place where people can make mistakes without being condemned, and where we often have to learn the hard way.

an alternative society—This view focuses on Jesus' teaching about the kingdom of God. In the Sermon on the Mount (in Matthew 5–7), Jesus taught his followers to follow an alternative lifestyle, rejecting the accepted behaviour of the culture around them. The church is therefore an alternative community. The people in it offer each other love and acceptance, and show the world a radically different way to live. This view puts a strong emphasis on the group.

a battery recharge—Others see the church as a place where they can go once, twice, or more times a week, to refuel spiritually. They receive the teaching and encouragement they need, and then go back out into their

> '*The* church is not made up of people who are better than the rest, but of people who want to become better than they are.'
> ANON

> '*The* church may become a beggar, it may act like a shopkeeper, it may make itself a harlot, as has happened and still does happen, yet it is always the bride of Jesus Christ.'
> KARL BARTH

> '*The* church is the church only when it exists for others. To make a start, it should give away all its property to those in need. The clergy must live solely on the free-will offerings of their congregations, or possibly engage in some secular calling. The church must share in the secular problems of ordinary human life, not dominating, but helping and serving. It must tell men of every calling what it means to live for Christ, to exist for others.'
> DIETRICH BONHOEFFER

> '*The* Christian church is the one organisation in the world that exists purely for the benefit of non-members.'
> WILLIAM TEMPLE

place of work in the world, fully equipped to meet the challenges they face as Christians.

So there are many different views about the nature and character of the church. Every Christian probably has his or her own particular emphasis.

This section of the notes explores what Jesus intended his church to be and how the first Christians followed in his footsteps.

Did you know?

The Christian church is the world's largest body. In 1991 it had over 1.78 billion adherents—33.1 per cent of the world's population.

The Church of England has two provinces (Canterbury and York), 44 dioceses, 11,052 full-time clergy and 13,099 parishes (1991 figures).

The Roman Catholic Church has one Pope, 160 cardinals, 754 archbishops, 3,246 bishops, 401,479 priests, 885,645 nuns, and just over one billion nominal members (1989 figures).

The oldest Christian church building in the UK was built in Colchester in AD320. Its remains are next to the modern police station! St Martins, Canterbury (AD560), is the oldest surviving church.

The world's largest cathedral is St John the Divine, New York. The largest in the UK is Liverpool's Anglican Cathedral. The largest church building in the UK is Westminster Abbey.

Taken from *The Guinness Book of Records 1993*.

---

1 *Defining the word 'church'*

When the writers of the New Testament wrote about the church, they were not thinking of buildings, prayer books, pews, overhead projectors, pulpits or collection bags and it wasn't only because these things hadn't then been invented.

They were thinking of people. The people of God.

The church is 'people' together

The Bible has a lot of things to say about the church, but it is all built on this simple point:

 KEY POINT The church is not a building. The church is 'people'.

It is a community of people whose sins have been forgiven, whose lives are committed to Jesus Christ, and whose loyalty is to his people—the church.

There are many different ways of describing the Christian community. Some of the most striking words used to describe Christians in the New Testament are:

Servants—'Live as free men, but do not use your freedom as a cover-up for evil; live as servants of God' (Peter, in 1 Peter 2:16).

Friends—'I have called you friends, for everything that I learned from my Father I have made known to you' (Jesus, in John 15:15).

Children—'To all who received him, to those who believed in his name, he gave the right to become children of God' (Jesus, in John 1:12).

Witnesses—'You will receive power when the Holy Spirit comes on you; and you will be my witnesses in Jerusalem, and in all Judea and Samaria, and to the ends of the earth' (Jesus, in Acts 1:8).

Ambassadors—'We are therefore Christ's ambassadors, as though God were making his appeal through us. We implore you on Christ's behalf: Be reconciled to God' (Paul, in 2 Corinthians 5:20).

Each of these descriptions is in the plural. As Christians we fit these descriptions because we are part of the people of God.

KEY POINT The church is not a static, unchanging institution. Instead it is dynamic. The church happens when people receive the new life of Jesus and gather together to become servants, friends, children, witnesses and ambassadors.

Which version of 'the church'?

If we want to talk about the church in its fullest biblical sense, how should we understand it?

The word 'church' is used in a number of different senses today:

the local church—there were also local churches in New Testament times (at places such as Philippi, Corinth and Rome)

the Methodist / Pentecostal / etc. church—today there are over 22,000 denominations in the world, with five new ones added every week*

the Protestant church—there are three main 'families' of the 'church' around the world: Protestant, Catholic and Orthodox—most denominations belong to one of these three traditions

the worldwide church—the 1.78 billion people who are adherents to the church across the globe, according to the *Guinness Book of Records*

For the New Testament, none of these descriptions match what the church is in its fullest sense. For Paul and the other New Testament writers, there is only one church. We might talk about the Baptist Church or the Church of England, but in reality there are not many churches, but only one church.

The church is the family of all true Christian believers, past, present and future.

* Statistics taken from *The World Christian Encyclopedia*, edited by David Barrett, OUP, 1982.

The church visible and invisible

Christian leaders down the centuries have talked about the visible church and the invisible church. They did this to make an important point:

The visible church—this is the church everyone can see. Today, some 1.78 billion people are visibly attached to the church worldwide.

The invisible church—not all of these 1.78 billion people are true Christians, however. The invisible church is the real church, the core of true believers, and we cannot so easily put numbers on it.

St Augustine once expressed this idea of the invisible church by saying that 'there are many sheep without, many wolves within'.

> '*H*e cannot have God for his father who has not the church for his mother.'
> CYPRIAN OF CARTHAGE, DIED ABOUT AD258

> '*T*he church is never a place, but always a people; never a fold but always a flock; never a sacred building but always a believing assembly. The church is you who pray, not where you pray.'
> JOHN HAVLIK

PAUSE FOR THOUGHT
Is there a better word than 'church' to convey what you mean?

In other words, there is no such thing as a solitary Christian. Unless we become partners with other Christians and serve God together as the church, we cannot hope to fit these descriptions of what Christians are.

The ekklesia—a 'called out' people

The New Testament idea of church did not include buildings or an institution. The Greek word which Paul and the other writers used for 'church'—*ekklesia*—simply refers to a body of people. This word *ekklesia* survives today in English in the word 'ecclesiastical'.

Martin Luther didn't like using the word 'church' at all. Whenever he mentioned the New Testament idea of *ekklesia*, he spoke about 'the community', 'the congregation'—or simply 'the company of God's people'.

Ekklesia was not a word which was invented by the first Christians. They took it from everyday life. In Greek society, you used *ekklesia* when you were talking about a public meeting. The word literally means 'called out', and citizens were called out by a blast on a trumpet.

In Acts 19, an emergency meeting in the theatre at Ephesus is described as an *ekklesia*. (The meeting was called to deal with a riot against the first Christians.) For the town clerk in Ephesus, the *ekklesia* was an official public meeting. It was part of the administrative process of the city. Many Greek cities were similarly governed:

In Athens—the *ekklesia* met twice a week to discuss civic affairs and was open to every male citizen over twenty-one years of age

In Sparta—the *ekklesia* consisted of the soldiers in the army—probably the only time that a military government operated democratically.

The *ekklesia* provided a forum where civic leaders could explain their plans, enlist popular support and listen to citizens' grievances.

The Old Testament and ekklesia

How did the word *ekklesia* become a religious word?

Around 200BC the Hebrew Old Testament was translated into Greek. This version of the Old Testament is known as the Septuagint, and it was used by Jewish people who had emigrated to other parts of the Greek-speaking world. It also came to be used by the first Greek-speaking Christians.

The word *ekklesia* was used to translate two Hebrew words, *edah* and *qahal*. In the Old Testament they were used for any meeting of the whole nation—for worship, reading the law, politics—and even when the people of Israel decided to sack Moses, replace him with new leaders, and not enter the Promised Land (Numbers 13:26—14:10)! *Ekklesia* was used by the Septuagint to describe all these meetings—and so for the first time this Greek word gained a religious dimension.

The Hebrew word *qahal* means 'to summon'. It was used for any meeting regarded as representative of the nation as a whole. This was especially true of situations where Israel was summoned together to meet with God (see Numbers 10:7; Deuteronomy 4:10; Judges 20:2; Psalm 107:32).

The Septuagint prepared the way for the specifically Christian use of *ekklesia*.

The New Testament and ekklesia

Why did the New Testament writers adopt this word *ekklesia* to describe Christians together? There were a number of very good reasons, and they tell us a lot about what the church is:

No spectators—in secular life, the *ekklesia* was a gathering of active participants. The citizens got together to hear the news, debate the issues, make decisions, take action... They were there for a reason. This was a great way to describe God's people meeting together. They gathered together for a specific reason:

- ▶ to worship Jesus
- ▶ to hear the scriptures and the teaching
- ▶ to break bread together.

And there were no spectators—every Christian had a part to play in the congregation.

An upside-down society—Christians chose a word which for an outsider possessed strong political rather than religious overtones. Why did they do this?

- ▶ perhaps they were saying that their faith wasn't simply an alternative to pagan temples, mystery religions and Jewish synagogues
- ▶ instead they were establishing a new society, with a new king, a different government and another way of living.

On the move—the word *ekklesia* had strong Old Testament connections. It reminded the first Christians of the time when the people of Israel had escaped from Egypt and were living in the desert under the leadership of Moses. It gave them a vivid picture of the church— they too had been:

- ▶ called out of slavery
- ▶ summoned to meet with God
- ▶ called to travel with him to a Promised Land.

They saw that the church was a dynamic community of people, experiencing the dramatic interventions of God, moving forward together.

The true Israel—the Greek-speaking Jews of the time met in 'synagogues'—a word which means 'gathering together'. So why didn't the Christians in Jerusalem simply establish a Christian synagogue?

- ▶ the first believers wanted to show that they were the new people of God
- ▶ they were the people with whom God had made a new agreement (a 'new testament').

Ekklesia was a good word to describe this, because it talked about being 'called out'. They had been called out from the old agreement to become a new Israel. In this way, *ekklesia* was used to show that the church had its roots in the Old Testament, but was something new and not just a Jewish sect.

A living organism—the word *ekklesia* was only used when Christians joined with each other as a community:

- ▶ those who were 'called out' were not just individuals, they were called to be partners together
- ▶ just as the congregation of Israel was called to be together (for example, see Psalm 35:18; 122:1–2), so is the church today
- ▶ this new *ekklesia* is drawn out of every tribe, family, nation and language (Revelation 5:9).

PAUSE FOR THOUGHT
How does the concept of ekklesia affect our image of today's church?

> '*T*o the average Briton the "church" is either the building down the road or an outdated institution.'
> MICHAEL GRIFFITHS

God's called-out people

The word *ekklesia* comes in two parts.

- ▶ *ek* = 'out of'
- ▶ *klesis* = 'a calling'

The church is therefore a called-out people, brought 'out of darkness into his wonderful light' (1 Peter 2:9). We are called by God to

- ▶ a new life (Ephesians 4:1)
- ▶ freedom and deliverance (Galatians 5:1)
- ▶ a relationship with God (1 Corinthians 1:9)
- ▶ a future inheritance (Philippians 3:14; Hebrews 3:1)
- ▶ the glory of Christ's kingdom (1 Thessalonians 2:12; 1 Peter 5:10)
- ▶ a new hope (Ephesians 4:1–4).

Getting it wrong

William Tyndale was the first person to translate the Bible into English from Greek and Hebrew manuscripts. As he worked, he consistently translated the word *ekklesia* as 'congregation'.

Some 80 years later, in 1611, the King James version of the Bible (also known as 'the Authorized Version') was translated. But this time the translators insisted on translating *ekklesia* as 'church'. They did this despite the fact that the English word 'church' and the Scottish 'kirk' more naturally stem from another Greek word *kyriakos* which means 'the Lord's house'.

Perhaps it is from this unfortunate translation that the building-centred concept of the church has come. For most people today, 'church' usually means a building rather than a congregation.

The church therefore consists of living people.

 KEY POINT **The church is an organism, not an organization.**

2 *According to the New Testament...*

We have seen where the New Testament word for 'church' (*ekklesia*) came from, and why the first Christians chose to use it. In this section, we look at how the New Testament describes the church.

In the Gospels

Jesus only speaks about 'the church' (*ekklesia*) specifically on two occasions and both of them are recorded only in Matthew. These are:

Matthew 16:15-20: 'on this rock I will build my church, and the gates of Hades will not overcome it.'

Matthew 18:15-20: 'if he refuses to listen to them, tell it to the church; and if he refuses to listen even to the church, treat him as you would a pagan or a tax collector.'

These two passages are rich in their teaching about the church:

strong foundations—establishing the church is an essential part of what Jesus came to do, and it is built on 'a rock', built to last (Matthew 16:18)

'my church'—Jesus says that the church is 'my church'; it has its focus in Jesus himself (Matthew 16:18)

spiritual power—the church is entrusted with the spiritual power of 'binding' and 'loosing' (Matthew 16:19)

authority—as a church the believers decide between right and wrong activity and exercise discipline over each other (Matthew 18:17)

'where two or three'—Jesus himself is present whenever two or three believers come together.

On two other occasions, Jesus sent out his followers to spread the good news. The way he did this pointed to the future mission of the church. These passages are:

Luke 9:1–6: Jesus sends out his twelve disciples

Luke 10:1–12: Jesus sends out 72 followers.

The disciples were given authority to drive out demons and cure diseases, and they were sent out to preach the good news and heal the sick.

Jesus was establishing a pattern for the future. The church of Jesus, as the 'new people of God' is in radical contrast to Old Testament Israel. Being part of God's people in the Old Testament had always been based on the Jewish race, law and covenant. You did not choose to join the Jewish community (except in exceptional circumstances)—you were born into it.

> **Entrance to the church is very different. It is not inherited at birth or earned by merit, but is the result of coming to faith in Jesus Christ. It is a gift of God.**

The rest of the New Testament follows on from Jesus by talking about the church in a number of different ways.

The church in the house

Because there were no church buildings (apart from the synagogues), Christians usually met together in their homes. Early in the morning on the first day of the new week, and probably at other times too, Christians in a town or city would make their way to the house of a Christian near them. In a large town, there might be several gatherings.

To take just three examples, the church met in a house in:

▶ Rome (Romans 16:5)

▶ Corinth (1 Corinthians 16:19)

▶ Colossae (Colossians 4:15 and Philemon 2).

When persecution against Christians grew, and the number of Christian converts rose, many local congregations were forced to seek alternative (and unlikely) accommodation. Many Christians in the city of Rome literally went underground by meeting in the subterranean cemetery known as 'the catacombs'.

The local church

As the Christian message spread out from Jerusalem, through Samaria and Judea, and then out to the Gentile

> '**W**here two or three come together in my name, there am I with them.'
> JESUS, IN MATTHEW 18:20

> '**F**or the first Christians, a "church" was not an organisation, local or national, it was not a community, though it was one of the things the Christian community did. A "church" was a meeting where Christian disciples met with Jesus, as members of God's household and citizens of the New Jerusalem, to receive Jesus' direction and to administer His kingdom rule in the cities where they lived.'
> MIKE JOBLING

PAUSE FOR THOUGHT
Is your home group a church?

world, local groups of Christians sprang up in many towns and cities.

The Book of Revelation, for example, is addressed to churches in Smyrna, Ephesus, Sardis, Thyatira, Philadelphia, Laodicea and Pergamum. All of these churches came from a relatively small area in what is now western Turkey.

Each of them:

Met together for mutual encouragement (Hebrews 10:25)

Remembered Christ's death and resurrection (1 Corinthians 11:23–24)

Maintained the essential doctrines of the faith (Romans 10:9–10; Hebrews 6:1–2; Acts 2:42)

Established orderly forms of church government (1 Timothy 3; Titus 1)

Shared in fellowship and prayer (Acts 2:42)

Cared for each other's needs (Acts 2:44–45 and 4:34).

The local churches did not see themselves in isolation. They:

▶ Possessed a spiritual unity in Christ (Acts 2:46; 4:32)

▶ Recognized that Christ was head of the church, and that each church was accountable to him (Acts 4:11)

▶ Shared in each other's needs (Acts 2:44–45 and 4:34)

▶ Received ministry from each other (Acts 2:42; 6:1–6)

▶ Recognized that the Spirit's message to one church was valid for others as well (1 Thessalonians 2:14; 1 Corinthians 4:17).

From the earliest days, some churches exercised influence and authority:

the church in Jerusalem was seen as something of a 'mother church' where important decisions were made (see Acts 15)

the church in Antioch was a key church in the early spread of the faith (see Acts 13:1–4).

While churches such as these exercised considerable influence and commanded respect, each local church had a high degree of individual freedom. There were no denominational headquarters in those early days because Christ alone was head of his church. This was to change later, but the early churches knew separation only on the basis of geographical location.

They remained spiritually one, under the leadership of the apostles, but at the same time were locally distinct and self-governing. 1 Corinthians 7:17 speaks of 'all the churches'.

The universal church

> **Although there were many local churches, they all saw themselves as small parts of the whole church throughout the world.**

The final reality of the church is not that it is local or regional—it is the universal body of people who have been redeemed by Jesus Christ.

> **KEY POINT The church includes the complete company of believers throughout history—the living and the dead.**

There was always meant to be one universal church which Christ promised to build (Matthew 16:8):

▶ as the invisible union of all true believers (Ephesians 2:19–22; Hebrews 12:22–24), the church is the body and house of Jesus Christ (Ephesians 5:23–32; 1 Timothy 3:5, 15)

▶ through the church, God makes his wisdom understood and reveals his glory (1 Corinthians 1:18, 24; Ephesians 3:10, 21; 5:23–32)

▶ Jesus himself reigns as head of the church universal

▶ he lives among all believers and will one day gather his church to reign with him—this is his brotherhood, the 'church of the firstborn' (Hebrews 2:10–12; 12:22–24).

In New Testament times, this unity was expressed when the churches from one region gave practical support to the churches in another. For example:

The church in Antioch—sends gifts to the Jerusalem church, which is threatened by famine—see Acts 11:27–30

The churches in Greece—give money to Paul to help impoverished Christians in Jerusalem—see Romans 15:25–26.

Christian believers had a dual loyalty:

▶ to the local body of believers

▶ to the church of Christ across the world.

This was not a foreign concept in the Roman world. All Roman citizens knew that, wherever they travelled, they remained part of the unity which was Rome. Wherever meetings were held they were eligible to be involved. They might travel to Ephesus, Caesarea, Spain or Italy—but they were still Roman citizens. On entering

> '**W**here three are gathered together, there is a church, even though they be laymen.'
> TERTULLIAN

> '**W**herever we see the Word of God purely preached and heard, there a church of God exists, even if it swarms with many faults.'
> JOHN CALVIN

a new town they automatically became part of its local society by means of their universal citizenship.

So it is with the church—except that our fellowship knows no geographical limitations, no earthly city, and will never fail or pass away.

Militant and triumphant

Christians have often thought of the church as two groups of people, joined together in a fellowship known as 'the communion of saints'. The two groups are:

the church militant—the body of Christians still on earth, engaged in spiritual warfare, carrying out the mission of Jesus

the church triumphant—the body of Christians who are no longer in the battle, but are with Jesus.

KEY POINT It must always be technically incorrect to speak of 'our church'. It is Christ's church or it is not what God intended it to be.

Did you know?

The church is mentioned in the New Testament

▶ in a city: 38 times

▶ in a province: 36 times

▶ the universal church: 20 times

▶ local but undefined: 16 times

▶ in a house: 4 times

Local churches in New Testament times

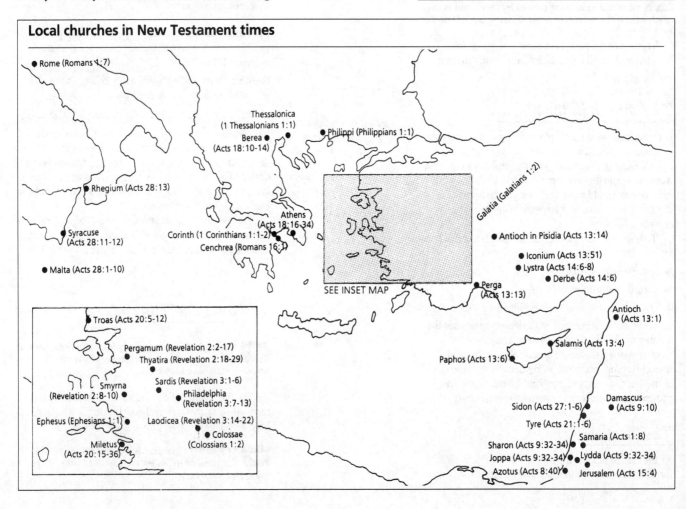

- Rome (Romans 1:7)
- Thessalonica (1 Thessalonians 1:1)
- Berea (Acts 18:10-14)
- Philippi (Philippians 1:1)
- Rhegium (Acts 28:13)
- Galatia (Galatians 1:2)
- Athens (Acts 18:16-34)
- Corinth (1 Corinthians 1:1-2)
- Cenchrea (Romans 16:1)
- Syracuse (Acts 28:11-12)
- Antioch in Pisidia (Acts 13:14)
- Iconium (Acts 13:51)
- Lystra (Acts 14:6-8)
- Derbe (Acts 14:6)
- Malta (Acts 28:1-10)
- Perga (Acts 13:13)
- SEE INSET MAP
- Antioch (Acts 13:1)
- Salamis (Acts 13:4)
- Paphos (Acts 13:6)
- Damascus (Acts 9:10)
- Sidon (Acts 27:1-6)
- Tyre (Acts 21:1-6)
- Samaria (Acts 1:8)
- Sharon (Acts 9:32-34)
- Joppa (Acts 9:32-34)
- Lydda (Acts 9:32-34)
- Azotus (Acts 8:40)
- Jerusalem (Acts 15:4)

Inset map:
- Troas (Acts 20:5-12)
- Pergamum (Revelation 2:2-17)
- Thyatira (Revelation 2:18-29)
- Smyrna (Revelation 2:8-10)
- Sardis (Revelation 3:1-6)
- Philadelphia (Revelation 3:7-13)
- Ephesus (Ephesians 1:1)
- Laodicea (Revelation 3:14-22)
- Colossae (Colossians 1:2)
- Miletus (Acts 20:15-36)

One church, many shapes

The New Testament sees the church as one people, sharing the same Holy Spirit, confessing the same Lord, united in one baptism. When we belong to Jesus, we are at one with all other true Christians, regardless of the differences of geography, culture and denomination.

Paul wrote about the church at every level . . .

▶ **universally**—'from whom his whole family in heaven and on earth derives its name' (Ephesians 3:15)

▶ **regionally**—'To the churches in Galatia' (Galatians 1:2)

▶ **municipally**—'To the church of God in Corinth' (1 Corinthians 1:2)

▶ **locally**—'Greet also the church that meets at their house' (Romans 16:5)

▶ **personally**—'To the holy and faithful brothers in Christ at Colossae' (Colossians 1:2).

'*S*ee how these Christians love one another.'
TERTULLIAN, BORN ABOUT AD160

Milestones in the story of the church

The New Testament and especially the Book of Acts records the story of the church in its first few years. It is one of the greatest stories of the Bible. The major milestones in the story include:

Jesus calls the 12 disciples—the people of Israel in the Old Testament were divided into 12 tribes, and Jesus called 12 disciples to show that he was establishing a new community of God's people—a 'new Israel' (see Mark 3:13–19, and especially verses 14 and 15).

Jesus sends out the 72—in a sort of preview of the church's mission, Jesus sent out 72 of his followers to prepare the way for his arrival in the local towns and villages (see Luke 10:1–12).

The day of Pentecost—after Jesus' resurrection and ascension, the Holy Spirit fell on the first believers who were meeting together in Jerusalem. Filled with the Spirit, they began to proclaim the good news. This day marks the real beginning of the church's mission in the world (see Acts 2).

The message spreads—the church was mainly confined to Jerusalem until Christians there started to face violent persecution. When Stephen, the first Christian martyr, was killed, the believers fled from the city, taking the good news with them (see Acts 8:1–8).

Mission from Antioch—the church in Antioch sent out two of its elders to take the good news of Jesus into what is now Turkey. The two elders were Saul (later known as the Apostle Paul) and Barnabas. This marked the beginning of several missions by Paul which took the gospel to the heart of the Roman Empire (see Acts 13:1–3).

A message for the whole world—the first Christians believed that the message of Jesus was only for the Jewish people. But when non-Jews ('the Gentiles') began to be converted, the church agreed that the good news was for everyone, regardless of race (see Acts 15:1–21).

Case study: *the church at Philippi*

In New Testament times, Philippi was a small town in Macedonia. It was here that the first Christian church was planted in Europe, when Paul arrived there around AD48.

Paul wrote his letter to the Christians in Philippi when he was in prison, on trial for his life. As he wrote to this church, he was not thinking of a building or institution, but a community of believers, living out their faith in a very dangerous world. For Paul, the church in Philippi *was* the group of believers.

About the Philippians . . .

▶ like most churches in the first three centuries they had no 'church' building to maintain

▶ they existed as a beleaguered minority in the midst of a hostile society

▶ their energies were directed to spreading the good news, teaching the faith, and caring for each other.

In addition, they had a structured leadership team of 'overseers and deacons' (Philippians 1:1).

Focus on relationships

Paul's letter to the Philippians is one of his most warm and personal. They had been good partners with Paul in the gospel and had given him a great deal of unselfish support (see Philippians 1:3–5 and 4:14–16). He spends much of the letter on the issue of their relationships:

▶ with one another
▶ with himself
▶ with other churches.

However, like most other churches of the time, the Philippian community faced big dangers. These were:

external persecution by the Roman state (Philippians 1:27–28) Paul tells them they should 'shine like stars' in a dark world (Philippians 2:15)

internal confusion from false teachers (Philippians 3:2–4) and personal rivalries (Philippians 4:2–3, compare with 2:2–4). Paul tells them to be mature and to 'stand firm' (Philippians 4:1).

KEY POINT Paul sees personal relationships as fundamental to the wellbeing of the church of Jesus Christ.

'*I*t is impossible for any that have it, to conceal the religion of Jesus Christ. Your holiness makes you as conspicuous as the sun in the midst of heaven.'
JOHN WESLEY

He truly sees the church as a living, breathing community where relationships are all-important. And so he:

▶ stresses their mutual sharing in the grace of God (Philippians 1:7)

▶ expresses his genuine affection for them (Philippians 1:8)

▶ emphasizes the value of their prayers for him (Philippians 1:19) and his for them (Philippians 1:9)

▶ stresses their relationship with Christ and the Spirit (Philippians 2:1)

▶ sees them as the fruit of his ministry (Philippians 2:16), his 'joy and crown' (Philippians 4:1)

▶ knows that they can rejoice together (Philippians 2:17–18)

▶ wants to see them soon (Philippians 2:23–24)

▶ longs that they might imitate his example (Philippians 3:17; 4:9)

▶ greets them as his 'dear friends' (Philippians 4:1)

▶ loves them and longs for them (Philippians 4:1)

▶ expresses thanks for their renewed concern for him (Philippians 4:10)

▶ appreciates the way they share in his troubles (Philippians 4:14).

It is this kind of relationship which lies at the heart of the Christian church. The partnership between Paul and the Christians he writes to, and between them all and the God they serve, is what the church—and the gospel—is all about.

This is why we now turn to look at these relationships in more detail, and to the spiritual principle which fires them and gives them life.

3 *The church as a partnership*

In its early days, the way Christians treated each other was a wonderful advert for the good news of Jesus. One Christian writer, Tertullian, was able to quote what pagans were saying about the church: 'See how these Christians love one another.'

Koinonia—*what it is*

The word *koinonia* was a Greek word from everyday life in New Testament times. It was used to describe friendship and co-operation in business, sports and personal relationships. Among Greek philosophers it became an ideal of brotherly love and co-operation— something to be pursued.

Paul and the other early Christian writers borrowed *koinonia* to express the quality of relationships which is needed in the local church. This word is normally translated as 'communion' or 'fellowship'. Along with its sister-words, *koinonia* occurs 46 times in the New Testament—which makes it a very significant term.

The New Testament takes this rich word and builds on it:

▶ for Christians, *koinonia* describes a strong, intimate, committed relationship between people

▶ but it is also more than this; *koinonia* is a relationship based on a shared participation in something of real importance to those involved.

> '**S**urely it is time for us to meet one another in penitent acknowledgement of our common failure to be what the church ought to be.'
> LESSLIE NEWBIGIN

> '**C**hristians claim that Jesus Christ is the Saviour of sinners, but they show no more signs of being saved than anyone else.'
> KRISHNA

Koinonia has usually been translated as 'communion' or 'fellowship'. However, these words have tended to devalue the rich meaning of *koinonia* as a word to describe relationships. The nearest English word for *koinonia* in everyday use is not 'communion' or 'fellowship', but 'partnership'. This partnership between Christians is based on something solid. It is based on our mutual participation in the love, service and life of Jesus.

Therefore our partnership is not based on what we do, but in whom we share!

So it is not our actions, structures and institutions which provide *koinonia*. We are already 'one' with all who are 'in Christ'. Instead, our *koinonia* is more concerned with personal relationships expressed in mutual commitment and joint action than it is about any kind of formal, institutional or structural unity.

Koinonia is used to describe our relationship with:

▶ the Father and the Son (1 John 1:3)

▶ the Holy Spirit (2 Corinthians 13:14)

▶ Christ in his suffering (Philippians 3:10; 1 Peter 4:13)

▶ the poor and hungry (Romans 15:26)

Therefore our partnership is not based first of all on what we do, but in whom we share. However, *koinonia* is not static—it leads to action, and a new quality of life.

Koinonia—*what it does*

What does *koinonia* mean in the New Testament? *Koinonia* . . .

▶ expresses partnership and working together (Luke 5:10; 2 Corinthians 8:23; Galatians 2:9; Philippians 1:7)

▶ involves practical action on behalf of those in need (Romans 12:13; 15:26; 2 Corinthians 8:4; 9:13; Philippians 4:14–15)

▶ involves sharing in both the witness and blessings of the gospel (Romans 11:17; 15:27; 1 Corinthians 9:23; Philippians 1:5, 7; Philemon 6; 1 Peter 5:1; 2 Peter 1:4)

The reality gap

🔲 **KEY POINT It is obvious that there is an enormous gap between what the New Testament is describing and what the church of today experiences.**

Christians are not perfect people. Some of our imperfections can be more obvious than others . . .

▶ **unfriendly**—we can fail to acknowledge, welcome and include strangers or those who have no obvious friendships.

▶ **insensitive**—it can be easy to produce glib answers in the face of human need, or to fail to notice when someone is troubled or hurt.

▶ **complaining**—if we feel ignored or rejected, it is easy to copy the people of Israel in the time of Moses and grumble about it.

▶ **introverted**—in the face of great human need, we can still find ourselves too caught up in the church to be involved in the rest of society.

▶ **gossiping**—verbal assassination still characterizes much of our church life.

▶ **insecure**—struggling for position and self-assertion we fail to move out of our own 'comfort-zones' to support others.

▶ **negative**—too often we are swift to see all that is wrong in a situation, instead of seeking to turn it around or applaud what is good.

▶ **proud**—the Pharisees believed that their obedience to the law counted as righteousness and sometimes we follow them instead of Jesus.

▶ **withdrawn**—it is easier to retreat to the back pews as a mere attender of church than to be an active member.

▶ **resentful**—we can become quick to register any apparent criticism and nurture thoughts of being slighted and put down.

▶ **unloving**—many people in today's world are looking for love. Often we fail to provide genuine expressions of Christian love and support to those in need.

This gap between what we should be and what we are can easily lead us into destructive ways of thinking about the church . . .

▶ **despair**—some people despair that the church can ever be as God intended it to be, and the heart goes out of their faith. Many of them give up entirely.

▶ **cynicism**—others become bitterly critical of the church and make it much harder for others to commit themselves to praying and working for change

▶ **escape**—others pretend the problems don't really exist instead they turn to an individualistic, highly personal faith that shuts out other people in the community.

It is clear that we have to be realistic about the problems of today's church—there is room for constructive criticism. But at the same time, we must have hope. We cannot move forward on our own. We need to take hold of the spiritual resources which God offers to us. These are explored in the next sections.

Adapted from Mark Birchall

The 'one anothers'

Of the 21 letters in the New Testament, only three are addressed to individuals. The rest are written to groups, which means that the word 'you' is invariably meant to be considered in the plural.

This fact is underlined when we consider how the writers emphasised mutual responsibility. They did this by using the phrase 'one another' . . .

▶ Romans 12:10a 'Be devoted to one another'

▶ Romans 12:10b 'Honour one another'

▶ Romans 12:16 'Live in harmony with one another'

▶ Romans 15:7 'Accept one another'

▶ 1 Corinthians 12:25 Express 'equal concern for each other'

▶ Galatians 5:13 'Serve one another in love'

▶ Galatians 6:2 'Carry each other's burdens'

▶ Ephesians 4:32 'Be kind and compassionate to one another, forgiving each other '

▶ Ephesians 5:19 'Speak to one another with psalms, hymns and spiritual songs'

▶ Ephesians 5:21 'Submit to one another'

▶ Philippians 2:4 'Look . . . to the interests of others'

▶ Colossians 3:13a 'Bear with each other'

▶ Colossians 3:13b 'Forgive whatever grievances you may have against one another'

▶ Colossians 3:16 'Counsel one another'

▶ 1 Thessalonians 3:12 'May the Lord make your love increase and overflow for each other'

▶ 1 Thessalonians 4:18 'Encourage each other'

▶ Hebrews 3:13 'Encourage one another daily'

▶ Hebrews 10:24 'Spur one another on towards love and good deeds'

▶ Hebrews 10:25 'Encourage one another'

▶ James 4:11 'Do not slander one another'

▶ James 5:16 'Confess your sins to each other'

▶ James 5:16a 'Pray for each other'

▶ 1 Peter 4:8 'Love each other deeply'

▶ 1 Peter 4:9 'Offer hospitality to one other without grumbling'

▶ 1 Peter 5:5 'Clothe yourselves with humility towards one another'

▶ 1 John 3:11 'Love one another'

▶ means mutual commitment in worship (Acts 2:42; 1 Corinthians 10:16)

▶ includes partnership in suffering (2 Corinthians 1:7; Philippians 3:10; Hebrews 10:33; 1 Peter 4:13; Revelation 1:9)

▶ is expressed in financial generosity (Galatians 6:6; 1 Timothy 6:18; Hebrews 13:16)

▶ ultimately means that we are in partnership with God himself—Father, Son and Holy Spirit (1 Corinthians 1:9; Philippians 2:1; 1 John 1:3, 6).

KEY POINT Every church has to ask itself serious questions about where it stands in terms of Christian partnership and relationships.

'True fellowship or koinonia is a dynamic sense of partnership, based on a common purpose, a personal relationship and a joint commitment.'
MARK BIRCHALL

PAUSE FOR THOUGHT
Is your church held together by its structures or a network of good relationships?

'The traditional picture of a static church, solid in its establishment, conservative in its attitudes, entrenched in familiar patterns of work and worship, is a gross distortion of the church as it is meant to be and as pictured in the Bible.'
DAVID WATSON

'To dwell above with saints we love, Ah, that will then be glory. To dwell below, with saints we know, Well, that's another story!'
ANON

---

4 *The Holy Trinity and community*

The Christian faith is not simply about 'me and God'. Instead, it shows how God created us to belong together. I belong to Christ and his community, and as a community we belong to God.

KEY POINT Because of this, *koinonia* is not just the icing on the cake for Christians. It is actually the cake itself.

This is why it represents perhaps the greatest challenge to the Western church today. Love in action has to be at the heart of the Christian good news, or it is simply not good news.

Overcoming obstacles

This idea of belonging to each other can be difficult. Christians have to struggle over a number of obstacles to accept this truth and start living it out:

In the church—until the printing press was invented, people depended on each other in order to learn. They did this either by observation or through personal instruction.

The introduction of books led to private study and solitary learning, which significantly influenced the way society behaved.

For the church, this resulted in an overemphasis on individual prayer, solitary study and private belief. At the same time, the place of shared spiritual experience, growth and discovery were all but ignored.

In our culture—as we saw in section one of these notes, we live in the 'Me' generation. Through its films, adverts, music and other media, our culture constantly promotes the need to fulfil our own personal desires and happiness. We have been conditioned to think primarily of ourselves.

In addition, we are increasingly isolated from others due to the impact of growing levels of mobility. New patterns of employment and education have weakened the extended family, local communities and networks of friendship. Our witness as Christians in the next years will increasingly be to show what true community and belonging really means. This too is difficult and costly.

In ourselves—at the deepest level, we have to struggle against ourselves, and our own sinful nature. The first casualty of sin is always our ability to relate to others—whether to God or other people. The Genesis story of the fall shows a series of 'aftershocks', where relationships completely break down.

We are alienated . . .

▶ **from God**—Adam and Eve hid from God (Genesis 3:8)

▶ **from each other**—they hid from each other (Genesis 3:7)

▶ **from myself**—Adam convinces himself of a half-truth (Genesis 3:10)

▶ **from people of other cultures**—at Babel, people are divided by the 'curse' of different languages (Genesis 11:5–9).

These are the powerful consequences of human sin, and we can see them today in everything from the divorce rate to the terrifying destruction in what used to be Yugoslavia.

Reversing the curse

The Christian good news is not simply that Jesus came to save me. It goes far deeper than that. Jesus came to break the chains of the fall. He came not only to put us back in touch with God, but to reconcile us to each other.

On the cross, Jesus threw the terrible momentum of the fall into reverse. The fall led to death, but Jesus' death led to new life—and his resurrection from the dead was the first sign of it. And so each curse of the fall was reversed.

We are reconciled...

To God—our sin is forgiven and our relationship restored (Colossians 1:22)

To each other—(Ephesians 2:19)—in fact, reconciliation becomes a special ministry of the church (2 Corinthians 5:18–19)

To myself—Jesus rescues us from our 'inner war' (Romans 7:21–25)

To people of other cultures—Babel is reversed when the language barrier is broken (Acts 2:1–6).

Walls of division are smashed down to the ground. As Paul said: 'There is neither Jew nor Greek, slave nor free, male nor female, for you are all one in Christ Jesus' (Galatians 3:28).

The church is therefore a community that teaches and experiences true reconciliation. However good (or bad) we are at doing this shows how good (or bad) we are at being the church.

The God of unbroken relationships

This is the theory. But we need more than a theory, and more than a system. Telling ourselves that we should be a community will not make us into a community.

> **KEY POINT** We need help from outside—the spiritual resources and spiritual power to change us into the true people of God.

Our first spiritual resource for recovering our sense of community is a surprising one: the doctrine of the Holy Trinity. For many people this idea of God as being 'three persons in one God' is just a dry old doctrine, dusted down perhaps once a year on Trinity Sunday.

However, many Christians today are beginning to rediscover that the Trinity is not just an idea, but a revolutionary vision of who God truly is, and a source of great spiritual strength. How is this possible?

First, we have to look at some theology. Christian teaching about the Trinity tells us two important things about the inner being of God. They appear to contradict each other.

God is one—the Old Testament insists that there is only one God (Deuteronomy 6). This one God is the creator and sustainer of all life, and of everything that exists. He is also a *personal* God. Where many of the pagan gods represented impersonal forces (Mars = the god of war, Isis = the goddess of fertility), God is personal—the God of Abraham, Isaac and Jacob. He relates to people.

> 'There can be no church apart from love.'
> ST JOHN OF KRONSTADT

> 'Let us love one another, so that we may with one mind confess Father, Son and Holy Spirit, the Trinity one in essence and undivided.'
> RUSSIAN ORTHODOX PRAYER

> 'It is love that fashions all things and holds them in unity. It is love that gives life and warmth, that inspires and guides. Love is the seal set upon creation, the signature of the Creator. Love is the explanation of his handiwork.'
> THEOKLITOS OF DIONYSIOU

> 'This is how God showed his love among us: He sent his one and only Son into the world that we might live through him.'
> 1 JOHN 4:9

God is three—the Bible's teaching seems to say that God is so much greater than we are, that he is super-personal. Within the one being of God there are three equal persons: Father, Son and Holy Spirit. These three relate to each other in self-giving love...

▶ **The Father** loves the Son and gives him glory (John 17:24)

▶ **The Son** loves and glorifies the Father (John 17:4)

▶ **The Spirit** brings glory to the Son (John 16:14) and searches out the deep inner life of God (1 Corinthians 2:10).

The deep truth about God is not simply that he is a personal God. He is also in himself a loving community of equal persons. This is why the Apostle John could say simply that 'God is love' (1 John 4:8). The love that exists between these three persons is eternally expressed so that at the heart of the universe there is not a solitary, lonely God, but a God who rejoices in relationships.

Living the life of the Trinity

How can the doctrine of the Holy Trinity help us today? It helps us by showing the reality of how God works in our lives. Jesus makes it possible for us to know the love of God, and the Holy Spirit brings us, individually and as a community, into that love.

The church lives as a community of love on earth not because it's the nicest thing to do, or even because God has commanded it.

> **KEY POINT** We live as a community because God himself *is* a community of love.

And because we are made in his image, we are only truly happy, or truly ourselves, when we live in love with God and with other people.

The love at the heart of the Trinity is a challenge to any Christian community...

The love of the Father—turns its back on bitterness and revenge, calling us instead to be reconciled to those who have hurt us just as the Father gave everything to bring us back to him (John 3:16)

The love of the Son—cuts across the 'Me' generation, calling us to put the needs of others before our own needs just as Jesus gave himself for us (Philippians 2:1–5)

The love of the Spirit—sends us out into the world, calling us to reach out in love to those who are in the dark and far from God just as the Spirit brought the good news to us (Luke 4:18–19).

It is the Holy Spirit who brings the love of God the Trinity down to earth and into our hearts. He does this by...

▶ making us part of the **body of Christ** (1 Corinthians 12:12–13) see pages 37–38

▶ showering the church with **special gifts** (1 Corinthians 12:1–11) see page 85

▶ giving the church **the gift of *koinonia***—'May the grace of the Lord Jesus Christ, and the love of God, and the fellowship (*koinonia*) of the Holy Spirit be with you all (2 Corinthians 13:14) see pages 34–35.

Why the Trinity?

The New Testament contains no explicit teaching about the doctrine of the Trinity. But it does contain the raw materials which the church later put together to form this uniquely Christian teaching about God.

The idea of God as Trinity arose mainly because of what the first Christians believed about God, and what they believed about Jesus. They believed that . . .

▶ there is only one God the uncompromising teaching of the Old Testament (Deuteronomy 6:4; 1 Corinthians 8:6)

▶ Jesus Christ is fully God he is God's beloved Son (Mark 1:11), the image of the invisible God (Colossians 1:15), and has always had the nature of God (Philippians 2:6).

Added to this, the New Testament teaches that . . .

▶ the Holy Spirit is a divine person and is frequently named alongside the Father and the Son (Matthew 28:19; 1 Corinthians 12:4–6; 1 Peter 1:1–2).

The doctrine of the Trinity was built on these foundations not because the church was fond of philosophy, but to defend the Christian faith from heresy. It became important to say whether Jesus was truly God, and how he and the Spirit related to the Father.

The church's final formulation, which was fixed in the fourth century, was that God is one substance or being, existing in the three persons of Father, Son and Holy Spirit.

No one can fully understand the doctrine of the Trinity and this is because it echoes the mystery of God himself. God is beyond human thought and imagination, he dwells in unapproachable light (1 Timothy 6:16). Our response to him is the same as that of the great figures of the Bible: to fall before him in worship and holy fear (Isaiah 6:1–5; Ezekiel 1:22–28; Acts 9:3–9; Revelation 1:12–18).

5 *The body of Christ*

KEY POINT Many of the most common New Testament expressions for the church are plural nouns like children, flock, saints, nation, disciples and people.

While 'saints' occurs sixty-one times in the New Testament, the singular 'saint' is used only once.

The Bible gives us many pictures of what the church is like. Take 1 Peter 2:9, for instance, which gives us four wonderful images of the church: 'But you are a chosen people, a royal priesthood, a holy nation, a people belonging to God, that you may declare the praises of him who called you out of darkness into his wonderful light.'

In the next three sections, we look at three images of the church . . .

▶ the body of Christ
▶ the bride of Christ
▶ the building of God.

They are images which not only tell us who we are, but how we should live as the community of God's people.

KEY POINT Apart from the Holy Spirit, the greatest gift God has given us is one another.

One body, many parts

'Now you are the body of Christ,' Paul tells the Christians in Corinth. 'And each of you is a part of it' (1 Corinthians 12:27).

> '*T*he body of Jesus Christ may well be sick or wounded. When has it not been? But as the body of this Head it cannot die.'
> KARL BARTH

> '*W*e believe in one holy, catholic and apostolic church.'
> CREED OF CONSTANTINOPLE, AD381

> '*C*ongregation of God" is equally the proper title for a small group meeting in a house, and for the whole worldwide family. This is because the real character of it is determined by the fact that God is gathering it.'
> LESSLIE NEWBIGIN

This description of the church as Christ's body appears in a number of passages . . .

▶ Romans 12:4–5
▶ 1 Corinthians 12:12–31
▶ Ephesians 4:16; 5:30
▶ Colossians 2:19.

The great thing about this picture of the church is that it is human and accessible. We can all understand it, and it shows that in the church God meets us on our level—the human level.

Paul's fullest description of the church as the body of Christ comes in 1 Corinthians 12:12–31. This passage gives us some deep insights into the church . . .

The body is Christ's—as the body of Christ . . .

▶ the church carries on the work of Jesus on earth
▶ it spreads the good news, prophesies, brings healing
▶ it carries out all the other types of ministry listed in 1 Corinthians 12:27–31.

We continue the ministry of Jesus in the world. Jesus said: 'As the Father has sent me, I am sending you' (John 20:21).

It is one body—whatever our differences of race, culture or sex, we are baptized by the Spirit into one body (1 Corinthians 12:13 and Galatians 3:26–28). There is therefore only one church.

The body is a living organism—

▶ the church totally depends on Jesus for its life and growth (Colossians 2:19)
▶ without him it is dead
▶ all the activity and organization of the church—baptism, the Lord's supper, preaching, the faith and love of Christians—none of these creates the church or guarantees its growth.

As Jesus said, in a parallel image: 'I am the vine; you are the branches . . . apart from me you can do nothing' (John 15:5).

Each member has a distinct role—

▶ although the church is one body, it has a wonderful unity, rather than a boring uniformity
▶ ears, hands, eyes, feet—each of them has a unique contribution to bring to the whole body (1 Corinthians 12:14–16)

Whose body?

Paul talks about the body of Christ. The church is not just a body but his body. What does this tell us?

The body of Jesus was born. Jesus became a human being to bring God's love to us. Because the church is Christ's body, it shows that God still relates to us on our level, and through us to the wider world.

The body of Jesus suffered and died on the cross and the church also follows Jesus by taking up the cross (Mark 8:34–35). Sacrifice and suffering are an integral part of the church's experience.

The body of Jesus was raised to life—the church is a living sign that the new life of Jesus is offered to the world. We not only proclaim this new life, but experience it for ourselves.

▶ each person in the church, whatever their gifts, is an essential part of the whole body, with a genuine contribution to make.

All the members work together—Paul's imagery becomes comical as he shows how anarchy might break out in the body. What if all the members wanted to be an eye? Or an ear? (1 Corinthians 12:17–20). If they had these crazy ambitions, then the whole idea of the body would be lost. Instead, the church can only be healthy when all its different parts work together.

The members do not fight—because the parts of the body all depend on each other, there should be no jealousy or superiority among them (1 Corinthians 12:21–25).

The body suffers and rejoices together—in other words, the members of the body do the opposite of fighting:

▶ they care for each other

▶ although there are many members in the body of Christ, there is no division (1 Corinthians 12:25–26)

▶ when one part suffers (through persecution or disagreement) the whole body suffers

▶ and when one part enjoys success, the whole body rejoices.

The head is Christ—while the whole body belongs to Jesus, Paul highlights Christ's role as the head of the church (Ephesians 4:15–16).

▶ he directs the development and growth of the body

▶ 'the body of Christ' is not an empty label—it really does belong to him

▶ we have not been left alone to act as Christ's body here on earth—he himself is leading us and it is his church not ours.

Each Christian believer is challenged to regard him or herself as a temple fit for God to live in (1 Corinthians 6:19–20; 2 Corinthians 6:16–18; 2 Peter 1:13–14). All of us corporately are called to be the body of Christ (Ephesians 1:23; 4:4; 1 Corinthians 12:13).

6 *The bride of Christ*

Paul wrote these words to the church in Ephesus: 'Husbands, love your wives, just as Christ loved the church and gave himself up for her to make her holy…' (Ephesians 5:25).

This picture of the church as the wife or bride of Christ is found in two main areas of the New Testament…

▶ Ephesians 5:22–33

▶ Revelation 19:6–9; 21:2, 9; 22:17.

Jesus is also described as a bridegroom…

▶ by John the Baptist (John 3:29)

▶ by Jesus himself (see Matthew 9:15; 25:1–13).

In the Old Testament…

This wedding imagery may be connected with the first miracle of Jesus. He began his earthly ministry at a wedding (John 2:1–11). His work closes at another wedding (Revelation 21:2), when as the bridegroom he comes to claim the church as his eternal bride.

> '*W*hat is terribly missing is the experience of "body life"; that warm fellowship of Christian with Christian which the New Testament calls *koinonia*, and which was an essential part of early Christianity.'
> RAY STEDMAN

> '*A*ny bride preparing for her wedding day has to see to many demanding details. Yet they should not be a burden to her, but rather expressions of her love for the bridegroom. As Christians, we have a glorious wedding day to look forward to. It is literally out of this world.'
> DAVID WATSON

> '*W*e must ask, "Do I fight merely for doctrinal faithfulness?" This is like the wife who never sleeps with anybody else, but never shows love to her husband… Our call is first to be the bride faithful, but that is not the total call. The call is not only to be the bride faithful, but also the bride in love.'
> FRANCIS SCHAEFFER

The roots of this idea lie in the Old Testament. Several passages picture Israel as a bride…

▶ God is her husband and delights in her (Isaiah 62:4–5)

▶ Israel becomes a whore, rejecting God's love and prostituting herself with pagan religions (Jeremiah 3:20; Ezekiel 16:32; Hosea 2:1–5)

▶ the marriage has gone wrong, but God will have compassion on his abandoned wife (Isaiah 54:1–8; Hosea 2:14–20).

The warmth and tenderness of their intended relationship is reflected in some of the Old Testament love songs (Psalm 45; Song of Songs 4:9–10). The wedding analogy also appears in two of Jesus' parables…

▶ the wedding banquet (Matthew 22:1–14)

▶ the ten virgins (Matthew 25:1–13).

John the Baptist

When John's disciples told him that Jesus was baptizing more people than him, John made an obscure reply: 'The bride belongs to the bridegroom. The friend who attends the bridegroom waits and listens for him, and is full of joy when he hears the bridegroom's voice. That joy is mine, and it is now complete' (John 3:29).

In those days the task of the best man was to keep the bride away from other men until her wedding day. John is expressing his delight at hearing what Jesus is doing. He sees himself as the bridegroom's friend or best man, who when he hears the voice of the bridegroom arriving at the wedding, knows that his task is complete.

In other words while he knows that he is the best man, the bridegroom is Jesus, and the bride is those who are coming to him.

Married to Christ

As Paul writes to the Ephesians he explains that the attitude of a husband to a wife should reflect the love that Christ has for his church (Ephesians 5:25). He also speaks of his betrothal of the Corinthian church to Christ (2 Corinthians 11:2).

The Bible points to our spiritual intimacy with Jesus Christ. With great daring Jesus uses the word 'know' (which is often used for the sexual relationship of a married couple) to describe our relationship with God (John 17:3). In return God delights in us, as a bridegroom rejoices in his bride (Isaiah 62:5).

Many commentators regard the Song of Songs not merely as a graphic example of Hebrew love poetry, but as a prophetic picture of the relation between Christ and his church.

The great missionary and founder of the China Inland Mission (now Overseas Missionary Fellowship), Hudson Taylor, wrote a book entitled *Union and Communion* which explores this theme. Detailed analogies are dangerous, but there is no doubt that the passionate, devoted relationship expressed in this song is a partial picture of the wonderful quality of Jesus' love for his church.

Jesus spoke of his first disciples when he told the Pharisees that they could not fast while their bridegroom was still with them (Luke 5:34). In stark contrast will be the days when the Lord is physically removed from his people. But then he will return to gather all his disciples, from throughout the ages, and we will unite as his church and bride at his return. At that final culmination of history the bride will meet her bridegroom (Revelation 19:7; 21:2, 9; 22:17).

7 The building of God

The people of God began as tent-dwellers, wandering nomads exploring the wilderness. During this period God chose to inhabit a tent—the tent of the Lord's presence. When the people of Israel settled in Canaan, King Solomon built a magnificent temple in Jerusalem for the Lord.

But the death and resurrection of Jesus ushered in a totally new era. Now the church is God's building, the place where he chooses to dwell. Paul insists that 'you are...God's building' (1 Corinthians 3:9). He asks the Corinthian church, 'Don't you know that you yourselves are God's temple and that God's Spirit lives in you?' (1 Corinthians 3:16). Indeed he goes even further and insists that 'If anyone destroys God's temple, God will destroy him; for God's temple is sacred, and you are that temple' (1 Corinthians 3:17).

So our God no longer dwells under canvas—he now lives in us, his people, his church. We, in turn, 'are being built into a spiritual house to be a holy priesthood, offering spiritual sacrifices acceptable to God through Jesus Christ' (1 Peter 2:5).

God's building project

> 🔊 **KEY POINT** The temple or house of God is no longer a building—that privilege now belongs to God's people. Therefore a building cannot be a 'holy place'; instead God's people are called to be a holy people.

God's choice of a tent in which to live among his people was important. It implied mobility and flexibility. For forty years God's people moved when he moved. Later on, the building of the Jerusalem temple signified the growing institutionalization of Israel's faith (2 Samuel 7:5–7; Acts 7:46–47). Stephen, the church's first martyr, denounced Israel's folly at his trial by saying 'the Most High does not live in houses made by men' (Acts 7:48).

The Old Testament temple has been superseded by a far more valuable building that our God is constructing. This building is described in a number of New Testament passages...

▶ 1 Corinthians 3:9–17
▶ Ephesians 2:19–22
▶ 1 Peter 2:4–8.

Paul calls it a 'holy temple', and Peter calls it a 'spiritual house'...

▶ it is being built from living stones (1 Peter 2:5)
▶ it is built on the foundation of the apostles and prophets (Ephesians 2:20)
▶ Jesus Christ himself is the cornerstone (Psalm 118:22; Acts 4:11; 1 Peter 2:6)
▶ it is to be 'a dwelling in which God lives by his Spirit' (Ephesians 2:22).

We then are the bricks of God's building. He is at work to mould and prepare us so that we fit together properly. It is this objective that Paul had in mind when he spoke of God's building project in 1 Corinthians 3:9–17...

> **'T**he church is never a place, but always a people; never a fold but always a flock; never a sacred building but always a believing assembly. The church is you who pray, not where you pray.'
> JOHN HAVLIK

▶ Paul has laid the foundation
▶ Cephas (Peter) and others have built upon it
▶ Paul refers to himself as a master-builder (1 Corinthians 3:10)
▶ he warns of the danger of shoddy workmanship by human builders
▶ this is God's project to be carried out by his servants— and they will be judged on the quality of their work.

A building for God

This building is not just inhabited by us. God has chosen not to dwell in man-made temples (Acts 7:48; 17:24) but to live, not only in heaven, but among his people (1 Peter 2:4–5; Matthew 18:20; John 14:23). Visitors will be able to see that God lives in us! (1 Corinthians 14:25).

The divine architect is not merely preparing a building for today. The dust, dirt and confusion of our current church life may resemble a building-site, but the finished product will be God's own glorious temple.

This then is our future inheritance: God's building, anticipated by Abraham and the martyrs (Hebrews 11:10–16) and described by John in his heavenly vision (Revelation 21:2–4, 22). Ultimately the new Jerusalem is the final destination for the church—the building of God.

8 Koinonia for beginners

The previous sections looked at the spiritual resources which are available to the church today. This section asks how *koinonia*—our quality of partnership as a community—can be worked out in practice, particularly in the local church.

This section provides a jumping-off point for us to look at ourselves. Its focus is the hallmark which should characterize God's company: that we love one another (John 15:12; 1 John 4:11). This is...

▶ the new commandment which Jesus gave us (John 13:34)
▶ the means by which everyone would be able to identify the disciples of Jesus (John 13:35)
▶ a love which cannot exist merely as a theory, but has to be shown 'with actions and in truth' (1 John 3:18).

> 🔊 **KEY POINT** Love between Christians cannot exist simply as an idea—it has to be demonstrated by how we live and relate to each other.

This section contains ideas for putting this into practice in six areas...

▶ friendship
▶ support
▶ forgiveness
▶ communion
▶ encouragement
▶ servanthood.

Friendship

The great Hebrew word *hesedh*, which means 'covenant love' is used in Proverbs to describe friendship. It describes those who are constant in their relationships with others (Proverbs 17:17).

📢 **KEY POINT** When the Bible talks about friendship it is not referring to casual and superficial acquaintances.

The great friendships of the Bible all bear eloquent testimony to the calibre of the relationships which we should enjoy together...

▶ David and Jonathan (1 Samuel 20:17)

▶ Ruth and Naomi (Ruth 1:16)

▶ Elijah and Elisha (2 Kings 2:2).

Above all, as those who obey Jesus, we are called his friends (John 15:14–15). This is a great privilege because this friendship is a form of partnership. Jesus reveals the Father to us and shares his plans. This is a model for our friendships in the church.

It is not enough to regard ourselves as Christian colleagues. We are all friends of each other because we share the friendship of Jesus. And even more we are brothers and sisters because we have the same heavenly Father. We are a family.

A major contribution of the 'new churches' has been this emphasis on developing personal friendships. Taking time to eat together in our homes, participate in hobbies and sports, and establish contacts between our children has all encouraged the process.

However, we have to guard against the loneliness some people may feel if they are intentionally or unintentionally excluded. For example...

▶ in some areas people will resist going into the home of another person—the home is a private place

▶ single people can easily feel rejected if all the emphasis is on the interrelationship between couples.

So a greater emphasis on corporate social activities and mutual participation in worship can be a key factor in encouraging the growth of friendships in the local church.

A church which wants to turn acquaintanceship into friendship could begin with some of the following ideas...

▶ Take every opportunity and any excuse to bring people together to eat. Pot luck meals; picnics; harvest suppers; every-member barbecues; a fondue night.

▶ Identify existing 'team' activities (for example PCC membership; children's work teachers; music or ministry teams) and give each of them opportunities to relax together in a social setting.

▶ Look for (invent!) projects that cause people to work together as a team. Paint the building; replant the church garden; organize an event; create special music/singing for a seasonal service. Link the activity with opportunities to meet at other times and to relax (and eat!) together.

▶ Provide an 'I need it' noticeboard, so that people can identify their genuine needs. School uniforms; a bedside table; a child's car seat; and so on.

▶ Use home group materials which place an emphasis on helping members to grow in friendship as well as in faith. Ideal materials can be ordered from Small Group Resources, 48 Peterborough Road, London SW6 3EB.

▶ Set up opportunities for church members to meet on a 'non-religious' basis. A keep-fit club; a badminton evening; a ten-pin bowling competition; a pre-Christmas coach trip to raid the French hypermarkets; a silly games night. Be creative.

> '*T*he lovely thing about being a Christian is that you don't have to be right: you have to be forgiven.'
> MICHAEL MARSHALL

> '*C*hristianity is a social religion. To turn it into a solitary religion is indeed to destroy it.'
> JOHN WESLEY

PAUSE FOR THOUGHT
What is the best and what is the worst characteristic of your local church?

▶ Publish or display a master 'you may borrow' list. Jump leads; wallpaper stripper; food processor; power saw; and so on.

▶ Look for ways to help people discover each other's tastes and history. For example, a 'bring your favourite album track' evening; a 'bring an object with a memory' evening...

Support

Friendship is often developed through mutual support. This support has to come in a number of different versions...

Practical support—love in action involves 'being there' for one another. Taking the initiative to provide practical help. On an individual basis this can mean anything from doing the ironing, cutting the grass, minding the children, and so on.

Some churches organize a Care Team—setting up a rota so that there is always someone on call to provide care such as emergency transport, urgent provisions, and so on.

Emotional support—the New Testament speaks of weeping with those who weep (Romans 12:15). Tears and emotional distress are part of a normal Christian life. We are called to stand with people in their pain—listening, caring, understanding, and not judging.

Spiritual support—spiritual survival and growth is essentially a 'one another' activity, according to the New Testament. It involves taking an interest in the spiritual lives of each other: nurturing (Ephesians 5:19); counselling (Colossians 3:16); encouraging (1 Thessalonians 4:18); owning up to sin (James 5:16). This view of support is drawn straight from Paul's picture of the body of Christ (see pages 37–38). It flies in the face of the cultural norms of our society. Individualism, self-sufficiency and independence are seen as signs of great strength. And yet the church is called to follow a different pattern.

The challenge we face is to live as a community and not a hierarchy, as an organism rather than an organization. Just as the eye cannot fulfil the functions of an ear, or vice versa—so we too need one other (1 Corinthians 12:25).

Nicknames

The closer people are in their relationships and the greater their level of camaraderie the more likely they are to call each other by nicknames.

This tells us something about the first Christians. Rather than being stuck at the level of mere acquaintanceship, they were close enough as friends to indulge in nicknames.

▶ Simon became 'Rocky' (John 1:42)

▶ James and John became 'Sons of Thunder' (Mark 3:17)

▶ Thomas became 'the Twin' (John 11:16)

▶ Simeon became 'Niger' (Acts 13:1)

▶ Joseph became 'Son of Encouragement' (Acts 4:36).

A way to measure the level of genuine friendship in a church is to count up the number of people known by their nicknames that can be used to their face.

By acting in this way we demonstrate what it means to be an alternative society. We avoid being totally caught up in ourselves by being committed to the needs of each other. As Jesus said: 'It is more blessed to give than to receive' (Acts 20:35).

Cutting the lawn

One Spring Harvest speaker returned home with her family after three weeks at the event. A few days later, she was at the informal regular meeting of wives from the local church.

She shared with them her concern at the number of domestic tasks she had encountered on returning home. Three weeks of family washing and ironing, the house to clean, the shopping to do as well as her responsibilities to the church and in the community.

Wistfully she commented 'If only I had come home to find that someone had cut the grass.'

She was given a sharp rebuke: 'Who do you think you are? None of us have our lawn mown when we're away enjoying ourselves on holiday.'

The comment is perhaps natural enough. But the Spring Harvest speaker could be forgiven for thinking that giving out spiritually for a minimum of twelve hours a day, over three weeks, had scarcely been a holiday.

Didn't someone once say something about 'bearing one another's burdens'? And if the grass had been cut, would the neighbours have seen a quality of church life that they might have missed before?

Forgiveness

Jesus taught his disciples to pray that God would forgive them in the same way that they forgave others (Matthew 6:12). In other words, if we are not very good at forgiving others, God might not be 'very good' at forgiving us!

Jesus also shocked his listeners by announcing that...

▶ we should love our enemies (Matthew 5:44)

▶ we should give up any ideas of revenge—because vengeance belongs to the Lord, and not to us (Matthew 5:38–39; Romans 12:19).

What Christians are left with is only one option—the option of forgiveness.

The gospel pushes us into a corner. As C.S. Lewis said: 'There is no slightest suggestion that we are offered forgiveness on any other terms. It is made perfectly clear that if we do not forgive we shall not be forgiven.'

However, we have strong reasons to forgive others...

▶ we forgive others because Christ forgave us our sins (Ephesians 4:32; Colossians 3:13)

▶ we forgive because of the example Jesus set on the cross (Luke 23:34)

▶ we forgive because Jesus told his disciples they should do this as often as 'seventy times seven'—in other words, endlessly (Luke 17:4).

As forgiven people we also need to forgive one another. Our relationships together mirror our relationship with Christ. Resentment, bitterness and alienation can be replaced by reconciliation and restored relationships.

Even if we are the 'wronged' party in a dispute, the message of the Bible is clear: we must make the attempt (the first move, if necessary) to resolve the issue before we bring an offering to God (Matthew 5:23–24).

> '**E**veryone says forgiveness is a lovely idea, until they have something to forgive...'
> C.S. LEWIS

> '**A** pat on the back, though only a few vertebrae removed from a kick in the pants, is miles ahead in results.'
> ANON

> '**M**ay the God who gives endurance and encouragement give you a spirit of unity among yourselves as you follow Christ Jesus, so that with one heart and mouth you may glorify the God and Father of our Lord Jesus Christ.'
> PAUL, IN ROMANS 15:5–6

However, we not only have strong reasons to forgive. We can also seek the power of the Holy Spirit to forgive what we might think is unforgivable. This is not easy for us, but it is possible.

Communion

Right relationships with each other result in a positive sharing together. The very service of communion refers to a partnership or *koinonia* in the body and blood of Christ (1 Corinthians 10:16). The communion...

▶ symbolizes our unity (1 Corinthians 10:17)

▶ promotes a relationship of mutual concern for the well-being of one another (1 Corinthians 10:23–33)

▶ is the sign of true *koinonia*—the intimate, personal, mutually-committed relationship which exists with Jesus and with each other.

That partnership goes beyond the individual act. Important as communion is, our *koinonia* is then to be further worked out in how we act towards each other...

▶ exhibiting practical financial generosity towards each other (2 Corinthians 8:2; 9:13; Philippians 4:16)

▶ avoiding the creation of unnecessary problems for each other (1 Corinthians 8:9–13)

▶ sacrificing our own interests for the benefit of others (Philippians 2:3, 20–21)

▶ caring for the needs of each other (Romans 14:19).

The early church vividly demonstrated *koinonia* in two ways...

▶ they met to eat bread and drink wine

▶ and they also shared in the *agape* or love feast—this was a fellowship meal where they shared food and conversation in celebration of their being 'all one in Christ Jesus' (Galatians 3:28).

Some churches still reflect this by eating together in fellowship meals which are part of a service, or by eating informally at picnics, barbecues, and so on.

Encouragement

Over the years, the church has gained a bad name for its use of the tongue. There is nothing new in this—James was aware of this danger 1,900 years ago (see James 3:3–12).

All Christians need to be aware of the power of the words they use. Words can bring healing—or they can deeply wound. Gossip, criticism, jealousy, quarrelling and backbiting all cause destruction not only to other Christians, but also to the church as a community (see 2 Corinthians 12:20). The results can be disastrous. By stabbing each other in the back, we wound the body of Christ.

There is an alternative. Our words can bring life. The New Testament writers encouraged the first Christians to encourage each other. This is because encouragement...

▶ **reinforces our community** as God's called-out people (1 Thessalonians 4:18; 5:14; Hebrews 10:25)

▶ **builds God's people up** in their faith (1 Thessalonians 3:2; 5:11)

▶ **strengthens us** to live as Christians in what we do and say (2 Thessalonians 2:16–17)

▶ **brings refreshment and unity** to God's people (Romans 15:5; Philemon 7).

Christians in the early church had a habit of giving each

other nicknames (see the box page 40). Joseph, a Levite from Cyprus, was nicknamed 'son of encouragement' (Barnabas in Acts 4:36). If we gave more evidence of this kind of lifestyle, then the church would be far more attractive to the people outside it.

There are many ways in which we can develop this vital ministry...

▶ acts of simple kindness

▶ prayerful concern

▶ identifying with the needs of others

▶ befriending those who are ignored

▶ speaking up for those who are being criticized...

...along with many more.

Perhaps the most important of all is the practice of speaking words of encouragement to one another. Paul specifically mentions this aspect when writing to the church in the town of Thessalonica. 'Therefore encourage one another and build each other up, just as in fact you are doing' (1 Thessalonians 5:11).

Despite enduring severe persecution, this church had learned how to encourage one another. Here was a church where the Christians had learned to speak well of each other. They concentrated on supporting each other.

The Greek word which Paul uses here is *parakaleo*. This word is...

▶ used to **describe encouraging speech**, exhortation, comfort or teaching

▶ used to describe functions that will enable Christians to **build each other up** in Christ

▶ also the root of a word used as **a name for the Holy Spirit**—'the paraclete', or encourager. He is the one who gives us the power to strengthen each other.

This same message was reinforced by the writer of the Letter to the Hebrews: 'Let us consider how we may spur one another on towards love and good deeds. Let us not give up meeting together, as some are in the habit of doing, but let us encourage one another—and all the more as you see the Day approaching' (Hebrews 10:24–25).

We live in a society which encourages us to promote ourselves. The Bible encourages us to promote the needs and achievements of others.

Servanthood

To a generation which worships at the altar of self-esteem, the church has a message of profound importance. It is the call to servanthood (Mark 10:44). Jesus put it in a riddle: 'If anyone wants to be first, he must be the very last, and the servant of all' (Mark 9:35).

The implications are profound. True servants of Jesus Christ must...

▶ wash each other's feet (metaphorically at least), in the same way that Jesus did (John 13:14)

▶ esteem each other as more important than ourselves (Philippians 2:3; Romans 12:10)

▶ drop the superficial mask of self-respectability in order to 'walk in the light' with one another (1 John 1:7)

▶ show sympathy and compassion towards others (1 Peter 4:8; Romans 12:15)

▶ be honest about our feelings, open and vulnerable to each other (2 Corinthians 6:11)

'**G**ossip, rumour, human tradition, criticism, isolationism, pessimistic and negative comments have spread like a creeping cancer throughout the church of Christ. As this cancer has grown it has proved to be an unpopular sin to denounce because we are all so guilty of it.'
CLIVE CALVER

▶ unselfishly serve the interests of others (1 Thessalonians 2:8; 1 Corinthians 10:33; Philippians 2:4)

▶ reject the temptation of ambition to 'lord it' over others (1 Peter 5:3)

▶ accept any task assigned to them (Luke 17:10)

▶ bridge the divides of class, race, gender or generation in order to demonstrate that they are one body in Christ Jesus (Romans 12:16; Galatians 3:28)

▶ be happy to take the lowest position with genuine humility (Romans 12:16; Luke 14:8–11).

It is this kind of *koinonia* partnership which will amaze and provoke our secular society. It is this kind of life that Jesus calls us to. He has never looked for 'lone rangers' in the kingdom—just for partners to fulfil his purpose.

'If one part suffers, every part suffers with it; if one part is honoured, every part rejoices with it. Now you are the body of Christ, and each one of you is a part of it' (1 Corinthians 12:26–27).

PAUSE FOR THOUGHT
What place does criticism have in the local church?

Booklist

Balchin, J., *What the Bible Says about the Church*, Kingsway

Bell, P. and Jordan, P., *Conflict*, Scripture Union

Berkhof, L., *The History of Christian Doctrines*, Banner of Truth

Bradshaw, T., *The Olive Branch*, Paternoster

Burton-Jones, J., *Caring for Carers*, Scripture Union

Clements, R., *The Church that Turned the World Upside Down*, Crossway

Cleverly, C., *Church Planting, Our Future Hope*, Scripture Union

Cohen, D. and Gaukroger, S., *How to Close Your Church in a Decade*, Scripture Union

Conner, K., *The Church in the New Testament*, Sovereign

Copley, D. and N., *Building with Bananas*, Paternoster

Davies, W., *Gathered Into One*, Faith Press

Dowley, T., editor, *The History of Christianity*, Lion

Fernando, A., *Reclaiming Friendship*, IVP

Finney, J., *The Well Church Book*, Scripture Union

Frangipane, F., *The House of the Lord*, Word

Gamble, R., *The Irrelevant Church*, Monarch

Getz, G.A., *Sharpening the Focus of the Church*, Scripture Press

Gibbs, E., *I Believe in Church Growth*, Hodder & Stoughton

Gillies, S., *Get The Most Out of Church*, Scripture Union

Griffiths, M., *Cinderella With Amnesia*, IVP

Griffiths, M., *Get Your Act Together Cinderella*, IVP

Harper, M., *Three Sisters*, Tyndale

Hobson, P., *A Voice in the City*, Scripture Union

Hughes, S., *Discovering Your Place in the Body of Christ*, Marshall Pickering

Kirby, G.W., *Why All These Denominations?*, Kingsway

Lancaster, J., *The Spirit Filled Church*, Sovereign

Lane, A., *The Lion Concise Book of Christian Thought*, Lion

Lovelace, R.F., *Dynamics of Spiritual Life*, IVP

Lukasse, J., *Churches with Roots*, STL

Nicholls, B., editor, *The Church: God's Agent for Change*, WEF / Paternoster

Robinson and Christine, *Planting Tomorrow's Churches Today*, Monarch

Scott, M., *Prophecy in the Church*, Word

Snyder, H.A., *Liberating the Church*, Marshall Pickering

Snyder, H.A., *The Problem of Wine Skins*, IVP

Snyder, H.A., *The Community of the King*, IVP

Snyder, H.A., *The Radical Wesley*, IVP

Stedman, R.C., *Body Life*, Regal

Tillapaugh, F., *The Church Unleashed*, Regal

Trudinger, R., *Master Plan*, Olive Tree

Wright, N., *Challenge to Change*, Kingsway

Youssef, M., *Leading the Way*, Marshall Pickering

Problems
Facing the hurts that are there

CONTENTS

Introduction: the church in difficulties

1   The problem of unity

2   The problem of relevance

3   The problem of change

4   Pain in the body

5   The problem of leadership

Booklist

Book of the seminar day:
Charles Colson, *The Body*, Word

Introduction: the church in difficulties

KEY POINT The church has always had problems—right from the very earliest days of the Christian faith.

Paul's letter to the Christians in Corinth (1 Corinthians) shows that today we don't face any problems that weren't being tackled even then. The New Testament has direct things to say about our difficulties with the church at the end of the twentieth century.

Many problems confront the church—each of us could come up with our own extensive list! This section of the notes explores just five of the big issues. The problems of:

▶ **unity**—why are Christians so divided?

▶ **relevance**—how can we show Jesus to our culture?

▶ **change**—how can we cope, or introduce change without chaos?

▶ **pain in the body**—how can we resolve problems in the church?

▶ **leadership**—how can we develop biblical patterns of leadership?

Meanwhile, in Philippi . . .

Many of the New Testament letters were written to deal with the problems of local churches. The church in Philippi had a fairly typical set of problems . . .

▶ disunity (Philippians 4:2)

▶ external pressures from a corrupt society (Philippians 1:28; 2:15)

▶ suffering for their faith (Philippians 1:29–30)

▶ the need for greater holiness (Philippians 1:27; 2:14)

▶ pride and selfishness (Philippians 2:3–4)

▶ a disruptive faction (Philippians 3:2–4)

▶ false teaching (Philippians 3:18–19).

This list from the first century describes many churches in the twentieth!

Finding a local church

Mark had just become a Christian, and he was looking for a good local church.

One Sunday he went along to the church nearest him, but he was shocked by what he found there. It wasn't just the savage gossip that he overheard before the service began—there were other things he hadn't expected to find. The sermon that denied the resurrection of Christ. The quarrelling that broke out during holy communion. The group of people who got up and walked out during the prayers.

After the service, someone filled Mark in on all the latest news about the church. How two members of the congregation were suing each other. How another man was having an affair with his stepmother. How the church was about to split four ways.

Mark went home and started to have serious second thoughts about his new-found faith.

Suppose that you could offer Mark some advice. What would you say to him? Perhaps you would tell him to try a different church. To look somewhere else. To find a New Testament church.

The problem is that the church Mark went to *was* a New Testament church. Mark was a citizen of the first century, and his local church was the church in Corinth.

'The church stands in the fire of the criticism of its Lord. It is also exposed to the criticism of the world and this criticism has never been altogether false and unjust.'
KARL BARTH

'In general the churches, visited by me too often on weekdays... bore for me the same relation to God that billboards did to Coca-Cola: they promoted thirst without quenching it.'
JOHN UPDIKE

PAUSE FOR THOUGHT
If your church was on trial, would you be a witness for the prosecution or the defence?

Not the church!

What do people think of the church?

Jesus I like, but not the church.

Outdated and irrelevant.

Full of unfriendly people

The biggest obstacle to my ever finding faith.

Boring!

Full of people with archaic values.

The services are irrelevant.

Always asking for money.

Can't even agree together about their message, but expect us to believe it.

Which church?

The church is a bit of a joke!

Adapted from Paul Weston, *Why We Can't Believe*

---

1 *The problem of unity*

In the previous section we examined the *koinonia* partnership which exists between Christians.

Theologically the truth is that committed believers are one body and one people. But while this may be true in theory we are not always so good at working it out in practice.

KEY POINT The scandal of Christian disunity remains a major stumbling block to non-Christians.

While we may believe that despite our differences, all true Christians are united, this is not how the external observer sees things. And for good reason—at the last count, there were some 22,000 different Christian denominations around the world.

Why has this happened? This section looks at the unity of the church, starting with Jesus himself.

What did Jesus mean by unity?

In the hours before his death, Jesus prayed for his disciples and for all who would later come to faith in him (John 17). Four times in this great prayer, Jesus asks his Father to grant the same request.

KEY POINT His longing is that his followers may be one, even as he and his Father are one (John 17:11, 21, 22, 23).

This unity has a purpose . . .

▶ to glorify Jesus (John 17:1, 5, 24)

▶ to protect his people (John 17:11–12, 15)

▶ that the rest of society may know who Jesus is (John 17:21, 23)

▶ that others may be able to recognize those who follow Jesus (John 13:35; 17:23).

This unity is not extended to the whole of humankind. It is restricted . . .

▶ to those who bear his name (John 17:11)

▶ to those who have been given to Jesus (John 17:2, 6, 9)

▶ to those who have believed in Jesus and in whom he now lives (John 17:8, 20–21, 26)

▶ to those who are loved by God and have received eternal life (John 17:2, 23)

▶ to those who know God and acknowledge his word as truth (John 17:3, 8, 17)

▶ to those who are sanctified by the truth and now go into the world to proclaim it (John 17:17–18).

For such people, their unity is generic. It is not worked for or earned—it is a simple fact. We have been born into God's everlasting family. Our *Creator* God has become our *Father* God. Sharing the same Father, we become brothers and sisters together. This is the message of Jesus—our unity is the gift of God for which he prayed.

Three ways of looking at our oneness

So how is our essential oneness to be worked out today? Three models have been suggested...

▶ **Uniformity**—it is argued, specifically by the Roman Catholic Church, that as there is one church, there can only be one model for it. Therefore, the Roman Church is the mother church, and all others are schismatics who must one day return to it.

▶ **Union**—the ecumenical argument is that the scandal of our disunity can only be remedied by differing churches moving towards a close union together. This union would be structural and necessitates inter-church consultation and agreement to overcome our differences and foster a climate for reunion.

▶ **Unity**—while some Evangelicals may be attracted by a desire for structural union, the vast majority are content to recognize the distinctives which exist over styles of worship and forms of church government. It is argued that Jesus made the acceptance of God's word as truth a non-negotiable prerequisite for unity.

Therefore Christians may choose to stay in different worshipping congregations—but all who own a commitment to biblical doctrines, the sole authority of scripture and saving faith in Jesus possess an inherent unity which cannot be destroyed by secondary causes of disagreement.

This unity is expressed by growing co-operation and partnership, while a variety of forms of worship and church membership are still maintained.

Unity among local churches

How can local churches express their unity together? This section looks at...

▶ differences between Evangelicals

▶ working with other Evangelicals

▶ working with non-Evangelicals.

Differences between Evangelicals

Evangelicals have suffered an identity crisis during the twentieth century in which many of us have forgotten who we are. Earlier in the century, the name Evangelical was often mocked and abused. Many withdrew into isolation—losing touch with one another, we also lost contact with the wider world.

Today the picture is radically different. Society seems to be rediscovering Evangelicals, and assuming that all who bear that label are automatically exactly the same as each other.

In recent years, media attention has been concentrated on Evangelicals to an unprecedented degree. Why has this happened?

▶ there have been major appointments of Evangelicals to key leadership positions within the different denominations

▶ 45 per cent of Protestant churchgoers in England describe themselves as Evangelical in belief

▶ high-profile events such as the missions of Billy Graham, March for Jesus and the growth of Spring Harvest (now the largest inter-church event in Europe) have captured public interest

▶ the indiscretions of a few American evangelists and their concentration on financial gain have also attracted media attention.

A MIXED PRESS

Much news coverage of Evangelicals has been critical. It is assumed by many in the secular press that British Evangelicals are...

▶ the same as their North American counterparts

▶ politically right-wing, constituting a moral majority of born-againers

▶ 'fundamentalists'—an American term with a different meaning from 'Bible-believing'

▶ a homogeneous mass, all believing and saying the same things.

Slowly, some journalists are realizing that the real picture is radically different, and much more complex. Simple assumptions that British Evangelicals are no more than a pale reflection of their North American counterparts are being shattered. Some progress is being made in educating public opinion that the word 'Evangelical' is most often used as a noun, to which many different adjectives can be attached.

Evangelicals can be Anglican or non-Anglican; Reformed or Arminian; innovative or traditional; Charismatic or non-Charismatic. The list of alternative descriptions is a long one!

KEY POINT Evangelicals are not duplicates of one another; they have an intrinsic oneness, but come in a multitude of different varieties.

So a reformed, Charismatic, new-church Evangelical can share a common bond with an Arminian, non-Charismatic Methodist Evangelical. Both are committed Evangelicals—but their distinctive areas of disagreement are also important.

This may sound complicated, but definition is crucial for a true picture to emerge. Four key areas which reveal distinctives between Evangelicals help us to understand how this 'same yet different' principle works.

1 CALVINIST AND ARMINIAN

▶ **Arminians** believe that everyone is free to choose for, or against, faith in Jesus Christ. It is possible for Christians to fall away from saving faith. God's election is his fore-knowledge, not selection.

▶ **Calvinists** hold the opposite position. They stress God's sovereignty in all matters. They believe that God's election is more important in a person's salvation than the exercise of human free will, and that once saved equals always saved.

Wesley and Whitefield

During the Great Evangelical Awakening, John Wesley and George Whitefield disagreed over the Calvinist–Arminian issue. Wesley was an Arminian and Whitefield a Calvinist.

Near the end of his life Wesley was asked by one of his more partisan supporters if he expected to see George Whitefield in heaven. It was a question expecting the answer 'no'.

Wesley replied: 'No, I don't, for George Whitefield will be so near the throne of Christ and I will be so far away.'

These particular issues have divided Evangelicals for centuries—and they still do so today.

Despite this tension, both groups stress the importance of personal conversion. Their central difference lies in who makes the first move; God or ourselves.

2 ANGLICAN AND FREE CHURCH

Up until a century ago in England, Anglicans enjoyed privileges denied to everyone in the Free Churches. These included...

▶ rights of burial in consecrated ground

▶ parliamentary representation

▶ civil service preferment

▶ many other advantages

This caused an inevitable sense of resentment on the part of Free Churches, which occasionally flared up into mutual hostility.

Today, with an increasing number of Evangelicals within the Anglican Church, the differences between these two major blocs of Evangelicals have diminished. However, several differences over important matters still remain. These include issues such as...

▶ infant baptism and believers' baptism (although not all Free Churches are against infant baptism)

▶ confirmation

▶ episcopacy (the authority of bishops).

However, the greatest rift lies in the fact that...

▶ the Church of England is established as the state church, while the Free Churches are separate groups of gathered congregations.

Over the last century, this gulf has diminished. Anglicans and non-Anglicans join together in diverse evangelistic and social initiatives. Mutual involvement in the vast variety of para-church societies and joint church activities, both local and national, have served to encourage a high degree of shared understanding and partnership across church boundaries.

Many similar tensions have existed between the Church of Scotland (the established, Presbyterian Church north of the Border) and the various Free Church denominations that exist alongside it. Here too, past divisions are being replaced by a growing sense of mutual understanding—even though fundamental differences remain.

3 CHARISMATIC AND NON-CHARISMATIC

For some years after the emergence of the Charismatic Movement in the 1960s it was popular to differentiate

'A younger generation of Christians has found traditional church structures too restrictive for the kind of fellowship and worship they are seeking. Leaders in the house churches are ready to admit mistakes have been made. The charge of being schismatic may be true in some cases, but more often than not it is a question of new wine not being able to exist in the old wineskins.'
GILBERT KIRBY

'The Pentecostal denominations which were to develop into such a major force in 20th Century Evangelicalism would perhaps shudder to be called the first Charismatics. They owed their origins to Azusa Street and similar outbreaks of spiritual power at the turn of the century. Fifty years later the Charismatics turned up on the scene like the bride who had missed out on the wedding!'
CLIVE CALVER

between Charismatics and Evangelicals, just as people had differentiated between Evangelical and Pentecostal in previous generations. It was argued that...

▶ the Charismatic emphasis emerged from a desire to see God's power visibly at work among his people today

▶ the Evangelical emphasis replaced an emphasis on personal experience with a commitment to understanding the truths contained in the Bible.

This division may make things look neat and simple, but it lacks objectivity. If Evangelicalism is not restricted to a particular denomination in the church, but transcends divisions about different styles of worship or forms of church government, then this verbal distinction becomes totally artificial.

There are some Evangelicals who would deny that Charismatics are true Evangelicals. Equally, there are some Charismatics who would hesitate to call themselves Evangelicals. But, even when added together, these represent only a tiny minority.

Charismatics and Evangelicals share a wholehearted commitment to...

▶ the authority of the Bible

▶ the need for conversion and holy Christian living

▶ other fundamental biblical doctrines.

The central position maintained by an overwhelming majority is that the true divide does not lie between Charismatic and Evangelical but between Charismatic Evangelicals and non-Charismatic Evangelicals.

How does the Holy Spirit work?

Initial fragmentation between these two groups revolved around the idea that the Holy Spirit worked in exactly the same fashion in the life of every believer. Some felt themselves to be regarded as no more than second-class Christians because they did not use certain spiritual gifts. Others felt that their experience was being reduced to the level of pure subjectivism, beyond the traditions of the church or the teaching of scripture.

Charismatic and Evangelical

	church members	% of total
Charismatic Evangelicals	424,100	41
Non-Charismatic Evangelicals	603,100	59

What is a Charismatic?

A Charismatic is someone who...

▶ has a crisis experience, or baptism, of the Holy Spirit—normally subsequent to their conversion, or occasionally simultaneous with it

▶ is enabled by the power of the Holy Spirit to exercise spiritual gifts such as prophecy, healing or speaking in tongues

▶ worships God in a characteristically spontaneous and joyful way.

Since those early days, more light and less heat has been generated in this debate. The majority of British Evangelicals will concede today that, while all receive the Holy Spirit at conversion...

▶ some proceed through a gradual and progressive sanctification

▶ others experience the Holy Spirit in a new, crisis experience which then matures in their daily lives.

In addition...

▶ some Christians use spiritual gifts

▶ others do not use spiritual gifts, but they do not deny their existence.

The days are long gone when Evangelical believers in Germany produced the Berlin Declaration of 1909 and claimed that spiritual gifts were demonic counterfeits. Pentecostal believers are welcomed as Evangelicals in the fullest sense. There is a growing link between Pentecostal denominations and Charismatics within other churches. They stand together in the belief that spiritual gifts have been used by a minority of Evangelical believers throughout the centuries of the Christian church.

It would be foolish to pretend that tensions and suspicions no longer exist. Evangelicals remain clearly divided on this issue. After all, there are no less than nine major views on the subject of the baptism of the Holy Spirit. It is important not to fall into the trap of trying to match our own spiritual hunger, experience or understanding to those of our neighbour. We cannot demand that everyone should walk the same spiritual pathway that we do.

Gradually there is a growing consensus that just as we all need the Holy Spirit, so Evangelicals need each other. We must stand together, despite our different perceptions about the work of the Holy Spirit.

4 NEW WINESKINS AND OLDER ONES

Few of us cope easily with change. The emergence of fresh patterns of team leadership, different styles of worship and new initiatives among Evangelicals have all contributed to a sense of transition and uncertainty.

While some have greeted such changes with enthusiasm, others have exhibited greater caution. A reluctance to comply with change has sometimes resulted in hostility and accusations of drifting away from biblical truth.

Nowhere is this trend more vividly illustrated than in the creation of a growing number of new congregations with a different style of leadership and worship.

The emergence of the new churches has caused consternation to many of their fellow-Evangelicals. Those who have maintained a faithful witness in a particular locality have felt threatened by the new churches...

▶ vigorous commitment to church-planting

▶ creation of new congregations

▶ robust evangelism

▶ clear commitment to Charismatic worship

▶ experimental view of the church

These emphases have often created both resentment and suspicion.

Two dangers have emerged...

▶ the new churches can make disparaging comments concerning the old which they have left behind

> '*E*ven the best Evangelical religion bears little resemblance to the experience of the Apostles. We have conditioned ourselves not to notice this... Is there any good reason why the Charismatic element in the New Testament should not continue throughout history? Should we play down evidences of a supernatural God in case they might disturb the weaker brother? Surely if God is working we should shout it from the housetops. And if our shouting upsets the apple-cart—Amen to that.'
> GAVIN REID, BISHOP OF MAIDSTONE

> '*A* work of God without stumbling blocks is never to be expected.'
> JONATHAN EDWARDS

> '*I*f the local church is restrictive and set in unyielding traditional ways, those within the body of Christ who are growing, expanding, developing and changing will shed their old allegiances like a butterfly emerging from a spent pupa case.'
> EILEEN VINCENT

Other Evangelical differences

These four issues do not constitute the only grounds for division among contemporary Evangelicals—far from it!

Evangelicals sincerely hold opposing positions on...

▶ feminism and the ordination of women

▶ the importance of socio-political and community involvement

▶ the nature, occasion and results of the return of Jesus Christ

▶ the current condition and future prospects of the church.

These all illustrate the fact that we are not as uniform in our perspectives as the popular media would have us believe!

▶ the older churches tend to forget that they were once new, and ignore the memory of how they were treated by those who were there before them.

Opportunities and dangers

Many within the new churches are fresh converts reached by positive Christian outreach. Others are more mature Christians. They saw denominational involvement as a product of their upbringing, rather than the result of firmly-held convictions, and so they were happy to try a new model.

Some older churches have learned valuable lessons from their new counterparts. For example...

▶ the emphasis on friendship

▶ cultivating contact during the week as well as in church gatherings

▶ the vocabulary of worship created in the new churches has tended to spread to the wider church.

A more conciliatory attitude is gradually emerging as each recognizes the Evangelicalism of the other. Symptomatic of this is the way that many more traditional churches will join in events such as Marches for Jesus, while new church leaders lend their support to more traditional Evangelical associations. This is all good for partnership, and mutual understanding can develop without always having to arrive at an agreement.

Nevertheless, problems do still exist...

▶ some claim to be more biblically sound in their doctrine

▶ others feel that spiritual life is strangled by rigid human traditions

▶ the particular danger of exclusivism is always present—those engaged in pioneering initiatives will often respond to hostility from existing Christian structures by withdrawing into themselves.

However, bridges are slowly being built, and a fresh sense of commitment to one another is being created against the background of constant change.

Working with other Evangelicals

Increasingly, Evangelical churches from different backgrounds are working together on a local level. A good example of this is the formation of Local Evangelical Fellowships, an initiative started by the Evangelical Alliance.

A Local Evangelical Fellowship is an association of local churches, societies and individuals in a defined community or region, who commit themselves to work together under the Evangelical Alliance basis of faith. This sort of partnership...

▶ provides a meeting point for local church leaders—who can share in mutual support, prayer and encouragement

▶ enables Christians to work together effectively—Christians together are able to witness to their community with greater power and with better resources

▶ builds up good relationships between churches—as Christians from different denominations and traditions come together, their suspicions are overcome and their faith is encouraged

▶ gives local churches a united voice—a coherent Christian voice carries weight with the media and

> *'In matters essential—unity.*
> *In matters non-essential—liberty.*
> *In all things—charity.'*
> WITSIUS

local authorities and makes campaigning more effective

▶ establishes a national link with other Evangelical churches—making individual churches aware of their wider belonging to the church nationally and worldwide

Local Evangelical Fellowships have worked together in many areas of the UK on specific projects. These include...

▶ Southampton: a pregnancy advice and care centre

▶ Bath: Christian books in libraries

▶ Merseyside: a Christian resources directory

▶ Wolverhampton: creative united mission

▶ South Wessex: a united church-planting strategy.

Working with non-Evangelicals

🖝 **KEY POINT Not all Evangelicals agree about the extent to which co-operation with non-Evangelicals is legitimate.**

▶ Some take the stance that co-operation at any level is tantamount to giving approval to all that non-Evangelicals believe and do

▶ Others feel able to work closely alongside non-Evangelicals, providing their own identity is not lost.

However, most Evangelicals are prepared to co-operate on issues of social need and justice. Others are also prepared to worship and study the Bible together.

Nevertheless, most Evangelicals are unwilling to engage in evangelism with those who do not share their belief and commitment to the central Christian truth of the need for repentance and faith in Jesus Christ alone for forgiveness and new life.

Unity and diversity

Evangelicals unite on primary issues such as...

▶ the divine inspiration of Holy Scripture

▶ the full deity and humanity of Jesus Christ

▶ the physical resurrection of Jesus from the dead

▶ the justification of the sinner by the grace of God alone.

Evangelicals agree to differ on secondary issues such as...

▶ infant baptism

▶ forms of church leadership

▶ beliefs about the millennium

▶ styles of worship and evangelism.

PAUSE FOR THOUGHT
Is your view of the 'baptism of the Spirit' a primary or secondary matter?

The 12 tribes of Evangelicalism

It is not an easy task to classify the various streams and groups of Evangelicals in the UK today. One suggestion points to twelve tribes with their own leaders, structures, ideas and heroes.

1 Anglican Evangelicals—about one in four who attend the Church of England are Evangelicals. Their focus is in the Anglican Evangelical Assembly and the Church of England Evangelical Council. Many are linked to the Church Pastoral Aid Society and Church Society. (Some of this group prefer to be called Evangelical Anglicans.)

2 Pentecostals—the three largest Pentecostal denominations are the Assemblies of God, Elim and the Apostolic Churches.

3 Ethnic churches—the so-called black churches of African or Caribbean origin. Mainly Pentecostal, they include an extensive number of denominations and churches in association with each other. The largest denomination is the New Testament Church of God. There are also many other ethnic churches in Britain including Asian, Chinese, Spanish, Portuguese and Iranian.

4 Renewal groups—Charismatic Evangelicals are a significant sub-section in all denominations. Some have their own identity, as with Anglican Renewal Ministries in the Church of England. According to the English Church Census, around 7,000 English Roman Catholics see themselves as

Charismatic or Evangelical.

5 Separatists—these are mainly Reformed (Calvinist) in their theology. They are not willing to be part of a denomination that includes non-Evangelicals. Some also separate from Evangelicals who are part of such mixed denominations. Key groups of separatist Evangelicals include the Evangelical Movement of Wales, the Free Church of Scotland, the Grace Baptists and the British Evangelical Council.

6 Reformed Evangelicals—Evangelicals of Reformed (Calvinist) persuasion exist within major denominations. For example, the (Anglican) Church Society and, more recently, the Proclamation Trust (a non-denominational organization which emphasizes biblical preaching and teaching).

7 Evangelical majorities—these are those in a denomination where the vast majority are Evangelicals. This includes the Salvation Army, the Presbyterian Church of Ireland and the Baptist Union.

8 Evangelical minorities—some Evangelicals are part of denominations where they are in the minority. This includes the Methodist Church, the Congregational Union and the United Reformed Church. Several have their own organizations within the denomination to foster their identity

and objectives. These include Headway in Methodism and the Group for Evangelism And Renewal (GEAR) in the URC.

9 Evangelical non-denominational groups—these are independent churches that are loosely affiliated together, but without denominational structure or identity. Wholly Evangelical, these include the Christian Brethren, the Assembly of God churches and churches within the Fellowship of Independent Evangelical Churches.

10 The New Churches—the title 'New Churches' has replaced the ineptly named House Church Movement. In the main, these are groups of churches linked under the leadership of someone they regard as an Apostle.

11 Independents—many Evangelicals are in churches which maintain a total independence, but are often happy to co-operate with fellow Evangelicals elsewhere.

12 Evangelical denominations—some small denominations are totally Evangelical—including the Free Church of England, the Churches of Christ and the Independent Methodists.

Taken from Clive Calver, Ian Coffey and Peter Meadows, *Who Do Evangelicals Think They Are?*

In a wider arena, many Christian initiatives have worked on the basis of seeking to be involved with individual Christians rather than seeking to make formal relationships with non-Evangelical denominations and groupings. This is particularly true where individuals are able to give assent to essential Evangelical belief while being part of denominational or local church structures that would not be willing or able to do so.

UNITY IN THE CHURCH NATIONALLY

It is easy to see that major differences exist between the different traditions and denominations of the church at a national level. One approach to tackling these differences has been to bring the churches back together in what is known as the ecumenical movement.

Because of Spring Harvest's Evangelical commitment, this movement will be analysed from that viewpoint.

However much we may want to see all true Christians united, the term Christian needs some amplification...

▶ can Evangelicals unite with those who deny the bodily resurrection of Jesus and the uniqueness of Christ?

▶ is it true that those who believe in the infallibility of the Bishop of Rome and the sole authority of scripture can co-exist together?

▶ are the traditions of automatic regeneration through baptism and the need for personal conversion truly compatible?

The answer to these questions has to be no.

Such a strident affirmation may make many of us feel uncomfortable. We do not like to emphasize differences in the church, but the only alternative is to submerge truth in a welter of compromise and uncertainty.

If the price tag for unity is to ignore—or even to destroy—Christian truth, then it is too high! The ecumenical movement is a ready-made vehicle for the expression of Christian unity, but it often falls into the trap of dispensing with the essential fundamentals of Christian belief.

The ecumenical argument is that Christians can unite together in basic harmony, based on a simple Trinitarian formula. Many Evangelicals have voiced serious disagreement with this appealing suggestion. The conviction that some doctrines, such as the authority of scripture and the deity of Jesus are beyond negotiation, lies at the root of their disquiet. Truth, it is argued, can never be sacrificed at the altar of Christian unity.

EVANGELICALS AND THE ECUMENICAL MOVEMENT

Evangelicals are different. They differ from the Roman Catholic Church, for example, on issues such as the authority of the Pope, the place of tradition, the priesthood—and many other important matters.

But their prime problem with the ecumenical movement lies in the idea of uniting with Protestants who embrace liberal theology. The problem here is that the liberal tradition takes issue with the following Evangelical essentials...

▶ there is no means to know God as Father through other faiths

▶ human beings are naturally sinful, our essential goodness having been damaged by the fall

▶ salvation comes only through the Lord Jesus Christ

▶ not everyone will be saved

▶ Jesus was born of a virgin, died, rose bodily from the grave and ascended to his Father

▶ all have the right to hear the Christian message—whatever their present faith or beliefs might be

▶ the Bible ultimately comes from God and is true in all that it affirms—including miraculous interventions

▶ a personal relationship with God, through conversion or growth in the faith, is essential to salvation

▶ the Bible is the final authority for all that we do

▶ only God can forgive sins.

EVANGELICALS AND UNITY

Here are two surprising facts about Christian unity...

▶ schemes for Christian union have frequently resulted in numerical decline for those churches which have joined forces together

▶ conversely, the uniting of those who hold to the same doctrines but operate in diverse denominations has frequently resulted in friendly relations and growth.

It was just this kind of pan-Evangelical spirit of sharing and fellowship which resulted in the formation of the Evangelical Alliance in 1846. In this context no compromise on essentials is necessary, and the result is a vehicle for mutual co-operation and support.

The objective of the ecumenical movement is far more ambitious. Instead of aiming at partnership between those who share common convictions, it aims at providing a base for union between all churches. This is not to suggest that the majority of UK Evangelicals are not associated with the ecumenical movement through their particular denominations...

▶ two-thirds of British Evangelicals are, in fact, members of denominations which have linked together in the Council of Churches for Britain and Ireland (the replacement body for the British Council of Churches)

▶ the remaining one-third are convinced that it is wrong to exist in structural partnership with non-Evangelicals, or to belong to a mixed denomination—one which contains Evangelicals and non-Evangelicals

▶ a small minority holds the view, known as 'secondary separateness', that no true Evangelical can join with Evangelicals who are prepared to link with such ecumenical structures or mixed denominations.

Fortunately, attitudes are softening. While bodies such as the Evangelical Alliance firmly distance themselves from ecumenical structures, there is a willingness to engage in dialogue and a desire to help non-Evangelicals understand the distinctive truths that Evangelicals believe.

The fact remains that Evangelicals are recovering a sense of unity rather than union. They are willing to work together on the basis of shared convictions rather than to seek to gain agreement on every issue. If such attitudes continue they may well survive long after schemes for church union have evaporated.

CHRISTIAN TOGETHERNESS

How then can we demonstrate our essential togetherness to a watching world?

> '*O*ur Alliance unites Charismatic and non-Charismatic Evangelicals, Anglican and Free Church Evangelicals, black and white Evangelicals, Calvinist and Arminian Evangelicals, ecumenical and anti-ecumenical Evangelicals—all stand shoulder to shoulder. Whatever our significant differences, we are united in the fact that we are all Evangelicals together!'
> PETER LEWIS

 KEY POINT Evangelical unity is rooted in doctrinal agreement—and also in shared experience.

Personal conversion to Christ lies at the heart of all Evangelical belief. We are one because we all know the same heavenly Father, through the death of his Son. Through the work of the indwelling Holy Spirit, this miracle of grace has occurred. We are one with him—and with each other.

But are we then excluding all those who do not call themselves Evangelical?

▶ many of those who feel comfortable in other traditions are clearly positive, committed Christians

▶ there are others who are uncertain about accepting any label at all except that of being a Christian

▶ others prefer a more meditative, contemplative tradition, yet love the same Lord as we do

▶ some with a more sceptical approach to the Bible clearly have hearts which are more obviously Christian than their heads!

Yet to pretend that differences do not exist would be a dangerous deception. To pretend that they do not matter would be worse! As Evangelicals we need a humble but positive approach—affirming the differences, expressing our position, and allowing the Living God to determine the final outcome.

Four key areas

What is it that makes the denominations different from each other? There are four key areas . . .

▶ particular doctrines held to be of critical importance within a specific denomination—for example, the use of spiritual gifts among Pentecostals, the baptism of adult believers by Baptists, etc.

▶ forms of church government

▶ styles of worship

▶ national, cultural and ethnic differences.

Unity and the worldwide church

KEY POINT For the first 1,000 years after the death of Christ, there were only minor splits away from the one 'Catholic' church. Since the year 1000 there have been two major splits, followed by countless other smaller ones . . .

Split 1—The first major division of the church took place around the year 1054. This division into Roman Catholic and Eastern Orthodox came about because of doctrinal disputes, the question of allegiance to the Pope, and an accident of geography. Despite the split, the Western and Eastern churches were still seen as essentially one church.

Split 2—This all changed in 1517 when a rebellious priest, Martin Luther, arrived on the scene to challenge the corrupt practices and traditions of the church. What followed is known as the Reformation. The Christians who split away from the Roman Catholic Church formed a new stream—the Protestant Church. Both sides in the dispute saw themselves as the one, true church.

Smaller splits—Once the church had been visibly divided, there was nothing to prevent it from happening again. Protestants began to split and split again into different church groups.

Roman Catholics argue that . . .

▶ the only true unity lies in the one, true and original church

▶ everyone should return to this church

▶ the church is under the leadership of the Pope, who is regarded as God's anointed successor to the first Bishop of Rome, the Apostle Peter.

Others agree that we need to return to the one, true and original church—but they disagree that the Roman Catholic Church is it. What we need, they say, is to reunite with each other.

However, the situation is not that simple. Our disagreements are not simply cosmetic. More fundamental issues are at stake.

It is tempting to consider the potential influence and status of one great superchurch. But we have to examine the real issues which divide us.

Separate denominations

The most obvious divisions between Christians for the casual observer are our different denominations. The denominations are there because Christians hold different views on four areas (see the 'Four key areas' box).

The differences in these four areas have created the groups we see today . . .

▶ Roman Catholics

▶ Anglicans

▶ Pentecostals

▶ Presbyterians

▶ Baptists

▶ etc . . . .

Each of these divisions has smaller divisions. For example, Pentecostals divide into . . .

▶ Assemblies of God

▶ the Apostolic Church

▶ the Elim Pentecostal Church

▶ the New Testament Church of God

▶ and many, many more

Geography, historic disagreements and ethnic considerations also intrude, so that Presbyterians in the United Kingdom become . . .

▶ the Presbyterian Church of Ireland

▶ the Church of Scotland

▶ the United Reformed Church

▶ the Free Church of Scotland

▶ the United Free Church of Scotland

▶ the Welsh Presbyterian Church, and so on . . .

We shouldn't underestimate the force of these many divisions. The differences between them are sincerely held—trivialize or ignore them at your peril.

Most denominations emerged because people felt strongly about the shortcomings of the church of their time. Christians tried to put right what they believed were omissions or abuses in their church. Very few people actually started out to create a new denomination—but that was often the end result.

For example, John Wesley was an Anglican. He would have hated to be known as the founder of the Methodist Church!

The changing face of denominations

The differences between denominations aren't what they used to be. Twenty years ago loyalty to your denomination was taken more seriously than it is today. However, a lot has changed in twenty years! To take just four examples of change which have affected most denominations…

▶ the renewal movement and new styles of worship

▶ the growth of Evangelicalism

▶ the emergence of new churches

▶ the rediscovered emphasis of social concern.

These and other changes have cut clean across the old denominational divides. The result is that many people now have a greater sense of loyalty to being an Evangelical or being renewed than to being a Baptist or a Methodist. This has led to a migration of people between the different denominations. Transfer growth has become a key factor in the strengthening of some churches at the expense of others.

Others have seized the opportunity to strengthen their commitment to their specific denomination. The development of Evangelical groups within particular denominations has been part of a process which began with the Keele conference of Anglican Evangelicals in 1967.

Significant changes have also taken place in the leadership of some of the major denominations. This has resulted in the promotion of Evangelicals to key positions

PAUSE FOR THOUGHT
Where does your church loyalty lie? If you moved into a new area, would you seek out a church of the same denomination, or go to an Evangelical church of whatever denomination?

'*T*here is no salvation outside the church.'
AUGUSTINE OF HIPPO
AD354–430

of prominence and influence.

Separate traditions

There are differences within the church which go deeper than groups and denominations.

KEY POINT The church contains a number of traditions. Each tradition has its own way of thinking, feeling and acting about the Christian faith.

Looking at these traditions exposes the most fundamental differences within the church.

In this section we are going to look at five of these traditions…

▶ Catholic

▶ Orthodox

▶ Liberal

▶ Broad Church

▶ Evangelical.

1 THE CATHOLIC TRADITION

This tradition is not confined to the Roman Catholic Church—it can also be seen in the Catholic wing of the Church of England, popularly known as 'Anglo-Catholicism'.

Catholics emphasize…

▶ the traditions and authority of the church, including

English churchmanship and denomination by adult attenders 1989

	Methodist	Baptist	URC	Independent	Afro-Caribbean	Pentecostal	Other	TOTAL Free Churches	Anglican	Roman Catholic	Orthodox	TOTAL Christian
Broad Evangelical	93,900	37,400	3,600	31,600	2,700	600	24,000	193,800	146,500	–	–	340,300
Mainstream Evangelical	16,800	79,200	2,400	64,300	10,500	7,400	40,200	220,800	39,500	2,500	–	262,800
Charismatic Evangelical	15,200	43,900	7,300	115,200	46,300	83,300	3,300	314,500	106,200	3,400	–	424,100
TOTAL Evangelical	125,900	160,500	13,300	311,100	59,500	91,300	67,500	729,100	292,200	5,900	–	1,027,200
Low Church	76,600	7,100	17,500	8,200	300	600	4,800	115,100	118,400	200	–	233,700
Broad Church	96,900	12,400	25,000	19,300	300	400	3,800	158,100	209,400	2,000	400	369,900
Liberal	81,900	17,800	54,600	16,900	1,100	200	5,000	177,500	223,300	9,100	–	409,900
Anglo-Catholic	500	100	–	17,400	100	–	–	18,100	139,400	3,900	100	161,500
Catholic	5,400	500	1,200	14,700	5,800	200	300	28,100	143,800	1,272,200	100	1,444,200
All others	8,900	1,000	2,400	5,200	1,400	2,500	1,600	23,000	17,400	11,300	8,800	60,500
TOTAL	396,100	199,400	114,000	292,800	68,500	95,200	83,000	1,249,000	1,143,900	1,304,600	9,400	3,706,900

Taken from Peter Brierley, *Christian England*, (London, 1991) Marc

the importance of 'orders'—priests and bishops

▶ a love of the sacraments which are seen as the chief way in which God's grace is transmitted to the believer (Catholics hold seven sacraments: baptism, confirmation, the eucharist, penance, extreme unction, orders and matrimony)

▶ a strong emphasis on personal prayer and meditation

▶ the continuity of the church with earlier ages—especially the early church Fathers.

The largest section of this tradition is, of course, the Roman Catholic Church. This ancient church has recently undergone a distinct shift in its theology, attitudes and practices. Over four lengthy sessions from 1962 to 1965 the Second Vatican Council introduced fresh thinking into the Roman Catholic Church.

While the Church remains an authoritative hierarchical institution, it now sees itself as a community of baptized disciples sharing in service to God and their neighbours.

In recent years there have been many signs of a fresh movement of God's Spirit in the Roman Catholic Church. In rejoicing at this we need also to recognize that non-Roman Catholics are still accused of apostasy by the official dogma of the Council of Trent (which was held in 1563!).

Roman Catholics remain officially committed to certain doctrines which are devoid of scriptural foundation. These include...

▶ the veneration of the Virgin Mary as the mother of God

▶ invocation of the saints

▶ purgatory

▶ the sacrifice of the mass

▶ the sacrament of penance

▶ papal infallibility.

Recently there has been a strong desire to see the reuniting of the Anglican and Catholic Churches, but the ordination of women has created genuine consternation among Catholics.

Three wings of the Catholic Church

The Roman Catholic Church is vast and complex (its membership is almost 1 billion). It would be simplistic to assume that all Roman Catholics are the same. Catholicism in Britain, for example, often differs from its counterpart in other European countries.

Catholics broadly divide into three sections...

▶ **Traditional Catholics**—the strongest element in the church. They maintain the absolute authority of the Pope and the traditions of the church. Extreme forms of this position exist in much of continental Europe, and can lead to the active persecution of Evangelical believers.

▶ **Liberal Catholics**—who follow modern rationalistic thought and are critical of the authority and accuracy of the Bible.

▶ **Charismatic Catholics**—people influenced by the Charismatic Movement and who emphasize personal commitment and faith. Many have a high view of the Bible and call themselves Evangelical Catholics.

PAUSE FOR THOUGHT

What should be the attitude of modern Evangelicals to the Roman Catholic Church?

'We know that our life is temporary, and we had better live with Christ and offer ourselves, and have true life in him. The pressures of life have brought us that really deep life of close relation with God.'

POPE SHENOUDA III, LEADER OF THE EGYPTIAN COPTIC CHURCH

---

2 THE ORTHODOX TRADITION

Orthodox Christians are in two families of churches, popularly known as...

▶ Eastern Orthodox—some 20 churches, including the Russian, Romanian, Greek and Bulgarian Orthodox Churches

▶ Oriental Orthodox—five smaller, but more ancient churches, including the Armenian, Coptic and Ethiopian Orthodox Churches.

The Orthodox...

▶ have a strong commitment to uphold the doctrines hammered out by the great councils in the early years of the church (although the Coptic and Ethiopian Orthodox Churches do not accept the decisions of the Council of Chalcedon and its creed)

▶ put a high value on the unchanging traditions of the church

▶ give priority to worship—approaching God through the liturgy, devotion and contemplative prayer.

The commitment to worship lies at the heart of the Orthodox Church. The very word 'orthodox' means to 'rightly glorify' God. Worship is even given priority over mission, which is understood as the invitation to all humanity to join the church's unceasing worship of the Father, Son and Holy Spirit.

Like Roman Catholics, the Orthodox hold conservative moral standards. Unlike Roman Catholics, they do not enforce a particular line on issues such as birth control. They believe that the Roman Catholic Church has deviated from the true faith of the church in its arrogant claims of authority for the papacy.

Orthodox spirituality has a very strong tradition of prayer. The Orthodox also use icons in prayer and worship as 'windows' into the spiritual world. Their emphasis rests on the believer encountering the mystery of God through the love and faith of a purified heart.

Nowhere is this more clearly displayed than in the holy communion. Here the eternal liturgy...

▶ is seen as a gate to righteousness for believers

▶ focuses on Jesus Christ who is believed to be present in the communion

▶ concludes with an act of consecration to live for Christ in the world.

Orthodox authorities have occasionally persecuted Evangelical believers, and they still do so in a number of countries. Such outbreaks of hostility are created by Evangelical determination to lead people to Christ and the refusal of the Orthodox to accept that this is necessary. Greece, Bulgaria, Romania and Russia have all seen recent outbreaks of persecution.

3 THE LIBERAL TRADITION

This tradition is the result of one brand of theological scholarship over the past 200 years. Liberals believe in...

▶ the freedom to question the authority of scripture—which they believe to be a fallible record of divine revelation

▶ rejecting miraculous elements of the New Testament

▶ using human reason to decide what in the Bible is (and is not) God's self-revelation

▶ a universalistic 'God of love' (as opposed to a God of judgment)

Nowhere is liberal thinking more clearly seen than in the teaching of the twentieth-century German theologian, Rudolf Bultmann.

Bultmann believed that...

▶ the Gospel records are highly biased accounts of the life of Jesus

▶ they tell us what the early church thought about Jesus, rather than who he really was

▶ all mentions of supernatural events fly in the face of human reason and therefore need to be cut out of the pages of scripture.

Bultmann set about doing this. He stripped the miraculous elements out of the four gospels in a process which he called 'demythologization'. He believed that only those stories or sayings of Jesus which would have been uncomfortable to the early church could be said to

'It is impossible to use electric light and the wireless and to avail ourselves of modern medical and surgical discoveries and at the same time to believe in the New Testament world of spirits and miracles.'

RUDOLF BULTMANN

be reliable.

By denying all intellectual constraints, liberal thinking has become extremely critical of traditional doctrines such as...

▶ Jesus' bodily resurrection

▶ Jesus' miracles

▶ the virgin birth.

Bultmann is now dead, but figures like Don Cupitt maintain the tradition. It is particularly present in the Anglican, URC and Methodist denominations.

4 THE BROAD CHURCH TRADITION

This tradition is highly inclusive. It urges the incorporation of all children of God because we share the one heavenly Father. Recognizing other faiths and

Development of Division

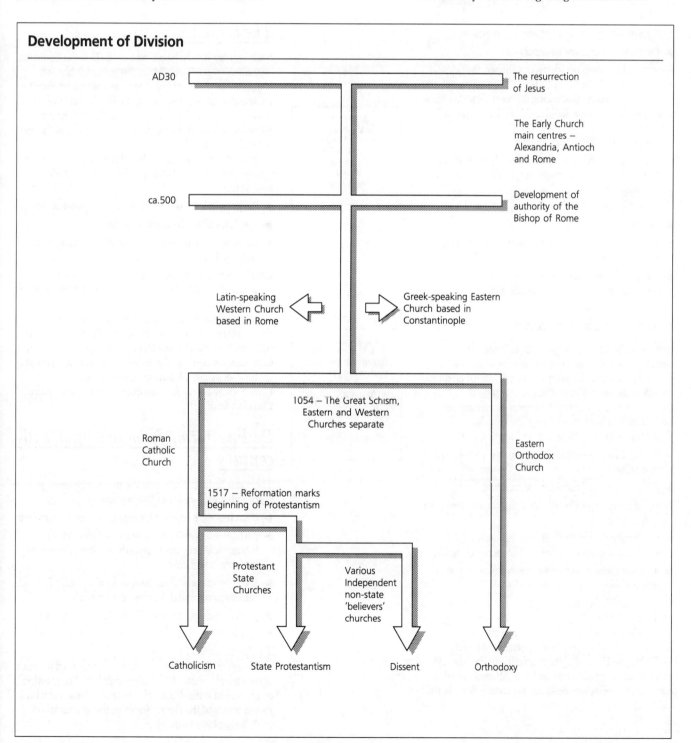

AD30 — The resurrection of Jesus

The Early Church main centres – Alexandria, Antioch and Rome

ca.500 — Development of authority of the Bishop of Rome

Latin-speaking Western Church based in Rome

Greek-speaking Eastern Church based in Constantinople

1054 – The Great Schism, Eastern and Western Churches separate

Roman Catholic Church

Eastern Orthodox Church

1517 – Reformation marks beginning of Protestantism

Protestant State Churches

Various Independent non-state 'believers' churches

Catholicism   State Protestantism   Dissent   Orthodoxy

traditions, it preaches the virtue of mutual tolerance and insists on developing unity with those of other religious convictions.

Approximately 10 per cent of the English adult population go to churches which are described by their ministers as Broad Church. The largest group in this tradition belong to the Church of England. They emphasize...

▶ a trinitarian creed

▶ the importance of the sacraments

▶ allegiance to the state church

▶ baptism as a means of entry into the church.

Broad Church membership recognizes the existence of other theological perspectives. It therefore finds a natural home in the Anglican communion which uniquely claims an unbroken continuity with two opposing traditions of the church...

▶ the pre-Reformation Holy Catholic church

▶ the sixteenth-century reformers.

In holding these two perspectives together, the prime emphasis of the Broad Church lies in a commitment to the church and its unity. Embracing different views is seen as a natural expression of the church in the richness of its diversity.

People in the Broad Church tend to...

▶ discourage extremism of whatever type—extreme spiritual fervour or extreme scepticism

▶ maintain a balance of tradition, rationality and commitment to church structures and practices

▶ emphasize the sacraments

▶ stress the corporate character of the church rather than individual conversion

▶ see the church's role in the affairs of state and in society as being of crucial significance.

5 THE EVANGELICAL TRADITION

Evangelicals represent 43 per cent of Protestant churchgoers in England (figures are not available for Wales, Scotland or Northern Ireland). Scattered among all the major denominations, Evangelicals regard themselves as standing in the orthodox, mainstream, biblical and apostolic tradition of the church.

Evangelicals emphasize...

▶ the need for a personal experience of conversion to Jesus Christ

▶ the authority and reliability of scripture

▶ the importance of Christ's atoning death on the cross to forgive our sins

▶ the significance of biblical doctrine as an infallible standard of truth to be believed by every Christian

▶ a strong commitment to justice, evangelism and mission.

Less predictable has been their return, in recent years, to their nineteenth-century roots of involvement in society. The last two decades have witnessed a growing Evangelical commitment to involvement in society.

As Spring Harvest is unashamedly an Evangelical event, it serves to illustrate both the differences and the common ground which exist among Evangelicals in the UK today.

> '*W*hereas Christ turned water into wine, the church has succeeded in doing something more difficult; it has turned wine into water.'
> SØREN KIERKEGAARD

> '*W*e have to be coopers first and make new barrels before the new wine harvest begins.'
> MARTIN LUTHER

> '*N*othing in the contemporary scene is more striking than the general regard which is felt for Jesus Christ and the general dislike of the organised church which bears his name.'
> STEPHEN NEILL

2 *The problem of relevance*

Which is more important to you...

▶ The problems we have with each other in the church?

▶ Or the problems our society has with the church?

It is a sad fact that many Christians concentrate far more energy on the first of these questions rather than the second. Many people in Britain have positive feelings about the founder of the church, but want nothing to do with the church itself.

KEY POINT **The gap between how people see Jesus and what they think of the church is a major problem for communicating the gospel in our culture.**

The evidence

Each Sunday nearly 90 per cent of the British population stay away from church. Many see going to church as being the same sort of experience as visiting an elderly uncle and aunt—it has nothing to do with real life. The result is that churchgoing today is at an all-time low. Attendance is down to a quarter of what it was in the mid-nineteenth century.

It is true that Evangelicals today can point to growth figures unprecedented at any point in this century, however...

▶ the growth level is only 3 per cent in a five-year period

▶ it follows after 100 years of decline!

▶ meanwhile, all other sections of the church are still diminishing.

Clearly there is no room for great displays of self-congratulation. Whichever way we look at it, we do have problems.

Some might suggest that this merely reflects the falling away of nominal churchgoers. There is certainly some truth in this, for the respectable aspect of being a Christian has been slowly eroded by the tide of twentieth-century secularism. However, it also reflects a loss of faith. Secular humanism has quietly replaced a nominal Christian faith.

Decline dating from the nineteenth century

There can be little doubt that the nineteenth century represented the heyday of Evangelicalism...

▶ churches were large and were often filled with people

▶ parliamentary reforms were carried through by Evangelical pressure to remedy working conditions for women and children

▶ social conditions were changed as the result of the campaigning zeal of leading Evangelicals

▶ preachers drew crowds far greater than the theatres

▶ missionary activities became a burgeoning industry.

The future looked full of promise.

However, the nineteenth century also marked the start of the church's slow slide from popularity. The growing confidence of critical biblical scholarship, coupled with a loss of status of the clergy (for example, in education) dealt body blows to the church.

Today we live in a society which is moving at a rapid pace...

▶ our culture loves to question and disturb traditional values

▶ the unusual and innovative come under the microscope of popular opinion—while orthodoxy is given scarcely a second glance

▶ truth is increasingly viewed as relative, and absolutes are dismissed

▶ scholarship appears to be valued on a Richter scale—the higher the level of outrageousness of the latest theory, the greater its media exposure

▶ modern marketing techniques focus on the fashionable, the new and the different—this means that our culture consistently underrates traditional and established values.

Little credit is ever given to being biblical—scripture, it seems, has little value. At a time when traditional positions face constant sceptical enquiry, experimental theology presents the media with a much more attractive proposition. Traditionally-held creeds or doctrines attract little exposure on the airwaves.

How did we get where we are?

The church's decline in influence and relevance can be traced to six major pressure points which have emerged in our culture...

1 Science and technology—the years since the industrial revolution have witnessed a major transformation in our society. Nowhere is this more evident than in science and technology.

The major difficulties in responding to changes in this direction are...

▶ the increasing tendency for modern technology to remove any sense of need for God

▶ relating the findings of science to scripture

▶ resolving ethical issues raised by new technology in areas such as genetic research.

2 Rationalism—the standard response to any mention of God is often to challenge his very existence...

▶ how do you know God is there?

▶ how can you be certain he is with you?

▶ how can you prove that Jesus rose physically from the dead?

These questions, and many others like them, all demand reasonable answers.

The five senses dominate our thinking. If God is there, then we must be able to perceive him with our senses. After all, they provide the yardstick by which we judge all things!

It is at this point that most Christians turn to the Bible. We believe that our certainties are reasonable and well founded. They are based on God's word to us in the Bible. In doing this, many Christians receive the same retort from the world that has existed since the beginning of time: 'Did God really say...?' (Genesis 3:1). The new thinkers view scripture not as God's message to mankind but as a human book about God. This distinction has proved to be very important indeed.

3 Liberal theology—it has often been said that through the centuries the greatest damage to the church

PAUSE FOR THOUGHT
What reason would your closest non-Christian friend or relative give for rejecting or ignoring the church?

> '*I*t is the contention of Evangelicals that they are plain Bible Christians, and that in order to be a biblical Christian it is necessary to be an Evangelical Christian. Put that way, it sounds arrogant and exclusive, but this is a sincerely held belief. Certainly it is the earnest desire of Evangelicals to be neither more nor less than biblical Christians... If Evangelical theology is biblical theology, it follows that it is not a new-fangled ism, a modern brand of Christianity, but an ancient form, indeed the original one. It is New Testament Christianity.'
> JOHN STOTT

> '*A*n Evangelical is someone who believes that the Bible is the Word of God; that Jesus is the Son of God; who holds to the traditional credal statements of the church and owns a commitment to Jesus Christ as their Saviour, Lord and King.'
> CLIVE CALVER

has come from the inside rather than the outside.

Sceptical theologians would have us believe that...

▶ because the Bible was written by human hands, it is therefore a purely human production

▶ the biblical writers were frequently biased about their writing and reporting

▶ scripture does not give us objective facts, history or truth—instead it is the record of events which have been filtered through the memory and perception of the biblical writers.

This point of view does not suggest that the Bible lies—it argues that the Gospel writers believed so strongly that Jesus was the Son of God that they simply interpreted events to give substance to their claims. We therefore have a book made up of saga, legend, myth, folklore and stories designed to help us view Jesus in the same way as the early church.

The impact of this kind of thinking is that many Christians become confused about their faith. And for non-Christians, watching yet another trendy theologian on television, the Christian faith seems to be falling to pieces.

4 Secularism—secularists argue that...

▶ whether or not a Creator God set the wheels in motion, the universe is governed by natural laws

▶ day follows night, summer follows spring—it is all an inexorable process

▶ an ever-present God is unnecessary, because the universe is a mechanistic, closed system, where one event naturally follows another.

Where does this lead? The secularist argues that God, if there ever was a God, has gone missing.

Belief in God is reduced to the level of personal preference. Once objective reality is dispensed with, then we are free to choose truth for ourselves! Each person's concept of God is OK for them. Each of us has our own road to God. Each viewpoint, or religious faith, is equally valid to the individual believer.

5 Escapism—a major reason for the church being seen as irrelevant to contemporary life has been the way past generations withdrew from the structures and institutions of society. This happened because of...

▶ A reaction to the social gospel—in the last century, major sections of the church caved in under the attack of liberal criticism of the Bible. They abandoned the gospel of proclamation and replaced it with social action, giving birth to the social gospel. Evangelicals then retreated from social action for fear of being seen to embrace this social gospel. They also became preoccupied with defending the Bible.

▶ An unbiblical understanding of worldliness—a wrong understanding of holiness and worldliness led to an over-emphasis on solitary piety. Christians abandoned the world of politics, the theatre, literature, and so on...

▶ A wrong use of prophecy—an emphasis on the teaching of the second coming and its imminence caused many to believe that the world was always going to get worse and that the only hope was for the return of Christ to bring everything to an end. As a result, they saw no need to be involved with the needs of society as a whole.

6 Social change—there was a time when the church was the heart of almost every community. It was the centre of social and moral life. This is largely no longer the case. Why did this happen?

▶ The growth of major cities and suburban areas. Only a minority of people now live in a village setting, under the shadow of the church's steeple.

▶ The increase of mobility of the population. This constantly tears people from their roots and relationships.

PAUSE FOR THOUGHT
If your church was removed from the face of the earth, what difference would it make to your local community?

Retreat into the ghetto

Against these powerful challenges, Evangelicalism has been perceived as being in total retreat. A belief in miracles, in God, in a faith which defies proof, and a cosmology which flies in the face of science—all these have become thoroughly discredited in the eyes of a modern world.

Because of the severity of the challenge, it is perhaps understandable that Christians have quietly retreated...

▶ having failed to win recognition or respect in the popular marketplace, Evangelical Christians have

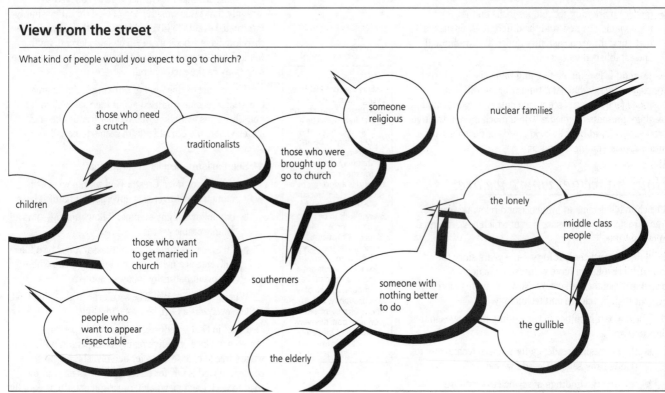

View from the street

What kind of people would you expect to go to church?

those who need a crutch · traditionalists · someone religious · nuclear families · those who were brought up to go to church · children · the lonely · middle class people · those who want to get married in church · southerners · someone with nothing better to do · the gullible · people who want to appear respectable · the elderly

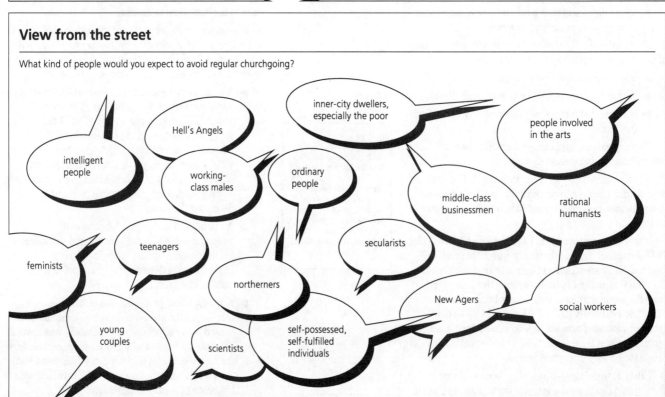

View from the street

What kind of people would you expect to avoid regular churchgoing?

intelligent people · Hell's Angels · inner-city dwellers, especially the poor · people involved in the arts · working-class males · ordinary people · middle-class businessmen · rational humanists · feminists · teenagers · secularists · northerners · New Agers · social workers · young couples · scientists · self-possessed, self-fulfilled individuals passively hid away in their own comfortable ghetto

▶ by dividing our secular labour in the workplace from our spiritual endeavours in the local congregation, we protect ourselves from the inevitable collision if the two worlds ever meet!

The problem with society does not lie so much in how we view living in a modern world, but in the fact that society regards us as being utterly irrelevant to it.

 KEY POINT Perhaps the biggest challenge facing the church today is that of cultural relevance.

Speaking to our culture

Every one of us is a creature of our society. Our culture, beliefs, values, customs and traditions—each plays a formative part in determining our response to situations that we encounter. Few of us recognize how much we are prisoners of our own cultural upbringing.

One distinct problem which we face in church life is that our cultural conditioning differs from that of the society in which we live. We use expressions, rituals and activities which are foreign to the people around us. The church forms an interesting sub-cultural island in the vast sea of secular society.

If we are actively to engage in communicating with those outside the church, then it is important that we speak to its culture rather than our own. In other words, we need to scratch where others itch rather than where we think they ought to be itching!

To do this effectively we must avoid...

▶ answering only yesterday's questions

▶ using 'the language of Zion'

▶ the idea that people will happily come to our territory on our terms.

In other words, we need to adapt culturally. While we carry God's changeless word, we seek to convey it to a changing world. Our message is unalterable, but our

> '*E*very day people are straying away from the church and going back to God.'
> LENNY BRUCE

PAUSE FOR THOUGHT
If you could change just one thing about your church to make it more accessible to non-Christians, what would it be?

> '*I* spent thousands of pounds down the years looking for fellowship down the pub. I walked into this church and found it for free.'
> A NEW CHRISTIAN, DESCRIBING HIS CHURCH IN SOUTH WALES

approach and methods should always be tailored to those we are seeking to reach.

How can we do this? One approach is to acknowledge that we share a common humanity with the whole of society. We are all God's creatures, and he has placed universal aspirations within each one of us. These are...

▶ the longing for love

▶ the longing for transcendence

▶ the longing for identity.

These deeply-felt longings provide common ground for us to address.

The longing for love

Many of the songs, films, poems and books of our generation proclaim the message which the Beatles articulated in the sixties: 'All you need is love.' This can be seen in many ways...

▶ feelings of loneliness, rejection, depression and despair are common in our world

▶ marriage is becoming an insecure basis to plan for life

▶ many look to cohabitation attempting to balance freedom with a loving relationship

▶ others have turned to communal living

▶ the majority still seek beyond themselves for more than they have found.

Few people turn to the church to discover an authentic, loving community. Yet that is what Jesus Christ designed the church to be. If people are looking for love, then more will depend on our actions than on our words. Far from feeling threatened by this suggestion, we should welcome it, for our preaching then becomes an explanation of our lifestyle.

This is consistent with biblical models...

▶ the example of Jesus with his disciples

▶ the teaching of Jesus and the apostles (see Matthew 18:20)

76% vote for God!

Many Christians have the misguided idea that people in society are no longer prepared to believe in God. This is far from the truth. One recent survey of 1,500 adults produced the following results...

Obviously, these figures need to be read carefully. The 76 per cent who believe in God do not all have the personal God of the Christian faith in mind. And among the 68 per cent who believe in a soul, there are many who also believe in reincarnation. However, these statistics hardly point to an absence of religious belief in our society!

76% believed in God

68% believed in a soul

49% believed in life after death

69% believed in sin

31% believed in hell

4% were atheists **4% were agnostics**

▶ the practice of the early church (Acts 2:42–47; 4:32)

▶ the whole concept of the people of God (see pages 76–78).

Proclaiming the good news, growing spiritually and living authentic Christian lives are best discovered in the context of the Christian community. To a world looking for love the local church must serve as a living model which will be magnetic to people outside.

The longing for transcendence

All around us we can see signs that people hunger for something beyond themselves...

▶ the growth of interest in New Age theories

▶ the pursuit of transcendental meditation, occultism, eastern religions, yoga, and drug-induced higher-consciousness

▶ the fantasies of science fiction

▶ the collapse of communism in the USSR

▶ the growing awareness of the emptiness of materialism and the redundancy of secularism in the West.

Each of us has a subconscious yearning for something beyond ourselves.

Many people appear to be prepared to search for truth. It is rarely the person of Jesus which stops them from turning to Christianity. Usually it is the character of Christians and popular perceptions of the church which create the stumbling block.

It is time seriously to assess the style of our church activities and the quality of our own lives so that people can start to look again at the church of Jesus Christ for life and reality. The world needs to see a people who are discernibly different, not in what we avoid but in what we accomplish.

The longing for identity

The message of Jesus was that people as individuals are important. He saw them as more significant than the religious institutions, structures and regulations of his day.

The very fact that human beings were created in the image of God explains why Christians regard this as an important issue. Auschwitz, Belfast, Sudan, Kampuchea and Sarajevo all bear eloquent witness to the awful atrocities which follow when people lose respect for human identity and significance.

Christian teaching on the dignity and worth of human beings is a necessary antidote to the opposite tendency within society. For when human beings are devalued, then society turns sour.

We can see this in many different areas...

▶ child abuse

▶ racial discrimination and hatred

▶ homelessness

▶ the removal of social benefits

▶ the pursuit of ever-higher standards of living

▶ runaway technology.

All of these are symptoms of the progressive dehumanisation of our culture. So many people are working with such determination to further themselves

> '*M*ainline Protestantism, from its structures to its hymns and gospel songs, has emphasised the individual over the community... Too often the church has been seen more as a mere collection of saved souls than as a community of interesting personalities. Christian growth has been a matter of individual soul culture rather than the building of the community of the Spirit. Saints who lived isolated, solitary lives were often placed on a pedestal above those whose lives were spent in true community.'
> HOWARD SNYDER

> '*I* would have liked to convince my father that I had found what he had been looking for, the ineffable something he had longed for all his life. I would have liked to persuade him that the search for God does not have to be in vain. But it was hopeless. He had known too many blind Christians, bleak moralists who sucked the joy from life and persecuted their opponents; he would never have been able to see the truth they were hiding.'
> BERTRAND RUSSELL'S DAUGHTER, WHO BECAME A CHRISTIAN

> '*C*hrist never gave any other commandment than that of Love, because he intended that this commandment be the test of his disciples and of true believers. For if good works and love do not blossom forth, it is not genuine faith, the gospel has not yet gained a foothold and Christ is not yet rightly known.'
> MARTIN LUTHER

The church—as some have seen it

'The church as an institution lacks Christianity.'
Anon

'If we wish to hear the call of Jesus, we must hear it despite the church.'
Karl Barth

'I became disillusioned with Christianity after many years of church attendance. I did not see many Christians (including the clergy) who actually followed the word of Christ.'
Anon

'The identification of a church and a state is about as farcical as a vegetarian joining the Butchers Union.'
Malcolm Muggeridge

'The church of Jesus Christ is the great new society which God is bringing into existence.'
Michael Griffiths

that they ignore the damage they inflict on others. The dignity and self-worth of others is rarely mentioned by today's ambitious individualists.

Society clearly has a problem, but few people who recognize the need for personal significance turn in the direction of the Christian church.

This is tragic, for there is no more profound expression of the value that God places on the life of an individual than the death of his Son on a cross.

Perhaps a clue as to the reason for the indifference of society towards the church is given by the example of Mother Teresa. She is the most popular Christian in our society. If our local church was getting its hands dirty in the way that she is, then maybe people would look to the church to recover human dignity and self-worth.

These suggestions are not pleasant. But this is what it means to be a disciple of Jesus in our culture...

▶ greater love between Christians

▶ more obvious involvement in the pain and hurt of our communities

▶ a lifestyle which displays the reality of the truth we have found.

This is not to suggest that the church should be moulded by society. Yet when our world echoes the demands of Jesus for his people, then we need to listen carefully. Perhaps society has a legitimate problem with us.

3 The problem of change

KEY POINT The issue of change vs. continuity has been a battleground for many churches in the past 20 years.

And it continues to be one of the most difficult challenges confronting the church today.

Some churches resist change to the last ditch. Others seek out new fashions and reinvent themselves every five minutes. Some churches are torn apart by change. Others contain a small group who fight the rest. In between these extremes, most churches try to maintain their balance...

▶ changing to meet the needs of people in the modern world

▶ keeping links with what has been valuable in the past.

Churches in change

The last twenty years have been an unsettling time for the church—but it has also been exciting. Many Evangelical churches have experienced the excitement of change, development and growth, reversing trends which had lasted for more than a century.

Some of the most obvious areas of change have been...

▶ new songs alongside older hymns

▶ many thousands of home groups

▶ leadership being shared in a team

▶ redecorated buildings, the loss of pews...

▶ a new emphasis on worship

▶ fresh initiatives in evangelism

▶ drama and dance groups in church services and on the streets

▶ new styles of worship, plus a rediscovery for many of spiritual gifts

▶ a growing commitment to social action

▶ fresh ways of teaching children

▶ involvement in the local community...

A growing number of churches have been changing in these and other ways. This is especially true in the Evangelical sector of the church. But where does it all leave us?

Are we happy with all the changes that have been made? Do we want to go on changing—or stop where we are? And what about the past—do we simply write it off? Or are we losing touch with our roots?

> '**L**ike a mighty tortoise
> Moves the church of God.
> Brothers, we are treading
> Where we've always trod...'
> PARODY OF 'ONWARD CHRISTIAN SOLDIERS'

> '**C**onstant change is here to stay.'
> ANON

PAUSE FOR THOUGHT
Are your instincts for change or continuity?

> '**B**y making imaginative use of change to channel change we can not only spare ourselves the trauma of future shock, we can reach out and humanize distant tomorrows.'
> ALVIN TOFFLER, *Future Shock*

A tale of two churches

These two imaginary churches show what might happen (and what sometimes does happen!) at the extreme ends of the spectrum of change...

▶ **St Wilfred's**—is like a time capsule from the seventeenth century. Readings are from the Authorized Version of the Bible, the congregation sings from Hymns Ancient and Prehistoric, and the vicar has clung on to the 1662 Book of Common Prayer wherever possible. The church council once considered installing microphones and amplification in the church, but it was considered too modern...

▶ **Tom & Jerry's Place** (formerly St Thomas & St Jerome)—the pews were ripped out several years ago, sermons were abolished and a giant dance floor, complete with a bar, was installed. The most popular meetings include the blessing of the filofax service, mid-life crisis counselling for the thirtysomethings, and the Super Nintendo youth fellowship. The leadership have just discontinued rapping prayer sessions because they are hopelessly old-fashioned...

A spectrum of change

Churches respond to the challenge of change in a number of ways...

Defiance—some churches still militantly resist any suggestion of change. While they suffer generally from dwindling congregations, they still insist that continuity with the past maintains a 'faithful witness'.

Fossilization—some churches have changed, and now are busy consolidating into a new pattern of tradition. Change is not continuing and the danger is that stagnation will set in.

Cosmetic change—some churches have changed in superficial areas of church life and stubbornly resist adapting in other spheres where more fundamental change may be essential.

Second thoughts—some churches have changed in so many areas and at such speed that they are now reviewing the situation and returning to some of the practices they had formerly discarded.

Trendies—some churches adopt the latest trend or fashion, or the emphasis of the most recent conference attended by their leaders.

Civil war—some churches contain a majority of people who see the need for change, alongside a minority who are determined to resist it to the last bullet.

Kamikaze change—some churches are committed to constant change and have cut all links with the past. Failing to manage the process of change has resulted in people becoming insecure and uncertain. There seems no secure foundation and the momentum of change continues unabated.

The picture of change in the churches is very varied. Local churches in a particular denomination do not line up in a uniform manner any more. A denominational label or style of church architecture does not act as a guarantee of what is going on inside the building!

There are several ways in which we can fail to meet the challenge of becoming a local church which is ready for the twenty-first century. We can...

try to recover from change—having adapted to the needs of people and our wider culture, we can now settle down and try to conserve our gains

imitate the secular world—adopting all the changes of our culture to become more acceptable, without any distinctive Christian understanding of what is happening

give up on the local church—finding change too difficult, we keep attending our church, but withdraw our involvement by putting our efforts and energies elsewhere.

Change can become idolatry

 KEY POINT Our culture is in love with change.

Think of all the words which are used on TV and in the media generally to describe change—they all paint the idea of change in exciting, positive colours...

▶ new, improved soap powder

▶ revolutionary

▶ newsflash

▶ new technologies

God and change

▶ God manages change in climate, fortunes and hearts—and he is even prepared to adapt his plans (Psalm 104:19; Ezekiel 36:26; Daniel 2:21; 5:18–21; 1 John 3:9)

▶ God calls for personal change (Mark 1:15–17; Luke 9:25; 18:18–30; John 8:11; 2 Corinthians 5:17)

▶ God introduces corporate change and renewal (Psalm 33:3; 2 Corinthians 4:16; Revelation 21:2)

▶ God will one day change all things (1 Corinthians 15:51–53; Revelation 21:1).

▶ shocking revelations

▶ radical new ideas.

In contrast, things which are older and might be resistant to change are often painted in dull colours...

▶ official church dogma

▶ the old order

▶ traditionalists

▶ the law of the Medes and the Persians

▶ the status quo

▶ backward-looking.

This is important, because as creatures of our culture we are often tempted to embrace change for the sake of change. The danger is that our love of change can easily become a form of idolatry.

The fact is that we do not have the right to change the local church. That is the sole prerogative of Jesus Christ. It is his church, not ours. Because he has purchased us through his blood we are his to own and rule.

We do not have a responsibility to introduce human gimmicks, methods or strategies into God's church and ask him to bless our humanly-inspired efforts. The obligation we do have is to ensure that leadership and congregation alike are giving time to listen for his direction.

To act in this way is a guarantee of spiritual blessing. Instead of asking for God to sanction our own endeavours we are simply co-operating with the changes which he initiates—and because he is a Creator God there are likely to be plenty of them.

God and continuity

God is the God of continuity as well as change...

▶ God's nature and truth do not change (Psalm 102:25–27; Psalm 119:151–152; Malachi 3:6; James 1:17)

▶ Our experience of him is rooted in his dealings with his people in the past, as 'the God of Abraham, Isaac and Jacob' (Exodus 3:5–6; Hebrews 11:9)

▶ He commands his people to remember the past and teach it to their children (Deuteronomy 6:6–7; 15:15; 32:7)

▶ God remembers and keeps his promises (Exodus 33:1; Numbers 23:19).

> '**A** person who has lived in many places is not likely to be deceived by the local errors of his native village; the person who knows the past has lived in many times and is therefore in some degree immune from the great cataract of nonsense that pours from the press and microphone of his own age.'
> C.S. LEWIS

The danger of change

American psychologists Holmes and Rahe have demonstrated that 'four out of five people who have experienced many dramatic changes in their lives over the past year can expect major illness in the next two years.'

Their research shows that an accumulation of 'life changes' create stress which has an physical and emotional impact on those involved. These life changes might include...

▶ retirement

▶ children leaving home

▶ new financial commitments

▶ illness.

KEY POINT While this research does not include the impact of changes within the church, the fact that change can inflict stress should not be overlooked so far as the local church is concerned.

Too much change, relating to too many issues, and over too short a time, is going to be unsettling at the least, and quite debilitating at the worst.

Continuity—dangers and opportunities

While our culture is in love with change, in recent years there has been a new emphasis on the value of roots. We need to hold these two together in balance. Change is important—but so too is continuity.

Learning from past mistakes—One of the most important aspects of history is that it tells us how to live in the present. When the church has a strong sense of its own history, it will be able to avoid some of the mistakes that have been made before.

Learning from past successes—We can also learn how the Christians who came before us responded to similar problems and opportunities. How did the church in the first few centuries cope with persecution? How was leadership organized in the first Baptist churches? And so on.

The value of our heritage—As Christians, we have sometimes been so obsessed with the new and different that we have failed to recognize the value in more traditional approaches. While we enjoy singing new songs, we are foolish to neglect some of the magnificent hymns of the past from Wesley, Watts and many others. It is worth reminding ourselves that time is a good test of intrinsic value. So that...

▶ the developments that are valuable today may not last until tomorrow

▶ some of the things that were valued yesterday might well be valuable today.

Contrary to what our culture tells us, new is not always better. Old is not always better either. It is more valuable to mix in the best of the old with the best of the new. In that way we will avoid simply introducing change for change's sake.

A passage in the Book of Ezekiel warns us about what can happen when we cling on to the past and ignore what God is doing. In a vision, Ezekiel sees the glory of the Lord leaving the temple in Jerusalem (Ezekiel 10). God was withdrawing his presence because of the sin of his people, and because of their superstition that the temple could never be destroyed.

Tragically this can apply to aspects of our church life which God has used in the past. He has moved on, but we continue as we always have, minus the power that was once there.

If we can have change for change's sake, we can also have the opposite danger: tradition for tradition's sake.

It is God's responsibility to turn his church upside down, and ours to co-operate with what he is doing. But it doesn't stop there. What God really has in mind is turning our world upside down (Acts 17:6)! This is the exciting work which God calls us to do with him.

Getting the balance right

The church today faces two opposite dangers...

▶ the danger of believing that the old must always be irrelevant and that the new is something to be pursued at all costs

▶ the danger of believing that change is always bad and that Christians must hold on to the heritage of the past at all costs.

The church needs to find a balance between valuing its Christian roots while remaining open to the changes which God wants to bring. While God does not change, he is prepared to do 'new things'.

KEY POINT The church must be clear about those things that should remain fixed and those which are open to change.

In particular there is a need...

▶ to draw on the richness of the Christian heritage and to enable today's Christians to recognize their links with those throughout history who have shared their faith

▶ to be open to God's Spirit and to recognize the need for changes which are essential to the life, worship and mission of the church.

For the church, change is most relevant at those points where...

▶ the prevailing culture has changed

▶ the Holy Spirit is instigating spiritual change

▶ lessons are being learned from other parts of the body of Christ.

Continuity and change

There is always a tension between continuity and change. Our guidelines should be to...

▶ recognize those things which are commanded in the Bible and which are not open to change

▶ consider which of our convictions and practices owe more to tradition than to scripture

▶ avoid compromise by adopting the standards and trends of society merely because they appear to be contemporary and popular

▶ make time and space to listen to God, asking him to show us where change is necessary

▶ ensure that we introduce structures and practices to translate theory into practice.

Managing change

One of the major issues facing local churches today is how those who can see what needs to be done can convince others of that fact and institute the change that is required.

The first step in any process of inaugurating change is that those who initiate it have a clear understanding of the need that they are addressing and where they wish to get to.

KEY POINT It is also important to understand the reasons why many people are resistant to change.

These include...

▶ they are genuinely happy with the way things are

▶ they doubt the motives and integrity of those who are making proposals

▶ they feel secure with the present—often because this links them with their past—and do not wish to risk the insecurity of the unknown

▶ they have not been consulted or involved in the proposals

▶ they see any admission of a need to change as also being an admission of their own guilt for creating what presently exists

▶ they are afraid of the consequences if the proposed change does not work

▶ they are right.

There are steps that can be taken in order to make sure that the change process takes place as painlessly as possible. These include...

Involve in the process those who are affected by the outcome—this must include genuine consultation in which those involved have a real opportunity to contribute, rather than seeing themselves as being talked round to the point of view of the leaders

Define the problem clearly—without agreement about the problem, there will never be agreement about its solution

Do not let people take sides—instead, ask them to work together in order to propose the best solution

Make sure that those involved are clear about the issues—they need to understand all the benefits of the proposals being made, and all the negative results involved in keeping things as they are

Give time for the proposals to be fully understood—remember, while some people 'see' things instantly, others are more naturally cautious towards new ideas and need time to feel comfortable with them

Institute change by way of a series of stages—this is often better than by way of taking one great step

Try to run the new in parallel with the old—choice is always better than conscription

Be prepared to put new ideas on trial—it helps to try something for a fixed period and then to evaluate the results

Give an assurance about monitoring the change—let people know that there will be opportunities to evaluate the change.

Twelve areas of change

Predicting areas of change for the local church is dangerous! Each local church is separately accountable to God, and sometimes owes respect to its denominational allegiance as well.

However, there are spheres of interest and activity that God seems to be introducing into the life of many churches. Twelve significant shifts in emphasis can be identified as important areas for the church at the close of the twentieth century. These are shifts towards...

▶ a recovery or re-emphasis of our commitment to the prime importance of scripture and biblical doctrines

▶ regaining the proper place and gift of biblical preaching and teaching

▶ questioning the cultural values of our world from a biblical/Christian perspective

▶ developing team ministry and greater involvement of the whole congregation, utilizing their gifts, ministries, talents and abilities

▶ creating a more caring Christian community which is able to be both 'natural' and 'supernatural' in proper proportion

▶ a more pastoral ministry, involving training and equipping small group leadership alongside counsellors and carers

▶ addressing family needs in changing ethical and cultural situations

▶ emerging from the ghetto-like mentality fostered in our own subculture and becoming more actively involved in our local communities

▶ a deeper understanding of Christian social action and political involvement, with more support for those who work in schools, medicine, politics...

▶ support for the poor, unemployed and deprived—both at home and in the Two-Thirds World

▶ mission in a post-industrial society

▶ a greater awareness and use of high-tech communications, including relations with the press and the media.

> '**G**od give me the courage to change the things I can; the patience to accept the things I cannot; and the wisdom to tell the difference.'
> ANON

Stories of change

The Bible contains many stories of how God brought about change in his people and in the lives of individuals. They mark some of the great turning points in the Bible...

▶ **Abraham** is called by God to leave his country, his people and his father's house to go to Canaan (Genesis 12:1–5)

▶ **Moses** is called by God at the burning bush to bring God's people out of Egypt (Exodus 3:1–10)

▶ **Simeon and Anna** prophesy over Jesus when he is first brought to the temple—marking the change from the Old to the New Testament (Luke 2:25–38)

▶ **Saul**, travelling to Damascus to persecute the Christians there, is struck down and confronted by Jesus who commissions him as the apostle to the Gentiles (Acts 9:1–6; 26:15–18)

▶ **Peter** receives a vision from God telling him that the gospel is not only for Jewish people, but for the whole world—marking a change in the mission of the church (Acts 10:9–16).

4 *Pain in the body*

Not only do all churches have problems, it is also probably true that...

▶ we all have problems with our church

▶ and our church has problems with us.

Although we can identify some common problems, each situation is unique and demands a unique response.

KEY POINT There is no blueprint which solves every problem perfectly, but we can look at some helpful steps which can be applied when we are confronted with a difficulty.

A common scenario in many churches is that members of the congregation have identified a need which the leaders are not attending to. How should the church proceed? These 12 questions might help to ease the logjam...

1 Am I right?—So often we can forge ahead without stopping to check our facts or our understanding of scripture. Only when we are convinced in this area should we proceed.

2 Do I have a right attitude?—We can get our facts right but still be wrong because of our motivation. If our aim is to harm or demean the leadership, or another group within the church, we should remain silent. If we are looking for selfish advantage or acting out of pride, hurt or resentment, we should wait until we have sorted out our motives.

3 Have I asked God about this?—Rushing into action without spending time with God praying through the issue is a recipe for disaster. We see things partially, whereas God sees the whole. If we are in the right, God can strengthen our convictions and grant us wisdom in moving forward.

4 Have I shared my concern with others?—A good check is to consult with other mature Christians who do not have a vested interest (such as friends outside the church). This is not a licence to gossip or stir up discontent on the backbenches (or back pews). Great care is needed to talk to the best person or persons. It may be with a home group leader, a deacon, PCC member, or with someone who is adversely affected by the problem. For example, the issue of lack of crèche facilities restricting the involvement of single mothers in a Bible study group could be raised with the group leader, or one of the women unable to attend.

5 Am I open?—Closed minds and hearts are devastating in disputes. The result is often division in the church. We must be open to God and to each other. God may redirect us through other people if we are prepared to see things from another perspective.

6 Am I flexible?—It is vital to be willing to compromise. Although some people compromise too easily, others are totally inflexible. Compromise over doctrinal fundamentals is clearly wrong, but in matters of practice it is often right. Idealists, beware! Your great goals may be wonderful and we all need to hear them, but are you taking account of the shortcomings of the rest of the church—or your own, for that matter?

7 Am I prepared to act?—Those who criticize most loudly are often those who are slowest to act when change becomes possible. If we speak up, we must also be counted when time and effort is needed to sort out the problem and its consequences. If we talk but do not act, we will not be listened to a second time.

8 Do I have an answer?—Frequently, we see the problem but not the solution. It may not be our role to provide the answer, as it may be beyond our direct responsibility, but leaders are generally much more disposed to listen if we have some possible remedies than if we merely highlight what is wrong. We need to be positive.

9 Have I thought this through?—Few 'people problems' are simple. Often there will be short-term and long-term consequences in introducing change. Some people may be hurt or misunderstand. There may be a financial cost to be borne. Although consideration of these matters is a responsibility of leadership, anyone concerned should consider the effects involved in their proposal.

10 Am I prepared to confront?—This can be tough for most of us. Our temperament and culture makes us shy away from confronting almost anyone—whether they are our juniors, peers or seniors. But in the case of sin, wrongdoing and injustice, the Bible teaches that those who have done wrong should be rebuked. This has to be done in the context of love (see Leviticus 19:17; Proverbs 15:31; 2 Timothy 4:2).

11 Am I willing to trust?—Often we find it hard to trust others in areas of our concern. It may be hard to hand over to the leadership the solving of a problem which has concerned us for a long time. Our emotions get in the way. Submission to leadership has gained something of a bad reputation in recent years (often with good cause), but the principle is right. Good leaders respond to genuine concerns brought to their attention because they want to help. Our trust will enable them to lead.

12 Am I willing to persevere?—It takes time to solve problems. In an instant society, waiting does not come easily to us—or cheaply. We may need to press on as gradual progress is made. Perseverance is a great Christian virtue. We need to exercise it inside the church as well as outside.

Principles for change

These 12 questions have been written from the church member's point of view—but they equally need to be asked by the church leader. Wrong attitudes can be as prevalent in a PCC, eldership or diaconate as in the body as a whole. Leaders, however, have the additional responsibility of implementing change.

There are a number of principles which can help here in guiding change...

Create a positive atmosphere—Encourage people to think positively rather than negatively, to build rather than destroy. The church in the UK has been riddled with people who can always give 12 reasons 'why not' rather than one reason 'why'. Leaders must encourage a positive spirit.

Commit the church to excellence—So often we settle for second (or third, fourth or fifth!) best in our churches. We make do rather than aiming for the best to the glory of God. Such a commitment encourages change.

Encourage trust—Leaders can encourage trust by being trustworthy and by fostering confidence. They must avoid any underhand activity which undermines this.

Show flexibility—Leaders must demonstrate a willingness to innovate, experiment—and even to fail! They need to shake off their image as coming from a conservative, older generation who find any change difficult.

Follow the principle of servanthood—If leaders seek to rule over the congregation and dictate progress, they will ultimately fail. We are all called to serve God. Leaders are called to serve God and the body of Christ. The degree of service is the hallmark of their leadership.

Practical steps for change

Alongside these principles for change, there are four practical steps which leaders can use in assessing change...

Test the waters—Leaders must know their own church. If they have a proposed course of action, they should informally and quietly sound out both the key people involved, and 'ordinary' members. What is their initial reaction?

Listen and respond to those who resist—Don't look on people as adversaries. Take note of their objections. Work on answers. Incorporate all the aspects of their concerns that you can, without destroying the initiative. Don't get into verbal dogfights. Facing their criticism can help you to refine your original proposal.

Convince individuals before talking to groups—Individuals often react negatively to any proposed change, but given time to think about it, they may warm to the idea. If the first they hear of a proposal is in public, they may feel obliged to hold to their original reaction for the sake of consistency—and this reaction might well be defensive or negative. Talk to those who are directly affected and to the key opinion-shapers in the church. Convince them, and you are more likely to convince the whole church, although it will all need time to think through.

Lead boldly—Do not be hesitant or fearful. Do not be put off by one or two vocal objectors if the majority support the change. If the change is for the good of the whole, it is better to persevere and lose one or two people than to draw back. If the church is a better place as a result, those who have left will probably soon be replaced several times over. Good change normally leads to growth.

We may never solve all our problems, but if leaders and congregations have the will to change and take action on some of these principles and practical steps, then we should see considerable progress.

The five principles and four practical steps outlined here are adapted from Kevin G. Dyer, *Must Brethren Churches Die?*, Partnership Publications.

> '*If* we go forward in the power of God, I am confident that in our generation we will see new, vibrant churches... experiencing not only the agony of change but the ecstasy of revival.'
> KEVIN DYER

The problem with my church is ...

Everything is done for adults. No one seems to do anything for the young people. That's why there aren't many of my age left in the church.

We've tried to introduce change into our church—but every time we were frustrated. So my wife and I have become involved in a para-church society—we put our efforts, energies and finance into that. We still go to church on Sunday mornings, but that's it!

The sermons are boring, the leadership bland —everything is concentrated on just not rocking the boat ...

Our church has a blindspot about the arts. We have so many gifted people but they are not given a chance. I'm afraid there's a cork in the bottle, and it is there at the top!

In a word—money—or rather the lack of it. There's so much to do, but our people don't tithe. They won't even give a decent weekly offering.

I never know what's going on. They only tell us when they want us to do something. Or when they need more money.

I guess I'm just lonely. My husband's away a lot at weekends on business. I hear all these sermons about fellowship and sharing—but it's hard to see the evidence of it. When he's around we get invited out, but when he's away I know what it feels like to be a single parent.

I'm single, and everything seems to revolve around those who are married. Family services, sermons on marriage, emphasis on children, but nothing laid on for all those of us who are single. People are friendly—but I only get invited to their homes when they need a baby-sitter.

We're really a more traditional church. People know what to expect when they come here. And now we've got this new minister, and he's started to change things. I've already complained about these Songs of Fellowship—but I can't make the minister see sense.

I just find it boring—the services are just drab and routine.

I'm shut in most of the time because of my age. The church has been a lifeline to me, and the vicar is truly wonderful. I shouldn't grumble really—but he is the only person who ever comes to visit me.

People are so unfriendly, they all get together in their cliques, but no one ever speaks to you. Unless you're one of the 'in crowd', you just don't seem to count.

Outside the church?

The frustration and pain of life in the church is reflected by one highly-motivated and committed Christian, Laurie Young. He recently wrote his story of how he left the church, in terms of its fellowship and meetings, but did not lose touch with God ...

'I assumed that I would be involved intimately with a group of Christians pioneering along with the house churches for the rest of my days. But the Lord (and it was he) led me a different way ...

'We debated the parables about the yeast and the bread. For the first time we saw that to affect the people in "the world" we would have to be "baked" with them and we would become intimately involved in the substance of their lives.

'That was nearly ten years ago. Since then my family, friends and I have been living very "normal" lives with very, very few Christian meetings (two in ten years). I have close friends who are Christians and some who are not. I have to say that I have found it a mixed blessing!

'I still love, know and worship God as much as I ever did ... There are many, many other Christians in these circumstances who are not measured because they are not part of a group ... So please do not assume that people who move out of a fellowship move away from God ...

'I'm sure Jesus said he came to let us live, not meet, abundantly.'

L.D. Young, *Alpha*, January 1992, Elm House Publications

Everyone seems to leave the work to someone else—that's why nothing ever gets done. Oh, you see everyone at 10.30 on Sunday morning, but by 12 o'clock they're gone for the week.

What's wrong with our church? I don't know. I don't go any more. I'm one of the growing number of Christians who love Jesus but can't stand the church. I meet with Christian friends occasionally for a meal together. I pray, read the Bible, love God, and enjoy the life he has given me . . .

It's all worship, worship and more worship. I'm not against it, but I would like some well-prepared, solid teaching. If we had a bit more of the Bible, related to real-life situations, then I'd have more to worship about.

As a church leader I sometimes feel that people don't see me as a person—or my family. It would be wonderful just to feel a bit more supported in positive, tangible ways.

We just aren't sure how to grow. We desperately want to go on with God, but there just seems to be a blockage in the congregation. They don't take the church seriously enough. For too many of us it is little more than a hobby.

People aren't really committed. You can see it in the lack of numbers at the prayer meeting. They'll come if it's entertainment, but not to pray.

We seem to be scared of spiritual gifts. We're always avoiding any chance that God might break out and do something surprising among us.

Everybody seems to want to get something. No one comes to give to others. Everyone wants to fulfil their potential, be blessed and encouraged. No one ever volunteers to make the coffee!

We are a bunch of junkies for 'personal words' or 'pictures'. If you receive a prophetic word for the week you're on a high. If you don't get anything it's a bad service.

We talk a lot, but we never seem to get around to actually doing anything. There's so much need in our community. I'm thinking of trying the Labour Party instead.

Things were great at the start, when the Spirit came, but now it all seems to be settling down—the leadership just aren't moving us further.

Our church is very spiritual, but not always very caring. I'm a single mother, but no one ever volunteers to babysit. Maybe I shouldn't expect it.

We're only a small fellowship. As soon as we've developed a good crowd of keen people, they all go off to larger churches with all their facilities, excitement and livelier worship. If people hadn't left, we'd now be a thriving church.

We are just too small to affect our village. Most local Christians commute to the big church in town.

5 *The problem of leadership*

Every society needs its scapegoats. In cricket it is the captain; in football the manager; in politics the prime minister—and in the church it is the leadership.

KEY POINT Leaders often find that the responsibility of leadership outweighs the privileges. They often find themselves blamed for everything!

Sometimes this judgment is not totally unfair, because leaders can be the cork in the bottle...

► relishing power
► resisting change
► restricting others
► repressing people.

On the other hand, leaders can be abused too. They can be...

► left with every responsibility in the local church
► regarded as the paid professionals on whom the 'success' of the church depends
► expected to be at the beck and call of every whim of their congregations.

A biblical concept

Despite the problems, leadership is a biblical concept. True leaders are...

► chosen by God (Haggai 2:23; Acts 9:15)
► humble (Exodus 3:11; Judges 6:15; 1 Samuel 18:18; Matthew 3:14)
► courageous (Acts 4:18–20; 7:51)
► incorruptible (1 Kings 13:8; 2 Kings 5:15–16; Daniel 5:17).

Leaders come in all shapes and sizes and have different characters and styles. This can be seen in the Bible itself, where leaders included...

► the faithful and strong leadership of Moses (Hebrews 3:5)
► the dictatorial King Rehoboam (1 Kings 12:13–15)
► the shrewd leadership of Nehemiah (Nehemiah 4:13–15)
► the cautious leadership of Timothy (2 Timothy 1:6–7).

Passive leaders such as Timothy were encouraged to 'fan into flame' their gift of God, while dictators were denounced for following a pattern that belonged to the world (Matthew 20:25–28; 1 Peter 5:1–5).

Leadership can often find that an obstructive Parochial Church Council, diaconate or church meeting can create great difficulties for them. The pressures of leadership were perhaps in the mind of Jesus when he trained his disciples for their first experience of Christian mission by teaching them about suffering and conflict as well as commitment (Matthew 10:5–42).

> *'I'm fed up when people stand up in church and say there are hurt people here. Why doesn't someone stand up and say there are bored people here. There would be a much greater response.'*
> SPRING HARVEST TEAM MEMBER

> *'It was the quality of the leaders that counted most, and Jesus and the Early church were quite revolutionary within their cultures in choosing and appointing some leaders who had the necessary qualities but would normally have been disqualified because they were women or uneducated or slaves (Acts 4:13; 21:9; Romans 16:13).'*
> ROY POINTER

Job description for local leaders

These descriptions show some of the different areas of leadership in the local church. They are for all the leaders of the local church—not merely for the minister or the full-time staff...

► **Visiting**—calling on members of the congregation in their homes. Door-to-door visitation in the neighbourhood. Factory or prison visits.

► **Community leadership**—involvement in secular community organizations so that the church is represented to show its concern by making a positive contribution.

► **Teaching**—expounding the scriptures and relating them to the contemporary world and daily life. Preachers and teachers are expected to give a considerable amount of time to prayer and preparation for Sunday sermons and in developing teaching programmes for groups within the church.

► **Congregation leadership**—serving as leaders in the congregation—those to whom members turn for advice and guidance on all aspects of the life and work of the congregation.

► **Counselling**—counselling individuals on personal and spiritual problems, couples planning to be married, those who are in hospital, other people with personal and vocational problems, especially bereavement.

► **Personal development and in-service training**—developing devotional life, plus pastoral, teaching and management skills. Keeping up-to-date in theological studies.

► **Administration**—one leader may serve as 'managing director' of the congregation, working with planning and finance committees. Ensuring that plans are implemented.

► **Denominational and ecumenical responsibilities**—carrying a fair share of denominational responsibilities, participating in ecumenical groups and other co-operative bodies.

► **Evangelism**—calling on the uncommitted people in the community, and sharing the good news. Preaching evangelistic sermons and engaging in evangelistic missions.

► **Leading worship**—planning and conducting public worship, and working with others who participate in leading corporate worship.

► **Team leadership**—serving with the lay leadership team—each with her or his own unique gifts and special responsibilities.

► **Enabling**—helping others to identify their own special call to service and ministry, and enabling them to respond to that call.

► **Training**—planning and executing a programme which trains leaders to teach groups, perform counselling and engage in evangelism.

► **Sacramental and priestly functions**—ministering the sacraments of baptism and holy communion. Conducting marriages and funerals. Spending time in prayer for and on behalf of the congregation and the community.

Taken from What Makes Churches Grow

Sharing Leadership Together

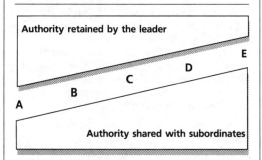

A. **Tells:** Leader decides then announces *his/her* decision.
B. **Sells:** Leader decides then tries to 'sell' *his/her* decision.
C. **Tests:** Leader presents *his/her* tentative decision, but asks advice before making *his/her* final decision.
D. **Consults:** Leader presents problem and obtains advice from the group before deciding.
E. **Joins:** Leader asks the group to decide within limits of given situation.

Diagram adapted from original by Warren G. Schmidt

According to the New Testament...

The New Testament reveals different models of leadership which existed simultaneously in the early church...

▶ the 'overseers' in Jewish churches were termed 'elders', and they followed the pattern established in the local synagogues of the time (Acts 11:30; 16:4; 21:18)

▶ meanwhile, a leader holding the same position in a Gentile church was termed a 'bishop' and functioned on the model established by contemporary local government (Titus 1:6–7).

The New Testament makes several key points about these leaders. They were to...

▶ exercise a caring ministry over their people (Acts 20:28)

▶ guard and guide the church, and to exercise discipline where necessary (2 Timothy 4:2)

▶ teach and prepare God's people for service (Ephesians 4:11–12)

▶ be growing in Christ (1 Timothy 3:6)

▶ be an example to others (1 Timothy 4:12; 1 Peter 5:3)

▶ be followed as long as they followed Christ (1 Corinthians 11:1)

▶ demonstrate Christian morality, spirituality and values in their daily lives (Acts 6:3; 1 Timothy 3:13).

The appointment of leaders in the New Testament was not determined by age, gender, marital status, race, culture or academic credentials. It was the quality of their daily lives which was regarded as being truly important.

The pattern adopted was not one of authoritarian rule. The church already had its head in Jesus Christ. Instead, leaders were to be servants, strengthening, building up and encouraging the body of Christ (Mark 9:35; 10:42–45).

> '*I*f the sixteenth century recovered "the priesthood of all believers"... perhaps the twentieth century will recover "the ministry of all believers".'
> JOHN STOTT

> *E*ncouragement from a senior to a junior devil: 'One of our great allies at present is the church itself. Do not misunderstand me. I do not mean the church as we see her spread out through all time and space and rooted in eternity, terrible as an army with banners. That, I confess, is a spectacle which makes our boldest tempters uneasy. But fortunately it is quite invisible to these humans.'
> C.S. LEWIS, *The Screwtape Letters*

Guidelines for leadership

It would take a whole week of seminars to tackle fully the problems faced by leaders in the local church and those problems that they actually create for everyone else. The following ten suggestions for the operation of leadership within the local church may provide an effective answer to some of these difficulties...

Guideline 1—a local church will never find one person who can fulfil every ministry simultaneously. The development of team leadership is essential.

Guideline 2—an interactive leadership is crucial, where leaders relate to one another, and team and people communicate hurts, needs and aspirations freely together.

Guideline 3—just as leaders pray for their people, so the congregation need to support and encourage their leadership prayerfully.

Guideline 4—leaders should always serve the people rather than attempting to impose upon them. Rather than being superior and remote, leaders should not withdraw from the congregation but take time together in social and informal contexts as well. The ideal model is of Jesus with the 12, because discipleship is a key function of leadership.

Guideline 5—we need to be actively involved in caring for our leaders. They are not working one day a week— many neglect the need to have a day of rest. By giving practical and financial support to the home and family of leaders, we give them more time to fulfil their duties to us. If they are married, they have a duty to their wives or husbands, and also to their families.

Guideline 6—avoid all forms of malicious gossip. Rumours do no one any good, and we need all to speak well of each other.

Guideline 7—leaders need to be prepared to apprentice and train younger leaders. The church needs to cultivate new generations of leadership.

Guideline 8—where conflict arises, do not be afraid to share openly with leadership. This is a prime area of responsibility for them.

Guideline 9—team leadership should be actively at work in releasing volunteer leaders for various spheres of church involvement—for example, for house group leadership, teaching, counselling, etc.

Guideline 10—leaders need time to exercise vision for the church. We need to encourage them in whatever ways we can to have adequate time with God and with the other church leaders—this will be a great investment for the church.

Growth brings problems

A church without problems has probably never existed.

As a church grows in finding new opportunities and new involvements, it will probably also see a growth in pressure and problems. In fact, this can be a hallmark of genuine growth.

God has given us each other in order that we can meet our problems together. As the church gains momentum our problems will not die away. But by God's grace we can surmount them—and our enemy will tremble!

The church is uniquely designed by God—not to be problem-free but to be victorious. Instead of struggling for survival we are called to move forward with victory assured.

Booklist

Allen, J., editor, *The Evangelicals*, Paternoster

Brierley, P., *Christian England*, Marc Europe

Calver, C., Coffey, I. and Meadows, P., *Who Do Evangelicals Think They Are?*, Evangelical Alliance

Cohen, D. and Gaukroger, S., *How to Close Your Church in a Decade*, Scripture Union

Dayton, E.R. and Engstrom, T.W., *Strategy for Leadership*, Marc Europe

Greenslade, P., *Leadership*, Marshall Pickering

Jansen, F.C., *Target Earth*, University of the Nations

Keeley, R., editor, *The Quiet Revolution*, Lion

Kirby, G.W., *Why All These Denominations?*, Kingsway

Marshall, T., *Understanding Leadership*, Sovereign World

Pawson, D., *Fourth Wave*, Hodder & Stoughton

Spriggs, D., *Christian Leadership*, Bible Society

Stott, J.R.W., *The Contemporary Christian*, IVP

Purpose

Discovering what the church is for

CONTENTS

Introduction: why the church?

1   **Back to the New Testament**

2   **Models of the church**

3   **A holy people**

4   **Biblical holiness**

5   **A royal calling**

Booklist

Book of the seminar day:
Stephen Travis, *I Believe in the Second Coming,*
Hodder & Stoughton

Introduction: why the church?

If the church is made up of **people** rather than structures, buildings and institutions...

If the church is rooted in a **partnership** which expresses its essential unity...

If the church is intended to encounter and overcome its **problems** in order to make clear its true identity...

Then we have to ask the biggest question of all: what is the **purpose** of the church? Why did God establish it? What purpose does he have for the church, both now and in eternity?

KEY POINT There is a yawning gulf between the church as God originally designed it to be and the church as it is now.

The church today clearly falls a long way short of what God intended.

For many Christians, this has led to disillusionment...

▶ some people settle for the 'reality' of how the church is now, and give up any attempt to change it

▶ others give up entirely and abdicate from the church.

Both of these options are dead ends. What we really need is...

▶ to start becoming the church God has called us to be

Only then will Christians be 'at home'—and our society might even start to become jealous of the alternative society we enjoy together!

To achieve this goal we must confront the question: 'What is the church for?'

1 *Back to the New Testament*

What was the church originally meant to be? It is not enough to search through church history to find the views which suit us best. In our search for the church's true purpose, we need to look behind our history and go back to scripture itself.

The church in the New Testament

The Bible does not pinpoint the exact nature, identity and practice of the church, but it does provide broad guidelines which we can work from.

KEY POINT The first thing to say is that the church represents the very summit of God's purpose, which was achieved through the ministry of Jesus Christ (Ephesians 3:11).

The church was...

▶ designed to reveal God's wisdom to heavenly powers

▶ God's 'eternal purpose' (Ephesians 3:10–11).

This means that the church is here for a number of reasons...

Worshipping God—While no specific form of worship or liturgy is given, we are to worship in spirit and in truth (John 4:20–24)...

▶ Singing, lifting hands, kneeling, speaking praise,

For more on worship, see page 84.

> '**W**hat is the chief end or purpose of man?' 'The chief end of man is to glorify God and to enjoy Him forever.'
> WESTMINSTER SHORTER CATECHISM

> '**T**he invisible church of Christ is catholic, not confined to any place or people. There is a striking contrast between (Jewish worship with its focus on Jerusalem) and the Christian church under the Gospel. There is now no local centre for the religious service of Christ's people—no holy place to which they must repair personally for their worship, or towards which, when at a distance, they must turn their face in prayer. Neither at Jerusalem nor in the temple are men now to worship the Father. Wherever on the wide earth there is a true worshipper, there is a true temple of Jehovah, and there he may be worshipped in spirit and in truth... The narrow barriers of a former economy have been thrown down; and in the gift of the Spirit to all believers, and in the fellowship of the Spirit co-extensive with all, there is laid the foundation of a church, no longer confined to our nation as before under the law, but worldwide and universal.'
> JAMES BANNERMAN

and the spiritual gifts were all used in worship (1 Timothy 2:8; Hebrews 13:15; 1 Corinthians 14:22–25).

▶ Prayer, thanksgiving, intercessions and praise were all to be included (1 Timothy 2:1), as were psalms, hymns and spiritual songs (Ephesians 5:19–20; Colossians 3:16).

▶ We worship in the energy of the Spirit and according to his word, in order to bring glory to God (John 4:23; Romans 15:5–6).

Serving God—because our worship inevitably must result in service (Matthew 4:10). This will be revealed in various ways...

▶ becoming the bride of Christ (Ephesians 5:23–32; Revelation 19:7)

▶ being built up in the faith (Jude 1–4)

▶ being involved in the work of ministry (Ephesians 4:9–16)

▶ sharing the good news of Jesus, and making disciples of all nations (Matthew 28:18–20; Acts 1:5–8)

▶ acting as salt and light in the world (Matthew 5:13–16).

Conquering the enemy—Jesus Christ builds a victorious church. Our battle is with demonic principalities and powers, and we are equipped to fight with spiritual weapons of warfare (Ephesians 6:10–20; 2 Corinthians 10:1–5). The church is therefore called to be both militant and triumphant (Matthew 16:15–20).

Growing together in love—(Ephesians 4:16) and to give glory to Jesus from generation to generation (Ephesians 3:21).

A blueprint in the early church?

The principles are very plain—but what we make of them is less certain. Many have therefore turned to the life and practices of the early church to see if they provide a blueprint for the church of today.

What was the church like in the beginning?

▶ in the early days, the believers continued to worship in the Jerusalem Temple, as Jesus had done, and they also broke bread in each other's homes (Acts 2:46)

▶ outside Jerusalem, they went to the local synagogues (Acts 14:1 and 17:2) as well as meeting in their homes.

The inclusion of Gentiles in the church, coupled with growing Jewish persecution, cut the first Christians' ties with the synagogues (Acts 18:4–6).

The general picture given in the Book of Acts and in the New Testament letters is one of small local communities of believers enduring hardship and seeking to support each other. Their aims seem to have been survival, growth and obedience to the teaching of the Bible.

KEY POINT For the first three centuries the churches had no buildings to maintain. Bureaucracy was kept to a minimum; the prime emphasis was on teaching and pastoral ministries.

They faced two threats...

▶ external persecution from the state

▶ internal undermining by teachers of false doctrine.

Far from destroying the church, these threats actually

strengthened it. They kept the church alert and in good condition.

Simple, straightforward worship

There was only a limited degree of uniformity between the local churches. Simplicity was their hallmark. Scattered New Testament references suggest that Christians met regularly to...

Read the scriptures and pray together

- ▶ public prayer and teaching were early features of church life (Acts 2:42)
- ▶ the scriptures were read aloud (1 Timothy 4:13)
- ▶ Paul urged that his own letters be not only read but exchanged with other churches (Colossians 4:16; 1 Thessalonians 5:27)
- ▶ fasting was also used (Acts 13:2; 14:23).

Sing hymns

- ▶ the New Testament itself may contain several early Christian hymns (Philippians 2:6–11; Colossians 1:15–20; 1 Timothy 3:16; plus some of the songs in the Book of Revelation)
- ▶ these passages are all Christological and may reflect the practice of composing hymns in rhythmic patterns to give glory to Jesus Christ
- ▶ regular singing was encouraged, and was paralleled in contemporary Jewish synagogue practice (1 Corinthians 14:26; Ephesians 5:19).

Use spiritual gifts

- ▶ these included both tongues and prophecy—indeed, the apostle Paul stressed that the believers should 'be eager to prophesy', and he added, 'do not forbid speaking in tongues' (1 Corinthians 14:3, 39)
- ▶ however, Paul also stressed that these should be carried out in an orderly and dignified fashion (1 Corinthians 14:40)—clearly, enthusiasm could equally result in people getting 'carried away' in the first-century church as it can today!

Repeat credal statements

- ▶ early statements of Christian belief were probably repeated in local church life (Romans 6:17; 10:9; 1 Corinthians 15:17; Philippians 2:11–16)
- ▶ as the years passed, more fixed forms of liturgy emerged—by the year AD225, one order for church worship began with...

BISHOP: 'The Lord be with you.'

PEOPLE: 'And with your spirit.'

BISHOP: 'Lift up your hearts'

PEOPLE: 'We lift them up to the Lord.'

Over 1,700 years later many of us would not find these words unfamiliar!

A focus on the sacraments

The patterns for baptism and communion were first set out by the Gospel writers and the apostles. These were generally followed in the early church, but it was perhaps inevitable that local variations would occur.

For communion—It seems to have been common for this celebration to have been linked with the *agape* meal, or 'love-feast'—when Christians shared food together.

> '*F*or as the bread of the earth, receiving the invocation of God, is no longer common bread but Eucharist, consisting of two things, an earthly and a heavenly; so also our bodies, partaking of the Eucharist, are no longer corruptible, having the hope of eternal resurrection.'
> IRENAEUS, SECOND-CENTURY BISHOP OF LYONS

> '*T*he sacrament of the Eucharist, which was instituted by the Lord at a meal-time and enjoined upon all, we take in assemblies before day-break, and only from the hands of the Presidents.'
> TERTULLIAN, SECOND-CENTURY APOLOGIST

For more on baptism, see page 84.

PAUSE FOR THOUGHT
Is the church in the book of Acts a model we should seek to follow today?

> '*T*hen they are brought by us where there is water, and are born again in the same manner in which we were ourselves born again. For, in the name of God, the Father and Lord of the universe, and of our Saviour Jesus Christ, and of the Holy Spirit, they then receive the washing with water.'
> JUSTIN MARTYR, SECOND CENTURY AD

For more on communion, see page 85.

This had resulted in abuses, which Paul tackled in his letter to the Corinthian church (1 Corinthians 10). However, the early church continued to emphasize the fellowship context for communion.

Justin Martyr, the second-century apologist, records that...

- ▶ thanks for the bread and wine is preceded by the Christians saluting one another with a kiss
- ▶ the meal is followed by a collection for the orphans, sick, widowed and disadvantaged among them.

For baptism—According to the *Didache*, a manual of church life written around the end of the first century...

'Baptise thus: having first recited all these things, baptise "in the name of the Father, and of the Son, and of the Holy Ghost", in running water. If you have no running water, baptise in other water; if you cannot baptise in cold water, use warm. If you have neither, pour water on the head thrice "in the name of the Father, and the Son, and the Holy Ghost". Before baptism, the baptiser and baptised should fast, and any others who can, and you must order the baptised to fast for a day or two.'

While local variations emerged in practice, the basic beliefs remained consistent. By the third century it was common for people to be sprinkled three times, accompanied by a liturgical confession of faith.

The secrecy which surrounded the sacraments caused Christians to be accused of cannibalism (eating the body and blood of Christ) and incest (the love feast). People were uncertain as to what Christians did, and so became very suspicious of them.

The expectation of persecution

Paul told the Christians in Philippi that they could expect persecution (Philippians 1:29–30). When persecution broke out, it was no big surprise—it was part of normal Christian experience (Romans 8:18; 2 Corinthians 1:6; 1 Peter 4:12–17).

Christians were often opposed by leaders in the Jewish community, or by leaders of the pagan cults. In the first few centuries of the church's life, hostility to Christianity became the generally accepted practice.

Letters written between Pliny, the Roman Governor of Bithynia, and the Emperor Trajan in the second century AD reveal that it was common practice to persecute Christians. They were regarded as atheists, for they rejected the normal gods and refused to worship anyone other than Jesus. Pagan temples were being deserted, and informers were employed to root out practising Christians.

Occasionally, there were periods of severe persecution. Christians prized their martyrs, and many believers sincerely sought to die for their Lord.

One of the most famous of these early martyrs was Polycarp, the aged Bishop of Smyrna. He boldly told the Roman consul who was trying to persuade him to renounce Christ: 'Eighty-six years have I served him, and he has done me no wrong: how can I blaspheme my King who saved me?'

Christian courage in the face of death amazed many pagan onlookers. It was tough to be a Christian, and faithfulness to Jesus was a crucial characteristic for the beleaguered church.

A developing hierarchy of authority

In New Testament times there seems to have been no fixed structure of church authority.

KEY POINT There was certainly no hierarchical system. No one person was in charge of a single community. Christ alone was head of the church.

But within a few years, later in the first century, things changed. For example, Ignatius, the Bishop of Smyrna, said that no eucharist was valid unless it was administered by the bishop. Why did this happen?

The church was under threat from a wide variety of false teachings. The authority of church leaders was emphasized to provide protection for the local churches. Christian creeds, charismatic practices and the apostolic tradition and succession were all emphasized. Gradually...

▶ the church leadership was given greater authority
▶ ordination received special priority
▶ no salvation was recognized outside the church.

These were originally intended as measures to help the church fight back against heresy.

To safeguard their flocks, the second-century bishops emphasized a number of external characteristics by which the true church could be recognized...

▶ the universal church consists of all the local units—they have no independent identity
▶ these are bound together by their loyalty and submission to the church as a whole
▶ the bishops rule as direct successors to the apostles and are the custodians of the true tradition.

Early sects challenged this. The Montanists, Donatists and Novatianists all reacted against the gradual secularization, worldliness and corruption of the church. Each of them made holiness the mark of the true church. The Montanists were ascetic in many of their practices and extreme in their belief that gross sins after baptism were unforgivable, but they highlighted a major problem.

It was a battle for survival. Thrown to the wild animals in the arena, burned as torches in Nero's gardens, plagued by Gnostic heresies and Jewish teachers seeking to impose rituals upon them, it was not an easy time to be a Christian.

The general picture was one of small communities of believers gathering together as 'the church' in a town, village or city. Through the early centuries the situation evolved into a struggle for primacy between the three major centres of the church...

▶ Alexandria in Egypt
▶ Antioch in Syria
▶ Rome.

The conversion of the Roman Emperor Constantine helped to ensure the ultimate triumph of the Bishop of Rome, and the eventual subservience of the church to the state.

The seeds were therefore already sown for future battles. Hierarchy, division and variety already existed. When people claim to be returning to the model of the early church, it is important to ask 'which one?'

'They are not to be sought out; but if they are accused and convicted, they must be punished.'
TRAJAN, ROMAN EMPEROR UNTIL AD117

PAUSE FOR THOUGHT
What does the early church's attitude towards persecution have to teach us today?

'Those who are truly his disciples receive grace from him... Some drive out devils... some have foreknowledge of the future... others heal the sick through the laying on of hands... and even the dead have been raised up before now and have remained with us for many years. Why, there is no numbering of the gifts which all over the world the church has received from the Lord and put into action day by day, in the name of Christ Jesus.'
JUSTIN MARTYR, SECOND-CENTURY AD

'For in the ordination of a priest the presence of the people is also required that all may know for certain that the man elected to the priesthood is of the whole people the most eminent, the most learned, the holiest, the most outstanding in every kind of virtue.'
ORIGEN, C. AD185–253

Back to the future

The past 200 years have seen a repeated chorus of 'back to the early church'. This has meant different things to different people...

▶ some want to copy the style and practices of the early church
▶ some want to apply the principles of the early church to our own time and culture.

Many have argued that there could be no finer purpose for the future than in regaining the heritage of the past. Different groups over the past 200 years have attempted to do this in a number of ways...

Independents—independent groups developed a strong emphasis on the systematic teaching of scripture and the autonomy of the gathered congregation of the local church. Congregationalists and Baptists upheld the principle of every-member involvement through the church meeting. The Baptists also emphasized the crucial significance of the adult baptism of believers. All of these were activities which claimed their roots in the earliest practices of the church.

Presbyterians—took as their form of church government the type which John Calvin had used in post-Reformation Geneva. Most would say that Calvin had only rediscovered a form of church government which had played a fundamental role in the life of the early church.

Methodism—John Wesley sought to recapture the sense of fellowship which typified the early church. Part of his genius lay in the way he created a disciplined Christian community from his converts. The great Evangelical Awakening of the eighteenth century pointed to the recovery of biblical preaching and an emphasis on personal conversion, both of which reflected the life of the early church.

The Salvation Army—they adopted uniforms and military music in their attempt to carry the gospel of Jesus Christ to ordinary people. General William Booth rejected the use of the sacraments, feeling that they created controversy and might deflect from the prime task of being soldiers for Jesus Christ.

The Brethren movement—its nineteenth-century founders sought to return to the early church in simplicity of worship, proper conduct and personal salvation. They rejected all forms of clergy and claimed that as disciples of Christ each man could minister as guided by the Holy Spirit. Each Sunday morning they met simply to break bread together and expound scripture.

Pentecostals—they pointed to the absence of spiritual fervour and gifts which had characterized the early church. They recovered the doctrine of the baptism of the Holy Spirit and reflected some of the characteristics of the early Montanists. Along with the Salvation Army and the Methodists, they placed great emphasis on the need for personal holiness.

Much of the doctrinal stress of the Pentecostals, coupled with the spontaneity and simplicity of the Brethren, has been carried through into the new churches.

All these attempts to recover the quality of life in the early church have developed into our modern denominations. None of them developed a comprehensive theory of the church to match that of the Roman Catholic

Church—which still concentrates its claims on standing in direct succession to the apostle Peter.

And the Church of England ...

But what about the Church of England? Many of the characteristics of the Free Churches such as biblical preaching and an emphasis on personal conversion could also apply to Evangelicals in the Anglican communion.

Yet most contemporary Anglicans do not trace their heritage back to the early church, they go further!

Their ideas centre around the fact that the concept of 'church' goes back to the biblical notion of a 'covenant' relationship between the God of Israel and his people. (A 'covenant' is an agreement between two parties.)

The Apostle Paul argues it like this in Romans 9–11 ...

▶ Abraham was called by God to be the founder of a great family of faith

▶ however, God's covenant people, Israel, rebelled against God and broke their agreement with him

▶ Jesus came not only to restore his people but also to include all the Gentiles who would be justified by faith in him

▶ God therefore redefines Abraham's family as the worldwide covenant family of faith.

Anglican evangelicals therefore trace their view of the church back in two stages ...

▶ first to Abraham, and the beginnings of God's people in the Old Testament

▶ then to the consummation of the covenant relationship in Jesus Christ.

They hold a clear commitment to scripture and the preaching of the word of God. From this twin root of word and covenant are traced the principles of authority, structure, ministry and sacraments, which they trace in an unbroken line to the early church.

While Evangelical Anglicans have often worked harder at their understanding of the church than their Free Church counterparts, Archbishop Robert Runcie urged that they put more effort into this endeavour. Speaking at the National Evangelical Anglican Celebration in 1988, he challenged Evangelical Anglicans to develop a clear doctrine of the church. This is a challenge that we still have to face.

The way forward?

Could we find a way forward in our understanding of the church if we simply combined all the special emphases of the different denominations? We might take ...

▶ Pentecostal power

▶ Independent preaching

▶ Salvationist evangelism

▶ Methodist structure ...

However, lumping all these qualities together is no substitute for building up a clear, coherent picture of what the church is called to be.

We still have a long way to go.

'*O*ur aim is that men should come together in all simplicity as disciples, not waiting on any pulpit or ministry but trusting that the Lord will edify us together by ministering to us as he sees good for ourselves.'
A.N. GROVES (BRETHREN)

'*T*he Apostle asks, What is the church? The church is "the body of Christ and members in particular". Christ is the head, we are the body, with the blood which flows through in this organic vital union. We are the branches in the vine and the life of the parent tree flows into us; it is a mystical vital union with Christ—saints in Christ Jesus.'
DR MARTYN LLOYD-JONES

'*T*he Methodist church discipline of the eighteenth century has no parallel in modern English ecclesiastical history.'
E. DOUGLASS BEBB

'*W*e Evangelicals are Bible people. We believe that God has spoken fully and finally in his Son Jesus Christ and in the biblical witness to Christ. We believe that scripture is precisely the written speech of God, and that because it is God's word it has supreme authority over the church. The supremacy of scripture has always been and always will be the first hallmark of an Evangelical. We deplore the cavalier and sometimes even arrogant attitudes to Holy scripture which are flaunted in the church today. We see these as derogatory to the Lord Jesus Christ whose attitude was one of humble, reverent submission to scripture.'
JOHN STOTT, *What is an Evangelical?*

---

2 *Models of the church*

KEY POINT There are invaluable lessons to be learned from the story of the church.

If we are dissatisfied with the church as it is today, we need to ask some questions ...

▶ how did we get where we are today?

▶ what did the Christians of the past believe about the purpose of the church?

This section outlines seven models of the church, as it has been seen by Christians down the centuries. These models are ...

1 Cyprian's 'one church'
2 Augustine's 'city of God'
3 Luther's 'community of believers'
4 Calvin's 'school of Christ'
5 The Anabaptists' 'separated communities'
6 The Puritans' 'purified church'
7 Anglicanism's 'established church'.

1 *Cyprian's 'one church'*

Cyprian was Bishop of Carthage in North Africa in the middle of the third century. He was the first Christian writer to present a detailed doctrine of the church, and his view was influential for many centuries.

Cyprian's teaching about the church came about because the church right across the Roman Empire was suffering violent persecution under the Emperor Decius (AD249–51). The Bishops of Rome, Antioch, Jerusalem and Caesarea were all martyred, but Cyprian went into hiding, from where he led the church using letters. Many of the clergy criticized his flight.

Decius ordered everyone to obtain a certificate stating they had sacrificed to the gods. Although some Christians avoided this by bribing officials, large numbers, including clergy, gave in and performed this act of pagan worship. Those who did not were executed or imprisoned.

When the persecution ended, large numbers sought readmission to the church. This led to some difficult questions ...

▶ should 'lapsed' Christians be allowed back into the church?

▶ who should decide whether or not they were fit to do so—the 'confessors' (those who had suffered for their faith), or the bishops?

▶ when should they be readmitted—immediately, or after a period of penance?

Cyprian, striving for unity, wrote *The Lapsed*, arguing that the bishops had the authority but should heed the recommendations of the confessors, and that there should be a period of penance. This policy was attacked from both sides: some said it was too liberal, some too strict.

Out of these struggles he wrote his most important work, *The Unity of the Church*. This work gives us Cyprian's view of the church. He argued that ...

▶ unity was a given fact—you could not divide the church, only leave it

▶ anyone doing so was committing spiritual suicide because salvation was only possible through the church

▶ the bishops were the key to unity—on the basis of Matthew 16:18 he regarded the bishops as the true successors to the apostles, given all their authority and functions

▶ each local bishop was supreme in his church, but together with all other bishops they were a college— the episcopate—who represented the unity of the whole church

▶ the baptism of all sects was invalid

▶ the Holy Spirit was only received through the church and its leaders, so there could be no forgiveness of sins other than through the church.

Cyprian also rejected the primacy of the Bishop of Rome.

In this way Cyprian formulated a concept of a church bound together by visible and external unity, presided over by bishops. This doctrine was the foundation of the Roman Catholic view of the church which continued largely unchallenged until the Reformation, over 1250 years later.

2 Augustine's 'city of God'

Augustine lived 100 years after Cyprian. He was born in what is now Algeria, was converted to Christianity after reading the Book of Romans and was baptized in Easter AD387. He became Bishop of Hippo in North Africa nine years later, and went on to become the most dominant influence on the medieval doctrine of the church.

The church had changed a great deal since Cyprian's time. There were two major changes...

▶ the Emperor Constantine had been converted to Christianity in AD313—he changed the status of the church from an illegal, persecuted sect to the official religion of the Roman Empire

▶ separatist churches (the 'Donatists') had grown up and now outnumbered the Catholic churches—Augustine opposed them vigorously.

Augustine's doctrine of the church was formulated against this background. The major attack of the Donatists on the Catholic Church was on its unholiness— this was why they had split away. Augustine's teaching on the church included these elements...

▶ He represented the true, universal, catholic church, whereas they were confined to Africa.

▶ They claimed they were the only Christians, and ignored the rest of the world. This made them guilty of schism, the opposite of love, and a sign that they did not have the Holy Spirit.

▶ On the unholiness of the church, Augustine pointed to Jesus' parable of the wheat and the tares. Only God knows who are genuine Christians—many in the visible church are only nominal followers. It is the 'position of the heart, not the body' that matters.

▶ The real church is holy because it is of Christ. The sacraments are valid, even if administered by one who is unholy, because they are given by Christ.

▶ He affirmed Cyprian's concepts of apostolic succession and authority within the one church.

The modern concept of the true church consisting of all believers of whatever church was inconceivable to those of Augustine's day.

Although the wicked could not be excluded from the visible church, they are separate from the righteous—

> '*If* a branch is broken from a tree, it cannot bud; if a stream is cut off from its source, it dries up... He who forsakes the church... is a stranger, he is an enemy. Without the church for your mother, you cannot have God for your Father.'
> CYPRIAN,
> *The Unity of the Church* c. AD252

> '*T*he Bishop is in the church and the church in the Bishop. If anyone is not with the Bishop, he is not in the church.'
> CYPRIAN,
> *The Unity of the Church* c. AD252

PAUSE FOR THOUGHT
Does your view of what is the true nature of the church reflect a local or global perspective?

> '*O*ne wonders why Luther's action had to be followed by consequences that were the exact opposite of what he intended. He wanted a real unity of the church and the West— the consequence was the disintegration of the church and Europe.'
> DIETRICH BONHOEFFER

> '*T*here are two kingdoms, the one is God's kingdom, the other the world's kingdom... Whoever would mingle the two would put God's wrath in God's kingdom and mercy in the world's kingdom—that would be putting the devil in heaven and God in hell.'
> MARTIN LUTHER

they belong to the house but are not in it. Eventually, they will be cast off like tumours in the body of Christ in the future pure church in heaven.

In his famous work, *The City of God*, Augustine also taught that...

▶ the church now—and not just in its future development—is to be identified with the kingdom of God

▶ the true church is the community of the pious, but it is also identified with the organized church

▶ he contrasted the 'city of God' with the 'city of the world': good vs. evil, spiritual vs. carnal, elect vs. non-elect

▶ he did not say that the 'city of the world' was the state, but he said that the state by its actions could embody it.

Ultimately Augustine's ideas produced an irreconcilable conflict and a disaster for the church. After his time, the institutional church came to be seen as the kingdom of God on earth. And the Bishop of Rome became the prince of an earthly kingdom. He gained secular power and authority.

▶ Christian duty to God became identified with services rendered to the church

▶ everything outside the church was seen as 'secular'— everything inside it was seen as 'spiritual'

▶ to withdraw from the world and become a monk, hermit or nun was the hallmark of special piety

▶ the institutional church became more and more powerful and involved in politics, economics and military affairs

▶ the church accumulated great wealth, an army and civil power in the name of the kingdom of God.

3 Martin Luther's 'community of believers'

Martin Luther was born in 1483. He joined a religious order and for many years struggled with the problem of how God could accept him although he was a sinner. In 1519 he came to understand the biblical doctrine of justification by faith in Christ alone. His beliefs brought him into conflict with the church, and he was excommunicated by the Pope in 1521.

Luther reacted against the concept of the church as an institution...

▶ he disliked the German word *kirche* ('church') because, as in English, it had come to mean the building or the institution

▶ he preferred to talk of *gemeinde* ('community') or *versammlung* ('assembly')

▶ he said the church was 'holy believers and sheep who hear the voice of their Shepherd'

▶ the true church was the invisible church of all the predestined, those who had responded in faith to the gospel—it was hidden from the world, known only to God.

In 1530 the Augsburg Confession, approved by Luther, described the church as 'the congregation of the saints, in which the gospel is rightly taught and the sacraments rightly administered'. Its three emphases were...

▶ **right belief**—the gospel unites the church, and not church structures

▶ **right teaching**—the word of God is decisive in all matters and must be proclaimed

▶ **right order**—there are only two sacraments, baptism and communion—both speak of the forgiveness of sins and are only effective through faith, not simply by being celebrated.

Luther's greatest innovation in the doctrine of the church was his teaching on 'the priesthood of all believers'. He abolished the division between clergy and laity into two separate classes. Christ has made us all priests, equally and together, with the responsibility to help one another.

4 John Calvin's 'school of Christ'

John Calvin (1509–64), a Frenchman, was the most influential of the second generation of reformers. He developed an understanding of the church which went beyond that of Luther. A church, to be a church, must...

▶ be holy

▶ preach the word

▶ administer the sacraments.

Calvin placed great emphasis on church discipline as part of the process of personal sanctification. He linked his doctrine of election to the local congregation. God will be present with his elect as they meet together. For Calvin there was an inevitable tension between the invisible church and its visible expression. Doctrinal error was a great danger to be guarded against.

His favourite pictures of the church were...

▶ a mother to nurture believers

▶ a school to teach believers.

He believed that the New Testament offices of apostle, prophet and evangelist had ceased with the end of the apostolic era. Only the office of pastor was left, and he emphasized this very strongly. The pastor was the preacher responsible for ensuring purity of doctrine. He also recognized elders and deacons, although laid much the greater stress on the former.

5 The Anabaptists' 'separated communities'

More radical than Luther and Calvin were the Anabaptists. The movement began in Switzerland with the public baptism in Zurich of a small group of believers on 21 January 1525. They were intensely persecuted from the beginning, by both Protestants and Catholics, but spread throughout Switzerland to Germany, Austria and Holland.

The reformers such as Luther and Calvin shared with Catholicism a belief in the Christian state, in which everyone is baptized and is part of the church. The Anabaptists came to reject this as being unbiblical. Their view of the church was radically different...

▶ they rejected the idea of a state church which forced everyone to belong to it

▶ they believed that Christian faith was voluntary (they tended towards free-will rather than predestination)

▶ the church consists of true believers who freely gather together and become separate from the world.

The Anabaptists were not a highly organized, unified group. However, in 1527, one of their leaders drew up a confession which came to be circulated widely among the different groups. The Schleitheim Confession contains

> '**W**e do not deny that the churches which Antichrist [the Pope] dominates by his tyranny remain churches. But we say that he has profaned them by his sacrilegious impiety, that he has afflicted them by his inhuman domination, that he has poisoned them with false and wicked doctrines, and that he has corrupted and, as it were, put them to death, so much that Jesus Christ is half buried, the Gospel strangled, Christianity exterminated, the service of God almost abolished. In short, all is so disfigured that there appears rather an image of Babylon than of the holy city of God.'
> JOHN CALVIN

> **C**alvin's church in Geneva is 'the most perfect school of Christ that ever was in the earth since the days of the apostles.'
> JOHN KNOX

> '**T**he church is... set forth to us as an object of faith to this end that we may have confidence that all the elect are conjoined through the bond of faith in one church and society, in one people of God, of which Christ our Lord is the leader and prince and head.'
> JOHN CALVIN

> '**I**n the primitive church the chalices were of wood, the prelates of gold. In these days, the church has chalices of gold and prelates of wood.'
> SAVONAROLA

seven articles which mark out the difference between the Anabaptists and the Reformers...

▶ baptism is for those who have repented and come to true faith in Christ—and not for infants

▶ believers who fall into error should be excommunicated after three warnings

▶ the Lord's Supper is a simple memorial service and is only for the baptized

▶ believers should be separate from the world and from public life, including military service

▶ pastors should be supported by their congregations

▶ Jesus Christ forbade the use of violence, so believers should renounce 'the unchristian devilish weapons of force'

▶ oaths are forbidden.

The purity of the church was very important to Anabaptists. Their rather harsh practice of excommunication (which they called 'the ban') was intended to act like strong medicine on offenders. Faced with vicious persecution by the outside world, the Anabaptists were determined to maintain purity and perseverance inside the church.

One of their most famous leaders was Menno Simons—a Catholic priest who slowly came to believe in salvation by faith. Like many Anabaptist leaders, he spent most of his life on the run from violent persecution. The communities he founded later came to be called the Mennonites, a tradition which is still strong in both Europe and the United States.

6 The Puritans' 'purified church'

The term 'Puritan' was first used in the time of Queen Elizabeth I. It became a label for a diverse group of English Christians who were dissatisfied with the extent of the English reformation. They objected in particular to...

▶ sections of the Book of Common Prayer

▶ ecclesiastical ceremonies, vestments, ornaments, organs and the sign of the cross

▶ prelates and ecclesiastical courts.

For the Puritans, everything in church life and worship had to be put to a rigorous test—is it explicitly commanded in scripture? If there was no express biblical warrant for any practice, it was rejected.

The Church of England had emerged during the Reformation, partly from conviction but primarily because Henry VIII required a divorce from his Queen. Some of the Puritans remained within the Anglican church, while others formed independent churches—Presbyterians, Congregationalists and Baptists.

During the reign of Queen Elizabeth, Puritans enjoyed the support of an influential minority within Parliament. Under the Republic of Oliver Cromwell they achieved positions of considerable importance.

Some of their concerns were...

▶ to eliminate all vestiges of 'popery' from the church

▶ personal holiness and Christian character

▶ effective church discipline and pastoral leadership

▶ personal revival ('reformation' was their term for this).

In 1620 the 'Pilgrim Fathers' led by John Robinson left Leiden in Holland for New England. They hoped to establish in the new colony churches that were built on the basis of scripture alone, and separate from the state. As a result, New England became a major centre of Puritanism.

After the restoration of the monarchy in 1660, and until the Act of Toleration in 1689, Puritans and other non-conformists were vigorously harassed, persecuted and imprisoned. One of the most famous of them was John Bunyan, who wrote *The Pilgrim's Progress* while he was in prison in Bedford.

The Puritans came to a number of distinctive views about the church...

▶ The church could only consist of the 'visible saints'—anything else was fatally compromised. In this, they followed the view of early church groups such as the Montanists, Novatians and Cathari, rather than Augustine's concept of the 'visible' and 'invisible' church.

▶ Most Puritans rejected concepts of ecclesiastical hierarchy and adopted a system of locally ordained ministry.

▶ The local church was regarded as autonomous, governed by elders whom they termed presbyters. It was a voluntary union of worshippers agreeing to a declaration of faith and submitting to biblical discipline.

▶ Their concept of the church was based on their belief that God called people out of the world and into the church. It was separate and distinct from society and state.

▶ New England Puritans emphasized the importance of a conversion experience. They believed the church was 'a society of visible saints'—although they accepted that the saints were not perfect, and that it was not always easy to tell who was truly converted. In practice, some Puritans found the latter so difficult to maintain that they reverted to offering communion to all worshippers.

7 Anglicanism's 'established church'

John Jewel and Richard Hooker were two leading figures in the English church shortly after the Reformation. They profoundly disagreed with the Puritan approach. They believed that the reforms allowed in the English church by Elizabeth I were not merely adequate, but were exactly how the church should be. Their writings helped to establish the Anglican view of the church.

Some of their key ideas about the church include...

▶ the English church had not separated from the apostolic faith

▶ a reformation of the church had been necessary, and provincial churches had the right to do so

▶ services should be held in the ordinary language of the people, and not in Latin

▶ the church is organic and not static—church government and administration changes to meet changing circumstances

▶ while the Puritans believed that there should be no ceremonies in the church which are not expressly found in scripture, Hooker believed that no ceremonies should be allowed which are expressly forbidden by scripture

---

> *T*he church is 'a company or congregation of the faithful called and gathered out of the world by the preaching of the Gospel, who following and embracing true religion, do in one unity of the Spirit strengthen and comfort one another, daily growing and increasing in true faith, framing their lives, governments, orders and ceremonies according to the Word of God.'
>
> THE PURITAN JOHN FIELD, 1572

> *'A*ll these people... were in one day, with the blast of Queen Elizabeth's trumpet, of ignorant papists and gross idolaters, made faithful Christians.'
>
> HENRY BARROWE, WRITING ABOUT THE CHURCH OF ENGLAND, 1605

▶ Hooker taught that church laws are established by scripture, tradition and reason—with scripture taking the first place.

3 *A holy people*

God has more for his people than heritage and structure—important as they are.

 KEY POINT **God has called us to live as his people in the world.**

Ultimately his purpose for the church in the here and now has to do with our lives.

The Apostle Peter described the church in this way: 'You are a chosen people, a royal priesthood, a holy nation, a people belonging to God' (1 Peter 2:9).

We cannot fulfil God's purpose, as his church, without fulfilling this vision—without beginning to pray and live as...

▶ a chosen people

▶ a royal priesthood

▶ a holy nation

▶ a people belonging to God.

A holy church?

The fourth-century Nicene Creed boldly states: 'We believe in one holy, catholic and apostolic church.' God's first intention for the church is that it should be holy. This was...

▶ the content of Jesus' prayer to his Father (John 17:17, 19)

▶ Paul's desire for the Corinthians (2 Corinthians 11:2)

▶ the fruit of Jesus' death for his people (Ephesians 5:25–27).

In the Book of Revelation, the major emphasis of the letters to the seven churches of Asia is on their purity and commitment to Christ. The final imagery is of 'the Holy City, Jerusalem, coming down out of heaven from God' (Revelation 21:10). Changing imagery (as the Book of Revelation often does), this is 'the bride, the wife of the Lamb' (Revelation 21:9). The consummation of all history is the union of Christ with his holy and glorious bride, the church.

Such startling images seem far removed from contemporary church life with all its problems of both open and secret sins.

How do churches cope with this?

▶ Some churches struggle to maintain a real degree of purity. They have a strong, disciplinary regime and often appear to be harsh and uncaring.

▶ Some churches do not believe it is possible to enforce holiness on a congregation. They accept the idea of a 'mixed multitude' of 'sheep and goats', leaving God ultimately to sort people out.

▶ Most churches lie between these two extremes. They place some limits on their members, especially over leadership and receiving communion.

If the New Testament churches had such great difficulties over this issue, we might well wonder what hope there is for us. How can we reconcile the demand of a holy God for his church to be holy with our glaring imperfections?

Israel: a holy nation?

For the first Jewish Christians this dilemma was not a new one. God had commanded that Israel be his holy people about 1,400 years earlier! At the giving of the law on Mount Sinai, he said to Moses, 'Although the whole earth is mine, you will be for me a kingdom of priests and a holy nation' (Exodus 19:5–6).

There were two emphases. They were to be...

▶ **separate**—different from the other nations surrounding them, because God had chosen them to be his special people (Deuteronomy 7:6)

▶ **a witness**—a light to the Gentiles, demonstrating practical godliness, true worship and right relationships (Deuteronomy 4:6–8).

God gave them the law so they knew what he required of them, and the sacrificial system so that when they transgressed there was a way to put things right with God. God had no illusions about the nation and assured them that his choice was not based on their own righteousness (Deuteronomy 9:6), but on his great love for them (Deuteronomy 7:8).

God's new holy people

Peter was the apostle to the Jews and one of the leaders of the Jerusalem church. Writing originally to Jewish believers living outside the boundaries of Israel (1 Peter 1:1–2), he uses the same images from the books of Moses of a holy nation and a kingdom of priests—and applies them to God's new society, the church. What had failed under the Old Testament Law—the establishment of a holy community—was to be fulfilled through the work of Jesus Christ. It was the same purpose, but a different vessel.

For all Jews there was a further dimension. In the time of Moses, worship centred on the tent of the Lord's presence (later the temple in Jerusalem was built to replace the tent)...

▶ the tent and the temple were symbols of God's holy presence at the heart of the nation

▶ the central part of the temple was the holy place, and behind the thick curtains was the Holy of Holies

▶ the Holy of Holies originally contained the ark of the covenant, a wooden box built at the time of Moses to contain the two stone tablets of the Law (Exodus 40:20) and Aaron's rod that budded (Numbers 17:10)

▶ this box was a unique symbol of God's covenant relationship with his people

▶ on top of the ark rested 'the mercy seat', a slab of pure gold, with golden angels fixed to both ends of it

▶ this seat itself was empty, symbolizing God's presence.

When the tent (Exodus 40:34–35) and the temple (1 Kings 8:10–11) were ready, the '*shekinah*' glory of the Lord came and filled the room. No one, not even the priest, could approach this place. If they did, they would be struck dead—such was God's awesome holiness.

Just once a year, on the Day of Atonement (*Yom Kippur*), the High Priest, dressed in special robes, was allowed to enter on behalf of the whole nation. He did this to...

▶ burn incense on hot coals, sending a cloud of smoke (a symbol for prayer) to cover the mercy seat

▶ sprinkle blood on the mercy seat and on the ground in front of it—this was to cover his own sins

▶ sprinkle the blood of a second animal (a goat) on the mercy seat—this was so that the nation might know that their holy God had forgiven their sins.

The Jewish Christians who read Peter's letter realized that this whole sacrificial system was a shadow of the ultimate sacrifice when Jesus offered himself for the sin of the people. No one could doubt that God was holy or ignore the necessity of personal holiness in order to enter his presence.

Two dangers

Now God, through his Son, has opened the way for us to know and love him. We are forgiven and Christ's righteousness is ours. However, there are two dangers here...

▶ **We can do what we want** (this is known as 'antinomianism')—some Christians believe that they are 'free' to live exactly as they like. Because our righteousness comes from Jesus, morality simply doesn't matter. What do you think? If forgiveness is automatic for us, then who needs restraints?

▶ **We are living under the law** (this is known as 'legalism')—other Christians behave as if Jesus came to bring 'Law 2'—an updated Christian version of Moses' Law. It's only by strictly keeping to all the points of the law that we can please God and gain his acceptance.

These two extremes—lawlessness and legalism—are both distortions of the New Testament teaching on personal holiness.

PAUSE FOR THOUGHT
Do you have a bias to lawlessness or legalism?

Sin in the church

KEY POINT It is easy to assume that everything is going well with our brothers and sisters in the local church.

Often we are convinced that others are immune to the temptations and problems which we ourselves encounter. We fall into the trap of believing that if people knew what we are really like, then they would move at least two seats away from us.

Sadly, the truth is often far worse! Today large numbers of local churches are waking up to the reality that respected members of their congregations are living double lives. Of course, all of us fall short of living as God intended—but a double life puts people into a different league. Shock waves of surprise, disappointment and sorrow greet the news that someone has been living a lie, with no one ever even suspecting it.

The bad news is compounded when the person has been a church leader: preaching, leading worship, teaching, praying with others, sharing the bread and wine as if there was nothing wrong.

The list of double lives is a long one. A shortened version of it includes...

▶ having an affair

▶ homosexual practice

▶ embezzling funds

▶ child abuse

▶ tax evasion

▶ violence in the marriage

▶ alcohol, drug and substance abuse.

This tragic catalogue reflects sins current in society which are increasingly invading the people of God. The situations which emerge add up to a nightmare for the local church.

A double life

Andrew was a highly-respected member of his church in a small town in Hampshire. He was a local solicitor, preached regularly in the church, played an active role in church leadership, and was generally liked and trusted by people both inside and outside the congregation.

But all the time, Andrew was leading a double life. As a solicitor, many people trusted him to invest or move large amounts of money for them. Over the course of three years, Andrew siphoned off this money into a number of personal bank accounts. He then used it to buy a large house, several cars and a number of exotic holidays.

When the police finally caught up with him, his double life was exposed. The shock waves were severe: a colleague committed suicide; one of Andrew's clients lost all his life savings and died because of the stress; Andrew's wife divorced him; the church was devastated.

In 1993, Andrew was sentenced to five years in prison.

The shock of deception

One of the most disturbing results of discovering secret sin in the life of a fellow-Christian is the realization that we have been deceived.

Discovering what has been done is traumatic enough, but the shock does not end there. Recognizing that it has been going on for a period of time makes people face the fact that they have been deceived.

Imagine how the young man felt who discovered that the minister who had preached at his wife's funeral was at the time having an affair. Such things—and worse—actually happen. Frequently a church believes it will never happen to them, and then it does!

We should not be surprised, for we have an enemy of our souls who is longing to destroy Christians and discredit the church. Jesus called him 'the father of lies' (John 8:44), for from the very beginning he lied (in the Garden of Eden).

What was Jesus' teaching about secret sins? He taught that...

▶ a believer who actively practises deception is a hypocrite—he was unsparing in his condemnation of this pretence (see Matthew 6:2–5; 7:5; 13:13–29; 22:18; Mark 12:5; Luke 12:56; 13:15)

▶ the light exposes darkness and reveals private sin (John 3:20)

▶ we should not be proud or legalistic about avoiding specific acts—a single thought can easily lead us into sin (Matthew 5:27–28).

The problem with deception is that the longer it goes on, the higher the stakes become. Exposure very often involves the downfall of the person involved. Jesus said that hypocrisy was like yeast—it spreads and infects the whole person (Luke 12:1).

Just as with overt sins, once a Christian's secret sins have come into the light, then it becomes the painful duty of the church to deal with the situation (Matthew 18:15–17).

Church discipline

Nothing can be less pleasant for a local church than to face the necessity of administering discipline. How should this be done? The New Testament lays down several guidelines...

▶ first to the offender alone—Matthew 18:15; Galatians 6:1

▶ then within the church—Galatians 6:1; Matthew 8:15–20; 1 Corinthians 5:1–5; 2 Corinthians 2:6

▶ as a last resort the church must confront and even excommunicate the person involved—Matthew 18:17; 1 Corinthians 5:5, 13; 1 Timothy 5:19–21.

All of this should be done in humility, recognizing our own sinful and weakened humanity.

These guidelines may sound harsh, but they are necessary for the well-being of the body of Christ. The intention should always be to achieve restoration, reconciliation and healing (Galatians 6:1; Hebrews 12:5–11; Revelation 3:19). After all, God judges and punishes—but in order to bring people back to him when they turn in repentance (1 Corinthians 11:29–32; 2 Corinthians 2:6–11).

With the Lord Jesus there is always the potential for a new start.

This is a continued emphasis in scripture—Abraham, Moses, David, Elijah, Jonah, Thomas and Peter all failed God in serious ways. Yet each was still used by God in a major way. With him there is always a way back, and the promise of forgiveness and a fresh start!

'Forgive us our sins...'

Jesus taught his disciples when they prayed to ask God to forgive them in the same way that they forgive others (Matthew 6:12; Luke 11:4).

This is very hard teaching. Forgiving others—even though we know our own need of forgiveness—can sometimes be very difficult. This is especially the case when we have been dragged down by the betrayal of another person.

It is easy to be tempted either to be...

▶ over-indulgent and too tolerant

▶ or to be harsh and judgmental.

The biblical pattern is that we should confront, expose and subdue sinful practice among us. At the same time

---

The Bible on greed, immorality, etc...

The Bible gives specific teaching about several types of destructive behaviour in the church. These are...

▶ speaking evil of others—see 1 Corinthians 5:11; Ephesians 4:31; 1 Timothy 6:4; 1 Peter 2:15

▶ immorality—see 1 Corinthians 5:1–5; Matthew 5:32

▶ greed—see Acts 5:1–11; 1 Peter 5:2

▶ extortion—see 1 Corinthians 5:11

▶ divisiveness—see Romans 16:16–18; 1 Corinthians 3:1–4; Ephesians 5:21

▶ drunkenness and disorderly conduct—see 1 Corinthians 5:11; 2 Thessalonians 3:6–15.

we should actively forgive and seek the reconciliation and restoration of the person who has done wrong. This is not a weak concept. It takes strength to oppose sin, and even more to forgive the sinner—see Mark 11:25; Luke 11:4; 17:4; Ephesians 4:32.

However hurt we may feel, we need to 'forgive as the Lord forgave you' (Colossians 3:13).

A climate of honesty

Prevention is better than cure. The rate of moral failure in some local churches is currently reaching epidemic proportions. How can we help one another to create a climate in our churches where moral failure is stopped before it has a chance to take root?

It is at this point that the issue of honesty becomes absolutely critical. We can ask ourselves a number of questions about our honesty in church...

▶ is there a 'version of me' which I keep specially for use in church?

▶ am I afraid to say what I really think and feel?

▶ do I let people think that I am a paragon of virtue?

▶ would I be shocked to discover that others are not paragons of virtue?

▶ do I have genuine friendships with the people of my church?

The danger of putting a veneer of virtue over our real characters is that someone will one day discover the chipboard underneath!

But honesty is liberating. It is good for us. Our churches need to create a climate of honesty where we are not afraid to be ourselves. There are three kinds of honesty that we need...

Honest to ourselves—Few spiritual failures happen overnight. There is usually an extended period of temptation and building up to the sin that finally occurs. Usually it will be in an area of inherent weakness—what the Puritans used to term 'besetting sin'.

Each of us is aware of areas in our lives which we find particularly difficult. We may have a weakness for anger, bitterness, lust, or hoarding money. This is where we need to be honest with ourselves. We need to recognize our points of weakness and seek out the protection, love and support we need.

Honest to others—This is where it gets difficult. Once we know our personal weaknesses, we need to share them with someone we can trust. Even if our particular weakness feels like the last area of our lives that we would ever reveal to others, we need outside help.

Many Christians today are finding the idea of a 'spiritual director' or 'soul friend' helpful—a mature Christian who will regularly listen, discuss and pray over your problems. Someone who will help you to be real with God.

Others find that sharing their joys and struggles with a close friend, or even a small group, brings the encouragement they need.

Greater honesty about ourselves will often reduce the level of superficiality in others. We can begin truly to understand and encourage each other—helping each other not to stumble and fall. This is what it means to be disciples of Jesus together.

The idea here is not that we should spend our lives sharing personal weaknesses and temptations with each other. It is that we should develop trust and respect with particular friends. Together we can help each other to make progress in God—and not fall! Rather than find that we shock each other, we may be surprised to find the level of mutual understanding that is swiftly achieved.

Honest to God—There is no point in being anything other than honest with God, because he knows us better than we know ourselves (Psalm 139:1–4; 23–24). And because Jesus lived a fully human life, he knows exactly what it is like to be faced by temptation—he understands us from the inside (Hebrews 4:15–16).

All of this means that prayer is a great spiritual resource for us when we are drifting into danger. It is only when we are honest with God that we can begin to receive the forgiveness and help that we need (1 John 1:8–9).

In conclusion ...

Secret sin is an awful fact of contemporary church life. Dealing with its implications and results is a major challenge. There are so often innocent victims to be comforted and helped—not just at the time of impact, but on a long-term basis. There is trust to rebuild and damage to repair.

Above all, we need to build honesty and trust, through personal friendship, which will help us to avoid the cycle of deceit and shock. This will not always work, but it will certainly help. And we need to practise forgiveness in such a way that the world will recognize the reality of Christian love and restoration (John 13:34–35). We may not always avoid sinning, but we can help each other to start again!

> **'**If we say that we have no sin, we deceive ourselves, and the truth is not in us. If we confess our sins, [God] is faithful and just, to forgive us our sins, and to cleanse us from all unrighteousness.'
>
> 1 JOHN 1:8–9, AV

4 *Biblical holiness*

Churches are deeply affected by the personal holiness of the people in them.

This was certainly true of the churches of the New Testament. The problems Paul tackled in his letters to the churches often came down to the personal holiness of the people in each church...

▶ false teaching was a problem because people taught it, others believed it and all were harmed by it

▶ moral impurity, disunity, lack of love and the other common problems of churches then and now are obviously the result of people's sin.

KEY POINT Paul frequently urges his readers to put things right, not only for their own benefit but also for the sake of the church.

There is a false version of holiness which we have inherited from Victorian Christianity. It says that holiness is a narrow-minded, kill-joy Christianity, obsessed with behaviour such as abstinence from alcohol, smoking, gambling, and even politics or public entertainment. Churches of this variety can rightly be accused of legalism, pharisaism or downright hypocrisy.

Biblical holiness is very different. As a holy people, the church is a community of all sorts of sinners...

▶ redeemed by Jesus

▶ serving God

▶ loving one another

▶ dedicated to the Lord

▶ filled with the Spirit

▶ confessing sins

▶ exercising forgiveness

▶ shining as lights in a dark world.

All these are true signs of a holy church. Biblical holiness does not ignore our weaknesses—it faces them.

Biblical holiness has to be explored from two different angles...

▶ **personal holiness**—because God calls us to be holy persons

▶ **community holiness**—because God calls us to be a holy people.

We now look at these in turn...

Personal holiness

At conversion, each of us is reborn by the Holy Spirit into Christ. We receive his holiness as a gift. This is our spiritual identity, but it needs to be translated into our daily lives.

Paul instructs the Philippians to 'work out your salvation with fear and trembling'. This is known as the process of sanctification, or growth in holiness. The once-and-for-all act of justification is the beginning and source of the life-long process of moral transformation.

 KEY POINT Holiness is not optional. It is not just for super-saints. It is a Christian essential.

Sanctification is both the responsibility of the Christian and a work of the Holy Spirit. It is the job of all Christians to...

▶ wholly dedicate themselves to God (Romans 12:1)

▶ forsake all else (Luke 14:33)

▶ take up their own cross (Luke 14:27)

▶ deny themselves (Mark 8:34)

▶ seek God's kingdom first (Matthew 6:33).

These all act as the hallmarks of a radical Christian lifestyle. They mark out the separation between self-centred worldly living and life in the Holy Spirit, via death on a cross.

Paul urges us to die to ourselves and our own desires (Galatians 5:24)—we are crucified with Christ. Sharing in his death, we will then share in his resurrection (Romans 6:8). It is one of the paradoxes of the kingdom...

▶ to gain we must first lose

▶ to live we must first die

▶ to rise up we must first go down.

How can we possibly do it?

Holiness is not something that we can 'achieve' on our own. We need help from outside ourselves.

Paul explains in Romans 6 that our dying with Christ has already happened (Romans 6:6) and needs constantly to be worked out (Romans 8:17). It is only through the power of the Holy Spirit that we can possibly do these things (Ephesians 3:16).

The Spirit...

▶ gives us the power to resist our sinful nature (Galatians 5:16)

▶ enables us to overcome our sinful desires and temptations (1 Corinthians 10:13), although the

struggle continues (Romans 7:14–25)

▶ begins to transform us to become like Christ (2 Corinthians 3:18)

▶ enables us to keep the spirit of the law which is now in our hearts (Hebrews 8:10)

▶ produces his fruit in us—love, joy, peace, patience, kindness, goodness, faithfulness, gentleness and self-control (Galatians 5:22–23).

Holiness starts to become a reality for us when...

▶ our obedience

is coupled to...

▶ the power of the Spirit.

This does not happen overnight. We may experience great breakthroughs with the Holy Spirit at different times, but overall our growth in holiness is a process that goes on throughout our lives.

Jesus called us to love God and our neighbours (Matthew 22:37–40). Holiness is ultimately all about loving God more than anything else. If we love him we will obey him, and this will be evident in our relationship with our fellow men and women.

Holiness is never harsh or legalistic if it is the result of the love of God...

▶ love is about giving, not getting

▶ love is the fulfilment of the law (Romans 13:10)

▶ we love not just because of the example of Christ, but because we have received his love ourselves (Ephesians 5:2)

▶ without love we are nothing (1 Corinthians 13:1).

The process of holiness

Holiness restores human beings to God's original design specification. The Holy Spirit gives us the moral character that we were always intended to have—human beings made in the moral image of God.

If righteousness is being put right with God, then holiness is being made whole. It is the ultimate liberation—not the ultimate enslavement!

But how does this happen? There are at least seven different views about this! They are not mutually exclusive, but the supporters of an individual idea usually regard it as *the* way. The last of the seven is regarded by many as being unbiblical.

1 REDIRECTING DESIRES

Taught by: Origen, Augustine, Gregory the Great, John of the Cross, Thomas Kempis, Francis de Sales, Richard Baxter, John Owen.

In brief: Our natural desires are redirected from earth to heaven. The inner life, through prayer, is the priority. Once desire for God has been established as central in our lives, everything else will follow from it. Satan will struggle to pervert our love of God through temptation and destroy our inner holiness. Honesty and purity of heart are the key to this.

Advocates of this view emphasize that...

▶ constant self-examination is necessary to guard against the danger of drifting away

▶ loving God is the greatest blessing and benefit to the individual

▶ in order to focus our desire clearly on God it may be necessary to strip away all distractions—mainly through periods of solitude.

Some believe that God withholds the sense of his presence for periods of time—this is known as 'the dark night of the soul'. God does this to intensify our desire and heighten our joy when we experience union with Christ.

Philippians 3:7–10 can be taken as Paul's own heightened desire to know Christ through his suffering and struggles. He counts everything as loss compared to knowing Jesus. A passion for God must always be at the heart of holiness.

2 CULTIVATING VIRTUES

Taught by: Medieval scholastics, Thomas Aquinas, Post-Reformation Anglicans.

In brief: This view focuses on ethical behaviour—developing a good character which is expressed through the practice of virtues. Aquinas believed in four 'natural' virtues common to humanity...

▶ prudence (wisdom and common sense)

▶ temperance (self-control)

▶ justice (including reliability, honesty and truthfulness)

▶ fortitude (courage).

He also believed in three supernatural ones which are unique to Christians...

▶ faith, hope and love (1 Corinthians 13:13).

In a Christian's life these three supernatural virtues work through the four natural ones, transforming and perfecting them. The conscience plays a key role in sensitizing the believer to what is right and wrong and directing a practical response.

PAUSE FOR THOUGHT
What are the strengths of the different views of sanctification? Which are most biblical? What has been true in your life?

> '*T*he Puritans' sharp-eyed discernment of the pervasiveness, repulsiveness and deadliness of sin sprang directly from this deep sense of God as holy. Their sensitivity to sin as an inner force, devious and wily, tyrannising the unconverted and tormenting the saints, was extraordinary. They remain Christianity's past masters in this particular field of understanding.'
>
> J.I. PACKER

3 FOLLOWING THE INNER URGES OF THE HOLY SPIRIT

Taught by: Martin Luther, other Reformers and Puritans.

In brief: It is the Holy Spirit who calls sinners to faith in Christ and changes our hearts at conversion. The Holy Spirit works from inside us to help us grow in holiness...

▶ he indwells every believer

▶ his power is at the centre of our lives

▶ he brings the presence of Christ into our lives

▶ he teaches us what is right and sensitizes us to good and evil

▶ he makes God's love real to us

▶ he stirs up the desire to respond to God through works of love.

Luther stressed that although we remain sinners we are accepted by God as being righteous. Our good works are not to merit salvation, but a response of thankfulness to God for our salvation. The motive is crucial.

The Holy Spirit only motivates us to do what is in accord with the written word. Urges that contradict scripture do not come from the Holy Spirit.

4 ESCAPING THE DOWNWARD PULL OF SIN

Taught by: John Calvin, the English Puritans.

In brief: This view puts forward two elements which are crucial for progressive sanctification...

▶ **mortification**—the process of constantly killing off sin whenever it breaks out in acts of self-indulgence or rebellion against God—achieved through the power of the cross

▶ **vivification**—the growth of all Christ-like habits or graces, particularly the ninefold fruit of Galatians 5:22–23, so that these become a person's habitual reaction to the pressures of life.

This view has a keen awareness of the parasitic nature of human sin. Sin is dethroned but not yet destroyed, and it constantly tries to re-establish its hold within. It is deeply rooted in our personalities. Sin never gives up. In the face of growing maturity or changing circumstances it will simply discover another angle!

It's no surprise then that those who hold this view see sanctification as a lifelong battle requiring vigorous action. Scripture is seen as the complete statement of God's moral law, and to be completely obeyed.

When the power of the cross is applied to a sinful desire, it kills it. Out of this apparently negative process can then flow great joy, peace and fellowship with other Christians and God himself.

5 A SECOND BLESSING

Taught by: John Wesley, the early Keswick Convention and some Pentecostals and Charismatics.

In brief: By faith we can receive from God an experience to lift us to a new plateau—an upgraded, higher-quality Christian life. The first blessing is conversion. The second blessing...

▶ enhances our sense of God's love

▶ enlivens our love relationship with him

▶ empowers us by the Holy Spirit so that we have the real possibility to overcome any temptation, all discouragement, apathy and defeat.

This represents 'entire sanctification', 'Christian perfection', 'Spirit-filling' or 'the higher life'. The terms may vary, but the concept remains the same.

John Wesley taught that Christian perfection is the rooting out of sin in the heart. No longer are desires perverted or motives mixed. It is experiencing now what we will all be like in heaven, with a perfect love of God. It is available to all who love the Lord, but is only received by those who...

▶ earnestly seek God for the blessing

▶ plead for his promise to be realized in believing prayer

▶ wait in anticipation for the blessing.

Whereas John Wesley taught that resident sin could be eliminated, the 'Keswick' teaching emphasized that this sin is merely countermanded. Consequently, the individual is empowered to act in the right way even if human motives are not always entirely pure.

Most Christians remain uncertain about the degree to which sanctification can actually take place in the life of the believer.

6 PRACTISING THE SPIRITUAL DISCIPLINES

Taught by: Medieval mystics, Ignatius of Loyola, William Law, Brother Lawrence, George Fox, Hannah Whitall Smith and Richard Foster.

In brief: We must use the spiritual disciplines, given to us by God, to receive God's grace and develop our Christian character. The disciplines anticipate our future struggles with sin and concentrate on preparing us to cope with them.

Richard Foster's highly influential book, *Celebration of Discipline*, gives three lists of disciplines...

▶ **the inward disciplines** of meditation, prayer, fasting and study

▶ **the outward disciplines** of simplicity, solitude, submission and service

▶ **the corporate disciplines** of confession, worship, guidance and celebration.

Others have added to these the idea of keeping a journal and monitoring our stewardship of resources.

The disciplines must remain God-oriented—a love response, not a means of seeking divine approval. The methods are God-given. Each discipline puts us in a place where we can receive the love and power which God longs to give us. The disciplines need concentrated effort, because half-hearted application is likely to produce discouragement and be self-defeating.

God provides us with these practical means in order that we may defeat the enemy. We ignore these disciplines at our peril!

7 SELF-EFFORT ALONE

Taught by: Pelagius, Celestius, Julian, Bishop of Eclanum, and much of pre-Reformation Europe.

In brief: Pelagianism is an ancient teaching that strongly emphasises human free-will. Pelagius taught that there is no such thing as 'original sin' passed down from Adam, but each child is born innocent—with the ability not to sin. It has been suggested that Pelagius and his followers believed that some people never sinned—for example, Abel and John the Baptist.

What marked humans from the rest of the animal creation is the gift of free-will. It is God's special gift of

PAUSE FOR THOUGHT
What is your own strategy for living a holy life?

grace and sufficient without anything else to keep God's commands. We simply choose to sin or not to sin.

▶ the negative side of this is that we remain without any excuse for our sin—after all, it was entirely our choice

▶ the positive side is that victory over sin is possible, even easy, by our own efforts.

In the Middle Ages this view strongly influenced the church. Before the Reformation many people believed that all they needed to do was observe the ordinances of the church. Penance was especially valued, for it was something men and women could do to win God's approval.

Pelagianism in various forms has consistently been condemned as heretical throughout church history for ignoring the true nature of human sin, and our utter dependence on God's grace. Its supporters stress the need to recognize our personal responsibility for the way we live.

All the other models of sanctification recognize the need for God's grace, the exercise of faith and the role of the Holy Spirit as well as our own efforts. To employ human energy alone can never be enough.

Community holiness

Having dealt with these different views, it is important to recognize that holiness is not simply about 'me and God'. It also has a corporate dimension.

In our present individualistic age we tend to read the New Testament as if it had been written to individuals. However, many of its exhortations are addressed in the plural to churches...

▶ worship in the church, including the Lord's Supper, spiritual gifts and the body of Christ—1 Corinthians 11–14

▶ the fruit of the Spirit—Galatians 5:13—6:10

▶ what it means to live together as the church—Ephesians 4–6

▶ living as 'God's chosen people, holy and dearly loved'—Colossians 3:1–17

▶ be holy!—1 Peter 1:13—2:12.

KEY POINT Holiness is not a solitary affair.

It is difficult, if not impossible, to fulfil God's commands and exhortations alone. We need to encounter God among his people, and to give, and to receive, the help, love and support of each other.

So what does it mean to say (with the Nicene Creed) that we believe in 'one holy... church'? Is the church holy because it is just a collection of individuals who are all striving to lead holy lives? Or is there a greater sense in which the church is holy?

The community of God's people is holy because...

It is God's community—and God himself is holy. The church has never, at any time, lived up to what God has called it to be—and yet it is holy because God makes it holy. The church's holiness can never come from us—it can only come from God himself.

The church is holy because it is the body of Christ, and Christ is its head. We may feel depressed or discouraged about the state of the church. But this idea that the church is holy because God is holy can be a great encouragement for us—we are called to live out together what we already are in Christ—a holy people.

It is the place where we encounter God's holiness—Because the church is God's community, it is here that we encounter him together. We are brought face to face with the love, power and holiness of God. This happens in a number of ways...

- We know the presence of Jesus among us—because he promised to be present whenever his people came together (Matthew 18:20).

- We encounter the living, active Holy Spirit—as he applies the scriptures to us, leads us into repentance and faith, and communicates to us the love and presence of God.

- We receive God's grace and strength to live holy lives—through the encouragement of each other, in the teaching we receive, in worship inspired by the Spirit, and especially by sharing bread and wine together.

Holiness can never be a private pursuit. It is something that takes place in the community of Christ.

It is a 'set apart' community—To be holy is to be 'set apart'. One of the root meanings of the word 'sanctify' is to set apart or consecrate. God's people, the 'called-out ones', are to be different from the world they have been called out of! What does this mean?

> '*T*he church is holy in its openness to the street and even the alley, in its turning to the profanity of all human life—the holiness which, according to Romans 12:15, does not scorn to rejoice with them that do rejoice and weep with them that weep.'
>
> KARL BARTH

- Some branches of the church (such as monks and nuns) have taken this to mean withdrawing from the world in order to avoid compromise, to draw closer to God, and to pray for the world.

- Others feel this takes separation too far, into isolation—they believe that being 'set apart' means having a radically different moral character to the rest of the world, being in the world, but not of the world.

- Still others agree with this last point, but add that the church is an alternative community of people, a truly 'holy' people—through our love and acceptance of each other we demonstrate how people were always meant to live together.

Whichever view you take, it is here that the concept of holiness begins to be lived out in real life.

It takes the presence of God out into the world—Our holiness should be a witness to the world...

- We are to 'shine as lights in the dark'. This does not mean shining our light at the world from a great distance, but taking the light and love of Christ out into the world.

- Our holiness is not meant to be self-righteous, creating a distance between us and non-Christians.

- Instead, as the church lives and works in the local community, its holiness should speak for itself, bringing hope to those who need it.

- Our model here has to be Jesus. He was sinless—and yet he showed the love, acceptance and 'otherness' of God to people who seemed to be far from him. Prostitutes, gangsters, beggars, terrorists, corrupt businessmen, people with unacceptable diseases—they all received from Jesus.

- True holiness always results in a renewed quality of human relationships. Our community is holy when it brings light to the world and seeks to serve those who most need the love of God.

Down-to-earth holiness

The Books of Exodus and Leviticus are full of teaching about the holiness of God and how it relates to the community of his people. Leviticus 19 is an important chapter for understanding what God's holiness means in the community.

It begins by making a direct connection between God's character and the character of his people: 'Be holy because I, the Lord your God, am holy' (Leviticus 19:2). It then goes on to spell out what this means in concrete terms, covering an astonishing range of areas in human relationships...

- respect your father and mother

- observe the sabbath

- leaving part of your harvest for disadvantaged people

- not stealing or lying

- not delaying the payment of wages to your workers

- not mistreating the deaf and blind

- not perverting justice

- not turning to mediums or spiritists

- showing respect for the elderly

- treating foreigners with love and respect

- using honest weights and measures

The early church was taught to follow this pattern of practical holiness by being radically different to the society around them. For example...

- they were highly committed to the teaching, fellowship, prayer and worship of the church (Acts 2:42–43)

- they shared their possessions and gave to those in need (Acts 2:44–45; 4:32, 34–35)

- they were taught to treat rich and poor in the same way (James 2:1–7)

- they renounced selfish ambition and followed the humility of Jesus (Philippians 2:1–11).

PAUSE FOR THOUGHT
How can we help one another to be more like Jesus in character?

---

5 *A royal calling*

KEY POINT As the people of God we are the church, and purchased by Jesus to fulfil a glorious destiny. We are designed to rule and reign with him for eternity.

There are two dimensions to this glorious certainty...

- the first is that we enter his kingdom in the here and now

- the second is 'not yet, but one day his kingdom will arrive in its glorious fulfilment'.

Christians are therefore called to live in the tension of already being God's children, but one day being transformed into all that he wants us to be (1 John 3:2). The church lives between the first and second comings of Jesus Christ.

As we wait for all that lies ahead, we still have a royal calling as the church to fulfil God's purposes here on earth. So what on earth is the church for?

The bottom line is this. The church exists to glorify God by its life and its actions. This is its ultimate purpose. Paul expressed it by saying: 'to him be glory in the church and in Christ Jesus throughout all generations, for ever and ever! Amen' (Ephesians 3:21).

But how does the church glorify God? It does this in three ways. By being a...

1 Worshipping community

2 Loving community

3 Witnessing community.

This section focuses on the ultimate purpose of the church by looking at these three areas.

1 *Worshipping community*

From a biblical point of view, everything the church does should bring glory to God: visiting the sick, providing counselling, preaching the good news, providing lunch for homeless people on Christmas Day...

However, praising together is the most important way in which the church brings glory to God. Worship is the focus of the Christian community, and everything else flows from it.

There are many ways in which Christians offer worship to God—in singing hymns and songs; through prayer and meditation; by speaking in tongues and prophesying; in the liturgy; by kneeling, standing, or even lying prostrate on the ground... But what lies behind it all? What exactly is worship?

While the Bible does not give a definition of worship, some of the New Testament words for 'worship' show us what it means...

▶ *proskuneo*—adoration, a word that literally means 'I come towards to kiss' (John 4:23; 9:38; Hebrews 1:6)

▶ *sebomai*—reverence and awe (Romans 1:25)

▶ *latreuo*—to serve (Philippians 3:3; Revelation 7:15)

Of all the words used for 'worship' in the New Testament, *proskuneo* is used most often (a total of 66 times). This tells us that at heart Christian worship means giving God our love and adoration.

Our worship can be shown in a number of ways...

▶ **through our words and songs:** 'Worship the Lord with gladness; come before him with joyful songs' (Psalm 100:2).

▶ **with our actions in worship:** 'Come, let us bow down in worship, let us kneel before the Lord our Maker' (Psalm 95:6).

▶ **by the way we live:** 'Offer your bodies as living sacrifices, holy and pleasing to God—this is your spiritual act of worship' (Romans 12:1).

Power of the Spirit

True worship takes place in the power of God's Spirit. This is because the Holy Spirit is the person who draws us close to God. Jesus said: 'God is spirit, and his worshippers must worship in spirit and in truth' (John 4:24). It is only by the Holy Spirit that we can declare that 'Jesus is Lord' (1 Corinthians 12:3).

The Spirit equips us for worship in two ways...

▶ **in our lives**—by giving us the 'fruit of the Spirit' (Galatians 5:22–23). He is the one who is able to make our lives holy and pleasing to God.

▶ **in our meeting together**—by giving us the 'gifts of the Spirit'. The rich variety of the Spirit's gifts are listed in several New Testament passages...

> '*I*t is since Christians have largely ceased to think of the other world that they have become so ineffective in this. Aim at heaven and you will get earth thrown in; aim at earth and you will get neither.'
> C.S. LEWIS

PAUSE FOR THOUGHT
Who benefits when you exercise your spiritual and practical gifts?

> '*A*dd together the word and the loaf and the sacrament is there.'
> AUGUSTINE

▶ 1 Corinthians 12:1–11

▶ Romans 12:6–8

▶ Ephesians 4:11–13

▶ 1 Peter 4:10–11.

These lists are not exhaustive—they give examples of God's generosity to us as a community. According to these four passages, the gifts of God's Spirit are given for specific reasons. They are not there simply for our own individual use, or for self-gratification. Instead, the gifts are given...

for the common good (1 Corinthians 12:7)—Paul teaches that there are many different kinds of gifts, and individual people receive different ones, but they are all given for the good of the whole church

so that we can love each other deeply (1 Peter 4:8)—gifts such as hospitality, service, pastoring, and contributing to the needs of others enable us directly to express love through giving and receiving

to show the unity of the body of Christ (1 Corinthians 12:12)—all three of the passages written by Paul are set in the context of teaching about the unity of Christ's body

so that the body of Christ may be built up (Ephesians 4:12)—the gifts of the Spirit are 'the living movements of Christ's body', as James Dunn put it—the gifts make us grow stronger and more mature as a community

to prepare God's people for works of service (Ephesians 4:12)—all the gifts have a decisive outcome: they prepare us to become servants of each other and of the wider world

to administer God's grace to others (1 Peter 4:10)—healing, prophecy, wisdom, teaching, evangelism, tongues—all the gifts communicate the love and power of God to others, but these do so in a direct way

so that in all things God may be praised (1 Peter 4:11)—ultimately, the Spirit gives to the church so that we may give praise to God: in our worship, our relationships, and in the way we live in the world.

Sacraments: signs of new life

Protestant churches believe in two sacraments: baptism and holy communion. A 'sacrament' has been described as 'a visible sign of an invisible reality'. Just as preaching puts the gospel into words, a sacrament shows the gospel in a visual way.

Baptism shows the gospel by using the symbol of water; holy communion by using bread and wine.

Baptism—Christian baptism goes back to Jesus himself. He was baptized by John in the River Jordan. After the Day of Pentecost, the church began to baptize all new believers in Jesus Christ (Acts 2:38).

Although Christians disagree about when and how baptism should be carried out, baptism has always been seen as a sign of entry into the Christian life, and into the church. The water of baptism powerfully reminds us of four great truths about the gospel...

▶ **Washing**—water suggests the washing away of sin. Baptism shows that God forgives us when we come to faith in Jesus.

▶ **Death**—this symbol is especially strong in baptism by total immersion. The believer goes under the water and is then raised up again.

Gifts of the Spirit

The list of gifts which God provides for his people is a long one. They can be put into the following three broad areas.

The 'extraordinary' gifts of revelation . . .

▶ discerning of spirits

▶ word of knowledge

▶ word of wisdom

▶ healing

▶ miracles

▶ faith

▶ tongues

▶ interpretation

▶ prophecy.

The 'ministry' gifts . . .

▶ apostle

▶ missionary

▶ pastor

▶ leadership

▶ administration

▶ evangelism

▶ teacher

▶ exorcism.

The 'general' gifts . . .

▶ service

▶ helping

▶ intercession

▶ motivation

▶ mercy

▶ hospitality

▶ encouragement

▶ giving

▶ celibacy

▶ martyrdom.

Adapted from Clive Calver, *The Holy Spirit*, used by permission of Scripture Union

---

Baptism symbolizes death to the old way of life, and rising to a new life with God.

▶ **Covenant**—the people of Israel had to pass through the Red Sea before they entered the Promised Land. Baptism reminds us of the new covenant God has made with his people. It is a sign of God's unbreakable promise to us.

▶ **The Spirit**—at Jesus' baptism, the Holy Spirit descended on him in the form of a dove. Baptism tells us that all those who come to Christ receive his Spirit, and are given the power to live a new life.

Holy Communion—according to the New Testament, sharing bread and wine is at the heart of our worship. It was the one act which Jesus commanded his followers to do when they came together for worship (Luke 22:19; 1 Corinthians 11:23–26).

Christians celebrate communion to . . .

'*F*aith and the Holy Spirit are not by-passed or somehow materialized, but the being baptized and the eating and drinking are faithfully accepting the gospel realities, sacramentally.'
TIMOTHY BRADSHAW

For more on lifestyle, and our koinonia partnership, see pages 39–42.

'*B*eing precedes doing. Whatever we do in the world has to flow out of what we are. The essence of the church— its reason for existence— is to be the new society that points to the coming kingdom.'
CHARLES COLSON

'*O*nce a man is united to God how could he not live for ever? Once a man is separated from God, what can he do but wither and die?'
C.S. LEWIS

▶ remember Jesus' death

▶ receive God's grace through communion with him, and with each other

▶ look forward to the time when he will come again.

Christians have disagreed about the meaning of communion. The differences centre around two questions: what happens to the bread and wine?—and what happens to the worshippers? These questions were vigorously (and violently) debated at the time of the Reformation.

Very briefly, some of the main views are . . .

▶ **The Roman Catholic Church** believes that the bread and wine are miraculously changed into the body and blood of Christ. They are worshipped by the congregation and offered as a sacrifice for the sins of the living and the dead. This view is known as *transubstantiation*—a 'change of substance'.

▶ **Martin Luther** taught that the glorified body and blood of Christ is really present 'in, with and under' the bread and wine—a view known as *consubstantiation*. This is different from the Roman Catholic view in that Luther believed that the body and blood co-exist in union with the bread and wine, rather than replacing them. This view is today held by Lutherans.

▶ **Ulrich Zwingli**, the Swiss Reformer, rejected any idea of change in the bread and wine. Instead he taught that they were symbols only. Physically, Christ is in heaven, but he is present in the service by his Spirit. For Zwingli, the whole point of the symbols was to enable us to remember the death of Christ. This view is held today by many Free Churches, and also by some Evangelical Anglicans.

▶ **John Calvin** emphasized that communion truly brings the believer into communion with God. The symbols of bread and wine are not just 'empty' symbols, but they truly enable us to feed on Christ and receive his grace in a spiritual way. This view is held by the Anglican Church, many Nonconformists and Methodists.

2 *Loving community*

Jesus declared that he had come to establish God's kingship in the lives of his followers—both individually and in their corporate life together.

The result of his teaching was revolutionary . . .

▶ enemies were forgiven (Matthew 5:44)

▶ barriers of race and class were broken down (Matthew 8:10–12; Luke 7:9; 10:29–37)

▶ women and children were affirmed in a male-dominated society (Mark 5:25–34; 10:13–16; John 20:15)

▶ Jesus' followers were called to serve each other (John 1:27; 13:5).

All of this was intended to serve as a model for his disciples in all generations. We can see this clearly in the life of the early church, where . . .

▶ they shared their possessions and cared for those who were in need (Acts 2:42–47)

▶ James taught there was to be no difference in the way they treated rich and poor people (James 2:1–4)

▶ Paul taught: 'There is neither Jew nor Greek, slave nor

The kingdom of God in the teaching of Jesus

Key words	Quotes	Description	Significance
Proclamation			
kingdom of God kingdom of heaven (Matthew) ... is among you ... is near	'Repent for the kingdom of heaven is near' (Matthew 3:2) 'I must preach the good news of the kingdom of God ... because that is why I was sent' (Luke 4:43) 'The time is fulfilled' (Mark 1:15, AV)	'The sphere of God's rule' and 'the degree to which that rule is accepted'. Initial pronouncements of Jesus. 'Manifesto' given at his home synagogue (Luke 4:14–30).	The core of Jesus' teaching. Practical implementation of God's rule in lives. Linked to ministry of John the Baptist. Fulfilment of OT prophecies. Both present aspect and future completion.
Entry			
repent and believe be saved born again	'Anyone who will not receive the kingdom of God like a little child will never enter it' (Mark 10:15) 'You are not far from the kingdom of God' (Mark 12:34) 'The kingdom of God is within you' (Luke 23:42) 'Unless a man is born again, he cannot see the kingdom of God' (John 3:3)	Entry into the community of the King is through repentance, faith and baptism. Nature of the kingdom lies in the heart, not an external state.	Kingdom entry is not a matter of heredity/birth, but through spiritual rebirth symbolized by baptism. Not a matter of keeping the law.
Power			
Preaching the good news Healing	'If Satan is divided against himself, how can his kingdom stand?' (Luke 11:18) 'My kingdom is not of this world. If it were my servants would fight' (John 18:36) 'The Law and the Prophets were proclaimed until John. Since that time ... the kingdom of God is being preached' (Luke 16:16)	Jesus' reign means war with Satan and his demons. Demonstrated in his casting out of evil spirits; explained in his teaching. Power of God over the elements also demonstrated and explained. Temptation is overcome.	God's kingdom is the opposite of secular power. Its weapons are love, faith and righteousness. Teaching cannot be separated from practice. The New kingdom was demonstrated as superior to the old covenant.
Personal ethics			
Love the Lord your God with all your heart ... and your neighbour as yourself.	'Blessed are the poor in spirit, for theirs is the kingdom of heaven' (Matthew 5:3) 'Seek first his kingdom and his righteousness' (Matthew 6:33) 'Ask ... seek ... knock ... ' (Matthew 7:7) 'Unless your righteousness surpasses that of the Pharisees ... you will certainly not enter the kingdom of heaven' (Matthew 5:20)	Law not abolished but its demands superseded. Ritual and sacrifice replaced. Prayer and giving emphasized. Righteousness a matter of the heart and mind not external acts. Many parables (e.g. the Good Samaritan) challenge values and set new standards.	The Sermon on the Mount contains the heart of Jesus' ethical teaching. It goes beyond the law and sets new standards for all who enter the kingdom.

Key words	Quotes	Description	Significance
Community ethics			
I am among you as one who serves.	'My kingdom is not of this world . . . My kingdom is from another place' (John 18:36) 'Render to Caesar that which is Caesar's and to God that which is God's' (Mark 12:17).	Covers all aspects of relationships, between believers (in the church), between believers and non-believers, church and state, male and female, rich and poor, young and old. Emphasis on love, integrity and justice. Jesus' teaching was integrated into his approach to others. Marriage, divorce, taxes and other civil institutions are included.	Jesus started a revolution within the conservative world of his day. He opposed political revolt and obeyed even unpopular laws to make it clear that his was an alternative agenda. Its fruit is seen in works of compassion and justice.
Discipleship			
Follow me	'I confer on you a kingdom, just as my Father conferred one on me' (Luke 22:29) 'Your kingdom come, your will be done' (Matthew 6:10) 'If you love me, you will obey what I command' (John 14:15)	Jesus' instruction of his followers was again linked to his example. His instructions in detail cover all aspects of life and faith. He emphasized both the cost and rewards to the follower and demonstrated the fruit that such a lifestyle would produce.	The church has always struggled with Jesus' call to discipleship. Its demands are great. A major temptation then and now is to believe with the mind without wholeheartedly following in heart and flesh.
Future fulfilment			
I will return	'...until the kingdom of God comes' (Luke 22:18) 'I have told you everything ahead of time' (Mark 13:23) 'Not everyone who says to me, ''Lord, Lord,'' will enter the kingdom of heaven' (Matthew 7:21).	Contrasting emphases: 'the kingdom is near' and 'the kingdom will come'. This future aspect is particularly clear in the 'kingdom parables', e.g. the master away in a far country, the ten virgins, the leaven, the mustard seed, the wheat and the tares. Apocalyptic passages (Matthew 24, 25) warn of future trials, but Jesus promises a personal return in glory.	The fulfilment of the kingdom is seen in stages: 1. With the arrival of Jesus and his message. 2. After his death with the establishment of the church. 3. At his triumphant return and instituting a perfect new age.

> '*T*his was a church that had a social conscience... its social programme was very much bound up . . . with the rapidity of its growth. But there was no ulterior motive in their involvement in the relief of poverty. It was no manipulative stratagem to win adherents. On the contrary, it was a spontaneous expression of the love for one another which the Holy Spirit had poured into their hearts.'
> ROY CLEMENTS

free, male nor female, for you are all one in Christ Jesus' (Galatians 3:28).

To become a Christian and enter the family of the church means to take on a completely different way of life.

3 *Witnessing community*

Out of the church's experience of God in worship, and its life together as God's people, it witnesses in the world to the life and light of Christ. The church is designed not only to be, but to grow.

Jesus said, 'I will build my church, and the gates of Hades will not overcome it' (Matthew 16:18).

How is this happening in the world today? Around the world, the church is seeing explosive growth in some areas and dramatic decline in others. Rapid growth is taking place in Two-Thirds World countries, while the Western world is seeing little or no growth...

▶ rapid growth is taking place in Kenya, Korea, Indonesia and Sudan

▶ slow growth is taking place in Australia, Greece, Sweden and the USA

▶ no growth or decline is taking place in Britain, Finland, Italy and Libya.

A faith for the whole world

During the 1980s, the numbers of Christians living in the poorer, southern hemisphere outstripped the number living in the richer, northern hemisphere. This represents a big change in balance for the church, because for many centuries Christianity had its heart in Europe. It means that Africa, Asia and Latin America are now the dynamic regions of the faith, witnessing great advances for the gospel.

KEY POINT The challenge for the church in the West is to learn from our fellow-Christians in the Two-Thirds World. They have a great deal to teach us.

The explosive growth of the church in the Two-Thirds World means that the church worldwide is expanding. Their gains make up for our losses. This means that 'on the ground' the church is seeing...

▶ in Africa—16,400 new Christians a day

▶ in South Asia—3,000 new Christians a day

▶ in East Asia—1,000 new Christians a day

▶ around the world—65 new congregations a day.

What does this mean for the church's mission in the world? In the past, the UK was seen as a 'sending' country—sending missionaries to spread the gospel in the 'receiving' countries of Africa, Asia and Latin America. But today, the situation is far more fluid.

African missionaries now come to bring the gospel to Britain. Caribbean Christians work in Nigeria. Indian missionaries go to Thailand. And of course, Christians in all countries spread the good news within their own culture. Tongan Christians, for example, take the message of Jesus from island to island in the South Pacific in their deep-sea canoes.

The missionary movement has become truly global and international. The whole church around the world is involved.

How can we learn from what is happening?

PAUSE FOR THOUGHT
What does the term 'kingdom of God' mean to you?

Statistics in this section are from David Barrett, editor, *The World Christian Encyclopedia*, Oxford University Press. Other material has been adapted from Robin Thompson, *The World Christian*, Lynx Communications.

Mission resources

Some key resources on mission around the world, with material on how the local church can become involved through prayer and action...

▶ *The World Christian*—highly visual workbook for people aiming to take the gospel from culture to culture (also available as part of the *Culture to Culture* study course run by St John's College, Nottingham): published by Lynx Communications and available in bookshops

▶ *W.O.R.M.*—World Outreach Resources Material. A catalogue of resources for communicating mission to all ages. EMA Youth Ministries, 37 Elm Road, New Malden, Surrey, KT3 3HB

▶ *FACTS Magazine*—published three times a year, with key articles on mission: 9 Anwyll Close, Caerleon, Gwent, NP6 1TJ

▶ *3rd Track*—strong, graphic materials for youth groups: Tear Fund, 100 Church Road, Teddington, Middlesex TW11 8QE

▶ *Jobs Abroad/Short Term Service Directory*—Resources and information available on Christian Service, Christian Service Centre, Holloway Street West, Lower Gornal, Dudley, West Midlands, DY3 2D2

▶ **Become aware** of the exciting growth in mission that is taking place around the world. See the 'Mission resources' box.

▶ **Thank God** for all that he is doing through his church around the world. This is an exciting time to be a Christian.

▶ **Join in world mission.** Each local church has a mission to its local area. In Britain today, there are many opportunities for mission: taking the gospel to a secularized society; to people of other faiths and cultures; to the outcasts and to complacent, rich people; showing the gospel in action through our words and our lives in the community.

The goal of the church's mission

What are the limits of the church's mission?

▶ Paul talks of God waiting 'until the full number of the Gentiles has come in' (Romans 11:25)

▶ Jesus tells his disciples in 'the great commission' to take the gospel to every nation (Matthew 28:18–20).

This word 'nation' (in the Greek it is the word *ethne*) probably means a 'people group'—a community sharing a common history, language, location, culture and identity. Many modern missiologists believe that the church's mission is to take the gospel to each of these groups.

There are thousands of such people groups around the world—some with only a few hundred members, others with over 1 million. Some 12,000 of these groups are said to be 'unreached peoples'. A lack of resources means that they are not hearing the good news of Jesus.

The ultimate goal of Christian mission on earth means that all people groups should hear and understand the gospel.

An exploding church

The Book of Acts gives us a vivid picture of how the early church grew from just a few followers of Jesus to many thousands of people across the Roman Empire. The development was phenomenal...

▶ 120 disciples (Acts 1:15)

▶ 3,000 added (Acts 2:41–42)

▶ Many more join the church—the men alone numbered 5,000 (Acts 4:4)

▶ Persecution scatters the church, every Christian plays their part in evangelism (Acts 8:1–4)

▶ Churches are established throughout Palestine and beyond (Acts 9:31–35)

▶ Gentiles become Christians—the evangelization of the nations begins (Acts 11:20–21)

▶ Growing churches are established in what is now Turkey (Acts 16:10–11)

▶ Paul and his companions reach Europe and more Gentiles become Christians (Acts 17:34)

▶ By Revelation 7:9 the numbers become uncountable!

Every nation, tribe, people and language

In the Book of Revelation, the apostle John wrote: 'After this I looked and there before me was a great multitude that no-one could count, from every nation, tribe, people and language, standing before the throne and in front of the Lamb' (Revelation 7:9).

If there was any doubt that God intends that people from every people group should share his destiny for humanity, this reference decisively answers it. We can see this by looking at each of the words used to describe the group...

▶ **nation** (*ethnos*) literally means 'company of people living together'—it was often used to describe the largest divisions of people, distinct national groups

▶ **tribe** (*phule*)—this originally referred to those with a blood relationship, but it came to be a term for a national or political sub-division, or an administrative unit

▶ **people** (*laos*)—often used of the Jews, this term refers to a political unit of people with a common history

▶ **language** (*glossa*)—the linguistic identity of a particular group.

The gospel is for the whole world, geographically, culturally, religiously and linguistically—to the ends of the earth and the end of the age.

Evangelism and mission lie at the very heart of God's purpose for the church.

The church and evangelism

As the local church grows in its worship, and as a community of God's people, its evangelism becomes more powerful and effective. This is clear from the teaching of the New Testament...

▶ Jesus asked his Father that believers might 'be in us so that the world may believe that you have sent me' (John 17:21)

▶ He also prayed that Christians would be one with each other 'to let the world know that you sent me' (John

'The church's task is not to save itself—Christ has already done that. It is rather to give itself in love and service—in fact to die for the world.'
TULLIO VINAY

'The church exists for mission as a fire exists by burning.'
EMIL BRUNNER

'Many churches do not share the gospel effectively because their communal experience of the gospel is too weak and tasteless to be worth sharing. It does not excite the believer to the point where he wants to witness, and (as the believer uncomfortably suspects) it is not all that attractive to the unbeliever. But where Christian fellowship demonstrates the gospel, believers become alive and sinners get curious and want to know what the secret is.'
HOWARD SNYDER

17:23)

▶ Paul taught that true worship convinces the unbeliever to say that 'God is really among you!' (1 Corinthians 14:22–25).

When the gospel can be seen as a living reality among God's people, the work of evangelists in the church is simply to point to the source of that living reality. This is what Peter did on the Day of Pentecost. He explained to the crowd the true meaning of what they could see was happening to the first Christians: 'Listen to me and let me tell you what this means...' (Acts 2:14).

Modern missiologists talk about the 'three Ps' of evangelism. This is a model of evangelism for the local church. Each part acts like a building block, preparing the way for the stage above it...

presence evangelism—brings into the local community a sense that God is present in the world, through the quality of the church's life and worship as the people of God

proclamation evangelism—once the community has sensed the presence of God in its midst, the gospel is proclaimed both by what the church says to the people outside it, and by the ways in which it serves them

persuasion evangelism—once the community has sensed God's presence and understood the gospel message, the church calls people to turn to Jesus Christ in repentance and faith—persuading them to become Christians.

Howard Snyder adds an essential fourth 'P' to this list...

propagation evangelism—those who respond to the gospel do not merely become individual disciples of Christ—they become an integral part of the Christian community, witnessing in their turn to the presence,

Church growth

These two inter-related emphases have had a significant impact on the church around the world in recent years. In brief, church growth looks at the factors which cause or inhibit growth. For example...

▶ What are a church's internal problems?

▶ Is there vision for growth?

▶ Are the members mobilized?

▶ Are they discovering and using their spiritual gifts?

▶ Is the leadership holding back the church or facilitating its expansion?

▶ Does the congregation understand the gospel?

▶ Can they communicate it in a culturally relevant way that the local people understand?

▶ Do we plan for growth?

Many of these questions have become familiar to the PCC members, elders or deacons of many local churches. Care must be exercised to realize that changing methods and structures do not guarantee growth. Neither human effort alone nor total reliance on the Holy Spirit without human planning and action are biblical. Growth demands both relying on the sovereignty of the Holy Spirit to work in people's hearts and the work and words of God's human messengers.

Church growth methodology should serve to encourage and continue growth. It is never the source of that growth.

proclamation and persuasion of the gospel.

The ultimate aim of evangelism is not to see individuals converted, or even to see individuals become disciples of Jesus. As Howard Snyder expresses it, 'the goal of evangelism is the formation of the Christian community.' Christ is building his church.

For ever with Christ

The Bible gives glorious promises about the end of time...

▶ the Lord Jesus will return for his people in visitation and vindication

▶ all wrongs will be righted in an unmistakable and irreversible act of divine judgment

▶ the dead will be raised to share in this universal

'*B*oth gospel proclamation and social action are equally important. They are like two blades of a pair of scissors. If either is missing, the cutting-edge is lost.'
DAVID WATSON

PAUSE FOR THOUGHT
Was the explosive growth of the early church normal for the church or exceptional?

'*S*tanding firm in one spirit, with one mind striving together for the sake of the gospel.'
PHILIPPIANS 1:27

'*B*e of the same mind, having the same love, being one in spirit and purpose.'
PHILIPPIANS 2:2

---

manifestation of God's presence and his reign of justice and peace.

The focus of heaven will be upon Jesus...

▶ he sits enthroned with his Father (Revelation 3:21; 22:1)

▶ angels, authorities and powers submit to his rule (1 Peter 3:22)

▶ he reigns as King over his people, and King of kings (1 Timothy 6:15; Revelation 15:3; 19:16)

▶ all the kingdoms of this world are to be subject to him (Revelation 11:15–19) because he has been chosen by his Father to be the 'heir of all things' (Hebrews 1:2)

▶ he therefore exercises authority over all things (Matthew 28:19–20; Hebrews 2:8; 1 Peter 3:22)

▶ all his enemies are to be placed beneath his feet (Hebrews 10:13)

▶ he will rule until the last enemy, death, has been destroyed (1 Corinthians 15:24–28)

▶ he is Lord of both the dead and the living (Romans 14:9).

Supremely he will act as head over the church (Ephesians 1:20–22; 4:15). First, however, he must act as our judge.

At his first coming Jesus arrived not to condemn the world, but to save it (John 3:17). On his return he will arrive with the task of passing sentence on all people. Having been invested with his Father's prerogative as Judge of all the world, he will come to raise the dead, condemn the guilty and vindicate his people (John 5:19–30; 6:39, 54).

This judgment has long been prophesied and is therefore expected by Christians who must be active in communicating a warning to unbelievers (Acts 10:42; 17:31).

The concept of God as 'the Judge' runs throughout scripture. His justice demands that he should put right all wrongs, punish offenders and establish his kingdom (Psalm 96:13; Ecclesiastes 12:14; Matthew 12:36–37; 25:46).

We all face this judgment...

▶ people are destined to die once, and after that to face judgment (Hebrews 9:27)

▶ we will have to give an account (Romans 14:11–12)

▶ it will judge our works (1 Corinthians 3:12–13)

▶ it will determine rewards (2 Corinthians 5:10)

▶ it will be on the basis of responsibility to the degree of revelation received (Romans 2:12–16).

One view is that there will be two judgments—often called 'the judgment seat of Christ' and 'the great white throne'. The former is to judge the believer—not regarding salvation but stewardship. And the latter to judge evil, Satan and his angels primarily, and then all unbelievers before they are cast into hell.

These two elements of the judgment are clear from scripture, even if their timing and location are not.

To paint the rest of the picture...

▶ Jesus will wind up the present age (1 Thessalonians 4:17)

▶ the dead will be resurrected (John 5:28)

▶ the living believers will rise to meet him (1 Thessalonians 4:15–16)

▶ Jesus comes to deliver the church (Matthew 24:13) and to judge the earth (Matthew 16:27)

Church planting

Church planting lays strong emphasis on the accessibility of the local church. The ideal is to have a worshipping community within walking distance of every home in a locality.

As soon as a church grows beyond a certain size it can divide and plant a new congregation. This has great advantages...

▶ each division brings the church closer to where the people—'churched' and 'unchurched'—live

▶ the church is less likely to have a remote, 'neutral' culture, which hopes to appeal to a wide range of backgrounds but is more likely to reflect the majority culture of the area

▶ instead, each congregation can have its own character—whether middle-class, Afro-Caribbean, suburban, inner-city, etc.

Recent initiatives such as DAWN (Disciple A Whole Nation) and the 'AD 2000 and Beyond' movement have tried on a global scale to promote aggressive church planting.

In many countries a different model of church planting is required...

▶ In Eastern Europe there are few evangelical churches. There may be a small group of 'evangelicals' who meet to pray and study the scriptures within an Orthodox or Roman Catholic church. They often face a dilemma concerning their identity and future direction—to stay as they are within their own church, to become a new independent fellowship or to seek to change the wider church to become more evangelically minded. In many areas of Eastern Europe, notably Albania, Bulgaria and Romania, there is an urgent need for church planting.

▶ In Western Europe, many para-church agencies, evangelical denominations or independent missionaries have engaged in church planting for the last 25 years. They have seen considerable success in countries such as France, Belgium, Spain and Italy.

▶ In the Middle East and large parts of the Islamic world, church planting has to take place in a more clandestine manner. New churches meet secretly in believers' homes for fear of the authorities. It is often difficult for converts to break openly with Islam, as this can lead to ostracism by their own family, loss of employment and housing, imprisonment or worse.

Yet despite this and restrictions on the availability and distribution of the scriptures, even in these countries new churches are being planted. We need to pray for them.

▶ he will destroy his enemies (1 Corinthians 15:22–28; Revelation 20:1–10)

▶ God's kingdom, in its fullest sense, will come (Luke 22:29–30; 2 Peter 3:13).

This, then, is the final destiny of the church. Jesus will be the centre point, reigning for ever, and we will be there with him. This is the 'not yet' side of the kingdom, but it is our ultimate purpose, for Jesus has promised that it will happen.

One day he will return: 'I will come back and take you to be with me' (John 14:3)—that is the destiny for which we are heading.

Booklist

Berry, R.J., editor, *Real Science, Real Faith*, Monarch

Bettenson, H., editor, *The Early Christian Fathers*, OUP

Bettenson, H., editor, *Documents of The Christian Church*, OUP

Bonhoeffer, D., *Letters and Papers from Prison*, SCM Press

Bradshaw, T., *The Olive Branch*, Paternoster

Bullock, A., Stallybrass, G. and Trombley, S., *The Fontana Dictionary of Modern Thought*, Fontana

Calver, C.R., *The Holy Spirit*, Scripture Union

Chilcraft, S.J., *One of Us*, Word

Clements, R., *The Church that Turned the World Upside Down*, Crossway

Cleverly, C., *Church Planting, Our Future Hope*, Scripture Union

Collins, G.R., *Christian Counselling*, Word

Colson, C., *The Body*, Word

Conner, K.J., *The Church in the New Testament*, Sovereign World

Cross, F.L., editor, *The Oxford Dictionary of the Christian Church*, OUP

Dobson, J., *Emotions, Can You Trust Them?* Hodder & Stoughton

Ferguson, J.O., *My People*, Oliphants

Foster, R., *Celebration of Discipline*, Hodder & Stoughton

George, T., *Theology of the Reformers*, Apollos

Gibbs, E., *I Believe in Church Growth*, Hodder & Stoughton

Guthrie, D., *New Testament Theology*, IVP

Hawthorne, T., *Windows on Science and Faith*, IVP

Hirsh, S. and Kummeron, J., *Life Types*, Warner Books

Hodgkinson, L., *The Personal Growth Handbook*, Piatkus

Hughes, S., *How to Live the Christian Life*, Kingsway

Hunt, D. and McMahon, T.A., *The Seduction of Christianity*, Harvest House

Hurding, R.F., *Roots and Shoots*, Hodder & Stoughton

Jones, G. & R., *Naturally Gifted*, Scripture Union

Keeley, R., editor, *An Introduction to the Christian Faith*, Lynx Communications

Keyes, D., *Beyond Identity*, Hodder & Stoughton

Kirby, G.W., *Why All These Denominations?* Kingsway

Lahaye, T., *I Love You, But Why Are We So Different?* Kingsway

Lahaye, T., *Spirit Controlled Temperament*, Coverdale

Lane, A., *The Lion Book of Christian Thought*, Lion

Lloyd-Jones, D.M., *The Puritans: their Origins and Successors*, Banner of Truth

McClung, F., *Holiness and the Spirit of the Age*, Word

McCrone, J., *The Myth of Irrationality*, Macmillan

McDonald, H.D., *The Christian View of Man*, Marshall Pickering

McDonald, H.D., *I and He*, Epworth

McGrath, J. and A., *The Dilemma of Self-Esteem*, Crossway

Meier, P.D., Minirth, F.B., Wichern, F.B. and Ratcliff, D.E., *Introduction to Psychology and Counselling*, Monarch

Milne, B., *Know The Truth*, IVP

Murray, I.H., editor, *The Reformation of the Church*, Banner of Truth

Nicholls, B.J., editor, *The Church: God's Agent for Change*, WEF / Paternoster

Packer, J.I., *A Passion for Holiness*, Crossway

Packer, J.I., *Among God's Giants*, Kingsway

Packer, J.I., *Keep in Step with the Spirit*, IVP

Payne, L., *The Broken Image*, Kingsway

Robinson, M. and Christie, S., *Planting Tomorrow's Churches Today*, Monarch

Sire, J.W., *The Universe Next Door*, IVP

Sire, J.W., *Discipleship of the Mind*, IVP

Skinner, B.F., *About Behaviorism*, Penguin

Snyder, H.A., *The Radical Wesley*, IVP

Stevenson, J., editor, *A New Eusebius*, SPCK

Stott, J.R.W., *The Contemporary Christian*, IVP

Toffler, A., *Previews and Premises*, Pan

Waitley, D., *Psychology of Success*, Irwin

Watson, D., *I Believe in the Church*, Hodder & Stoughton

Wheeler Robinson, H., *The Christian Doctrine of Man*, T&T Clark

Whitney, D.S., *Spiritual Disciplines for the Christian Life*, Scripture Press

Wichern, F.B., Ratcliff, D.E. and McRoberts Ward, R., *Self-Esteem, Gift From God*, Baker

Winter, R.D. and Hawthorne, S.C., *Perspectives on the World Christian Movement*, William Carey

INTRODUCTION TO PHILIPPIANS

Philippi was a Roman colony, on the Egnatian Way—the great northern east-west highway. It was occupied by Italian settlers following Octavian's great battles, first against his former ally Antony. The colonists were proud of their special rights and privileges and intensely loyal to Rome. In Philippi, as in the province of Macedonia as a whole, women enjoyed high status. They took part in public and business life—a situation which is reflected in the church.

The church

The church was founded about AD50, during Paul's second missionary journey (see Acts 16:12-40). When Paul, Silas and Timothy left, Luke, the doctor, stayed on. Philippi was a medical centre, and may possibly have been Luke's home town. He no doubt did much to put the group on its feet and continue the evangelistic outreach. The letter reveals a church taking its share of suffering (1:29), and in some danger of division (1:27;2:2). There may have been some leaning to a doctrine of perfectionism (3:12-13). And the arrival of the Judaizers (see on 3:2ff.) introduced a new threat. But Paul loved this church and rejoiced over its progress.

The letter

Paul wrote from prison (1:12). If this was in Rome (Acts 28:16, 30-31), the date was about AD 61-63. But conditions are harsher than they appear in Acts; judgement is imminent and there is a real possiblity of death. Timothy, but not Luke (to judge by 2:20-21), is with him. It may therefore be that the imprisonment is an earlier one not recorded in Acts. A good case has been made out for Ephesus, which would make the date of writing about AD 54. We cannot be certain either way.

There are several reasons for writing. Paul wanted to explain why he was sending Epaphroditus back. He wanted to thank the Philippians for their gift. He had news for them. And what he had heard about them made him long to encourage and advise. Further news reached him while he was writing that made it imperative to add a word of warning (3:1b).

PHILIPPIANS

A free translation by Clive Calver and Steve Chilcraft

To the Philippians

From Paul and Timothy, slaves of Christ Jesus, to all the saints in union with Christ Jesus who are at Philippi with their overseers and deacons: we wish you the grace and peace of God our Father and the Lord Jesus Christ.

I thank my God for every memory of you, constantly praying with joy each time I pray for you, because of your partnership in the gospel from the first day until now.

I am confident that he who began a good work in you will carry it on to completion until the day of Christ Jesus. It is only natural for me to feel like this, because I have you in my heart; you all share in God's grace with me, both in my imprisonment and in defending and confirming the gospel. For God is my witness how much I long for you all with the heartfelt compassion of Christ Jesus. And this is my prayer, that your love may overflow more and more with knowledge and insight so that you may discern what is best. By this means you will be pure and blameless until the day of Christ, having produced the harvest of righteousness that comes through Jesus Christ—to the glory and praise of God.

Now I want you to know, brothers, that what has happened to me has actually helped to advance the gospel, so that it has become obvious throughout the praetorian guard and to everyone else that I am in chains for the cause of Christ. Because of my imprisonment most of the brothers and sisters in the Lord have grown in confidence and dare to speak the word of God with greater courage and without fear. Some proclaim Christ out of envy and rivalry, but others out of goodwill. These are motivated by love, knowing that I have been placed here for the defense of the gospel. The others preach Christ out of selfish ambition, not with pure motives, intending to increase my sufferings while in prison. What does it matter? In every way, whether in truth or in pretence, Christ is preached. In this I rejoice; yes, and I will continue to rejoice. For I know that through your prayers and the help of the Spirit of Jesus Christ this will result in my deliverance.

I eagerly expect and hope that I shall never fail in my duty, but will have sufficient courage so that now, as always, I will magnify Christ in my body, whether I live or I die. For to me, living is Christ and dying is gain, but if I am to go on living in the body, this will mean fruitful work for me, and I do not know which I prefer. I am torn between the two; I desire to leave this life and be with Christ, which is far better; but for your sake it is more necessary that I remain alive. Since I am convinced of this, I am confident that I will remain and stay with you all to add to your progress and joy in the faith, so that when I come to you again your praise to Christ Jesus will overflow on account of me.

Only conduct yourselves in a manner worthy of the gospel of Christ, so that whether I come and see you or hear about you in my absence, I will know that you are standing firm in one spirit, with one mind striving together for the sake of the gospel, without being intimidated by your opponents. This is a clear sign to them that they will be destroyed, but that you will be saved. And this is God's doing, for you have been granted the privilege not only of believing in Christ, but of suffering for him as well, experiencing the same struggle you saw I had and now hear I still am fighting. Therefore, if you have any encouragement from being united with Christ, any comfort from his love, any partnership in the

Spirit, any inner compassion and sympathy, make my joy complete: be of the same mind, having the same love, being one in spirit and purpose. Don't do anything from selfish ambition or empty conceit, but in humility regard others as more important than yourselves. Each of you should look not only to your own personal interests, but also to the interests of others. Your attitude should be the same as that of Christ Jesus: he always possessed the nature of God, but did not regard equality with God as something to be exploited. He emptied himself, taking the form of a slave, being born in human likeness. And being found in appearance as a man, he humbled himself and walked the path of obedience all the way to death—even death on a cross! For this reason God raised him to the highest place and gave him the name that is above every name, so that at the name of Jesus all beings in heaven, on earth, and under the earth should fall on their knees, and every tongue should confess that Jesus Christ is Lord, to the glory of God the Father.

So then, my dear friends, as you always obeyed me when I was with you, now evermore in my absence keep on working out your own salvation with fear and trembling, because it is God who is at work in you, enabling you both to will and to act in line with his good purpose.

Do everything without complaining or arguing, so that you may be pure and innocent, children of God without fault among a crooked and depraved generation, in which you shine as lights in the world, by your holding fast to the word of life, so I can boast on the day of Christ that I did not run or labour in vain. But even if my life's blood is to be poured out as a drink offering on the sacrificial service coming through your faith, I am glad and share my joy with you all; in the same way you should be glad and rejoice with me.

I hope in the Lord Jesus soon to send Timothy to you, so that I also may be encouraged by news of you. I have no-one else like him who will be genuinely concerned for your welfare. Everyone else is concerned only with his own interests, not with the cause of Jesus Christ. But you know how Timothy has proved his worth, how as a son with his father he has served with me in the work of the gospel. So I hope to send him to you as soon as I see how things go with me. And I am confident in the Lord that I myself will come soon.

Still, I deemed it necessary to return Epaphroditus to you—my brother, co-worker and fellow soldier, your messenger, the one you sent to take care of my needs—because he was longing for all of you and has been very upset because you had heard that he was sick. He was indeed so ill that he nearly died. But God had mercy on him, and not only on him but on me too, to spare me sorrow upon sorrow. Therefore I am all the more eager to send him, so that you will be glad when you see him again, and that I may be less anxious. Welcome him, then, with great joy in the Lord, and honour those like him, because he risked his life and nearly died for the sake of the work of Christ, in order to give me the help that you yourselves could not give.

Finally, my brothers and sisters, rejoice in the Lord! It is no trouble for me to write the same things to you again, and you will be safer if I do so.

Look out for the dogs, beware of those workers of evil, watch out for those who mutilate the flesh. For it is we who are the true circumcision, who worship God through his Spirit, who glory in Christ Jesus and who have no confidence in the flesh, though I myself have reasons for such confidence.

If anyone thinks he has reason to trust in external ceremonies, I have more: circumcised on the eighth day, an Israelite by birth, from the tribe of Benjamin, a pure-blooded Hebrew; as far as the law is concerned, a Pharisee; as to zeal, a persecutor of the church; as far as a person can be righteous by obeying the commands of the law, faultless.

Yet whatever advantages I had, these I have counted as loss for the sake of Christ. More than that, I consider everything as a loss compared to the surpassing greatness of knowing Christ Jesus my Lord, for whose sake I have suffered the loss of everything. I regard them as refuse, in order that I may gain Christ and be found in him. I do not have my own righteousness, gained from obeying the law, but one that comes through faith in Christ, the righteousness which comes from God on the basis of faith. I want to know Christ and the power of his resurrection, to share in his sufferings, and become like him in his death, in order that I myself will be raised from death to life.

Not that I have already obtained all this, or have already become perfect, but I press on to take hold of that for which Christ Jesus took hold of me. Brothers, I do not regard myself as having laid hold of it yet; but this one thing I do: forgetting what lies behind and straining forward to what lies ahead, I press on toward the goal to win the prize of God's call through Christ Jesus to the life above. All of us who are spiritually mature should share the same viewpoint; if you think differently God will make this clear to you. Only let us live up to the same standard as we have followed until now.

Brothers and sisters, join in imitating me and take careful note of those who follow the example we gave you. For many live as enemies of the cross of Christ. I have often told you about them, and now even repeat it with tears. Their destiny is destruction, their god is their stomach. They are proud of what they should be ashamed of, their minds are set on earthly things. We, however, are citizens of heaven, and it is from there that we eagerly await a saviour, the Lord Jesus Christ, who, by the power that enables him to bring everything under his control, will transform our weak mortal bodies so that they will be like his glorious body.

Therefore, my brothers and sisters, you whom I love and long for, my joy and crown, stand firm in the Lord, dear friends!

I urge Euodia and I plead with Syntyche to agree with each other in the Lord. Yes, and you too, my loyal partners, help these women, for they have struggled beside me in the course of the gospel, together with Clement and the rest of my fellow-workers, whose names are in the book of life.

Rejoice in the Lord always. I will say it again: Rejoice! Let your gentleness be evident to everyone. The Lord is near. Stop worrying about anything, but in everything, by prayer and petition, with thanksgiving, let your requests be made known to God. And the peace of God, which surpasses all understanding, will guard your hearts and your minds in Christ Jesus.

Finally, brothers and sisters, whatever is true, whatever is honourable, whatever is right, whatever is pure, whatever is lovable, whatever is admirable—if anything is well spoken-of as excellent and praiseworthy—think about these things! Put into practice what you have learned and received, what you heard and saw in me, and the God of peace will be with you.

Now I rejoice greatly in the Lord that at last you have renewed your concern for me. I do not mean that you stopped caring for me, you just had no opportunity to show it. I am not saying this because I am in need, for I have learned to be content whatever the circumstances. I know what it is to have little, and what it is to have more than enough. I have learned the secret of being content in all circumstances. Whether I am well-fed or hungry, whether I have too much or too little, I can do anything through the one who gives me strength. Yet it was good of you to be my partners during the troubles.

You Philippians know very well that when I left Macedonia in the early days of preaching the Good News, not one church shared with me in the matter of giving and receiving, except you alone. For even when I was in Thessalonica, you sent me help more than once to meet my need. Not that I am looking for a gift, rather I want to see profit credited to your account. I have been paid in full and have more than enough; I have all I need now that Epaphroditus has brought me your gifts. They are a fragrant offering, a sacrifice which is pleasing and acceptable to God. And my God will fully satisfy all your needs according to his riches in glory in Christ Jesus.

Now to our God and Father be the glory for ever and ever. Amen.

Greetings to all the saints in Christ Jesus. The brothers who are with me send their greetings. All the saints greet you, especially those in Caesar's household.

The grace of the Lord Jesus Christ be with your spirit. Amen.